# RIDING BUFFALOES AND BRONCOS

# Riding Buffalo

## Rodeo and Native Traditions

### ALLISON FUSS MELLIS

UNIVERSITY OF OKLAHOMA PRESS : NORMAN

# s and Broncos

## in the Northern Great Plains

This book is published with the generous assistance of
The Kerr Foundation, Inc.

Library of Congress Cataloging-in-Publication Data

Mellis, Allison Fuss, 1970–
    Riding buffaloes and broncos: rodeo and native traditions in the northern Great Plains.
Allison Fuss Mellis.
        p.   cm.
    Includes bibliographical references and index.
    ISBN 0-8061-3519-0 (hc.: alk. paper)
        1. Indians in rodeos—Great Plains.    2. Indian cowboys—Great Plains.    3. Crow Fair—
History.    4. Indians of North America—Cultural assimilation—Great Plains.    5. Indians of
North America—Great Plains—Ethnic identity.    6. Indians of North America—Great Plains—
Social life and customs.    I. Title.

E78.G73 F87 2003  .
305.897'078—dc21

                                                                                    2002032364

1   2   3   4   5   6   7   8   9   10

To my parents, Tim and Carol Fuss,
with all my love and gratitude

# Contents

# Illustrations

## PHOTOGRAPHS

## MAPS

# Preface

TEN YEARS AGO AS A NEWLY MINTED COLLEGE GRADUATE with a tightly packed Honda, I veered off southeastern Montana's Highway 90 and my life's direction changed. Turning onto the narrow stretch of Highway 212, isolated parts of which locals told me had only recently been paved, I drove past the historic Little Bighorn Battlefield. Soon after, my heart quickened as I read the road sign announcing my arrival on the Northern Cheyenne reservation—and fell as I began to notice bouquets of flowers dotting the roadside, memorials to loved ones whose cars had not made it home. Driving on, I approached a trading post on my right, and on my left, a one-room post office surrounded by a cluster of homes tucked into the rolling northern Great Plains. Having finally reached my destination—the small reservation town of Busby, population 409—I was pleased and, admittedly, slightly apprehensive. Only two weeks earlier, Roger Turns Plenty, representing the Busby School of the Northern Cheyenne Tribe, had hired me over the phone from my hometown of Memphis to come to Montana to teach second grade.

On the Northern Cheyenne reservation, I discovered an American Indian community creatively adapting to meet its socioeconomic and cultural challenges. They had done so with the fortitude and hope of a people rooted in family and evolving tribal traditions. I witnessed this most strikingly on a couple of occasions: one, the federal holiday Native American Day; the other, the Crow Fair and Rodeo. Even though people joked, "Every day is Native American Day on the rez," they still seized the opportunity to celebrate by staging a colorful parade through town. My second grade class decorated its float with the theme of the Northern Cheyenne creation story "The Great Race" and wore costumes depicting the various animals that had competed in that epic contest that determined whether animals or humans would rule the earth. That afternoon, we rode around town on the back of an adorned flatbed pickup truck, with my students waving at their "aunts" and "uncles," some exchanging greetings in their Native language.

The friends, each of them wonderfully unique, whom I eventually made in Busby have remained a valued part of me. They range from my bright second graders (including Tyler Medicine Horse, Leroy Pine, Jon Fire Crow, Davida Old Bear) to my dedicated teaching colleagues (among them Sharon Bear Comes Out, Jack Kobizar, Frank Rowland, Ginny Weeks, and my teaching aides, Mabel Killsnight and Betsy Swank) and my generous neighbors Tom and Jane McMakin.

It was remarkably apparent that over a century after the United States federal government had relegated them to this reservation, the Northern Cheyennes had made it into their tribal home, part of their evolving Indian identity. Subjected to the Indian Office's aggressive policy of assimilation, they had managed to subvert its goals, often by using the very instruments it had provided, to remain a distinctive "nation within a nation." A visit to the Crow Fair and Rodeo on the neighboring Crow Indian reservation revealed that the Crows had accomplished a similar feat. Since 1904, the Crows had transformed their government-sponsored agricultural fair—designed to detribalize them and make them into independent farmers and ranchers—into The Teepee Capital of the World. They had remade Crow Fair and Rodeo into a tribal and intertribal event where Crows and other Native peoples gathered to revel in being Indian. This meant enjoying the parades, the powwows, the fry bread, and, of course, the all-Indian rodeo. Privileged to have experienced the people and cultural celebrations of the Northern Cheyenne and Crow reservations, I began this project.

# Acknowledgments

A NETWORK OF KNOWLEDGEABLE PEOPLE AND ORGANIZA-
tions has contributed to the formation of this manuscript. Many
archivists, librarians, and staff members provided particular assistance in
accessing manuscript collections, periodicals, and rodeo ephemera. These
include: Doug Archer, University of Notre Dame, Notre Dame, Indiana;
Michael Brodhead, National Archives, Regional Archives System—Central
Plains Region, Kansas City, Missouri; Leonard Bruguier and Margaret
Quintal, American Indian Research Project, University of South Dakota,
Vermillion; Jodie Foley and Ellie Arguimbau, Montana Historical Society
and Archives, Helena; Terry Grey, Sinte Gleske University, Rosebud, South
Dakota; Eric Halverson and Anne Mejias-Mariani, Big Horn County
Library, Hardin, Montana; Jennifer King, reference archivist, American Her-
itage Center, University of Wyoming, Laramie; Julie Lakota, Oglala Lakota
College Archives, Kyle, South Dakota; Magdeline Medicine Horse, Little Big
Horn College and Archives, Crow Agency, Montana; Geri and Dennis
Sanders, Hardin Photo Service, Hardin, Montana; and Harry Thompson,
Center for Western Studies, Augustana College, Sioux Falls, South Dakota.
Others helped me at the South Dakota Historical Society and Archives,
Pierre; the Montana State University Library, Bozeman; the National
Archives, Regional Archives System—Rocky Mountain Region, Denver; and
the Greenough Family Rodeo Collection, Carbon County Museum, Red
Lodge, Montana.

I am also grateful to the many Indian rodeo cowboys and cowgirls with
whom I have corresponded and conversed over the past decade. Each of these
lively and informative interviews and letters has enlightened this book. Yet, I
owe particular thanks to Clem McSpadden of Chelsea, Oklahoma, one of the
founders of the Indian National Finals Rodeo, for readily responding to all of
my sundry questions. Great Plains Indian Rodeo Association president, Kelli
Powers Ward and secretary Bobby Jacobs, and American Indian Rodeo Cowboys Association secretary Avalina Jim also provided useful information in

the early stages of my research. Crow Indian cowboys Pius, Charles, Shawn, Curtis, and Hank Real Bird and other members of the Real Bird family of Medicine Tail Coulee in Garryowen, Montana, as well as Marlon Passes and Lloyd Pickett of Crow Agency, Montana, not only welcomed me into their homes and families' histories but graciously contributed their time and recollections to my research.

The magnanimous people and resources of the University of Notre Dame, where I received my doctorate, and of the United States Naval Academy, where I am now an assistant professor, have nurtured both this project and me. My dissertation director, Walter Nugent, provided unwavering enthusiasm and astute advice that have encouraged this manuscript from its inception as a seminar paper in 1994 to its development as a dissertation and finally into its current form. I am also grateful to my dissertation committee, including Thomas Blantz, C.S.C.; Gregory Evans Dowd; and Sharon O'Brien for their careful reading and informed suggestions. Friends and colleagues in the History Department at the United States Naval Academy, including our chair, Mary DeCredico, and the "works-in-progress" crew—among them Richard Abels, David Peeler, and Nancy Ellenberger, who perceptively critiqued chapter 1 over wine and cheese—as well as, Wilson D. Miscamble, C.S.C.; James Carroll, C.F.C.; and Brian Shanley, O.P. have consistently lent me their valuable insights and moral support throughout this process. Indeed, Fr. Bill Miscamble, former chair of the History Department at the University of Notre Dame, has remained a mentor to me since I had the privilege to be his teaching assistant and benefit from his excellent example as a teacher, historian, and steward. Most recently, he generously read this manuscript in its entirety and offered his typically shrewd and candid commentary.

I have also had the good fortune of working with a collection of talented and amiable people associated with the University of Oklahoma Press. I am ever grateful to Albert L. Hurtado, professor and Travis Chair at the University of Oklahoma, for bringing my manuscript to the press's attention on the advice of Walter Nugent. From my first meeting with Jeff Burnham at the Western History Conference in Portland, Oregon, to my ongoing first-rate relationship with his successor, Acquisitions Editor Jo Ann Reece, and her editorial assistant, Shelia Buckley, and most recently with Assistant Editors Julie A. Shilling and Jennifer Cunningham, the University of Oklahoma Press's staff of editors has capably guided this first-time author through each of the potentially harrowing stages of publishing a monograph. I am also appreciative of the anonymous readers and, especially, of copyeditor Mike Mollett, whose meticulous reading of this manuscript and intelligent suggestions have surely improved it.

Several sources provided financial support for this project. The Zahm Fund, the History Department, and the DeSantis Fund at the University of Notre Dame largely funded a number of research trips throughout the northern Great Plains and Canada. The Buffalo Bill Historical Center in Cody, Wyoming, granted me a fellowship to attend their Larom Summer Institute in Western American Studies in the summer of 1994. There, I met Linda R. Mac-Cannell, who had been photographing American Indian rodeo cowboys, and I began to consider the history and cultural significance of rodeos among Northern Plains Indian communities. Finally, the Naval Academy Research Committee (NARC) grant has provided me with essential summer funding, as I worked to augment and revise this monograph in its final stages. I am indebted to each of these people and institutions.

Above all, I want to thank my dear family, including my newlywed husband, Jon Mellis; my parents, Tim and Carol Fuss; my sisters and brothers-in-law, Stephanie and Tim Hayes and Jennifer and Tom Pierotti; and my precious nieces, Camille, Catherine, and Virginia Hayes, and Stephanie and Elizabeth Pierotti. Their steadfast support and sense of humor have remained my greatest wellspring of encouragement. I have always felt supremely fortunate to have not one but two big sisters in Stephanie and Jennifer. My treasured friends and confidants, they have graced me with their love, insight, and resolute faith in me, as has Jon, whose surprise incentives have happily encouraged me to meet more than one fast-approaching deadline. His penchant for history and adventure have also made him a prized research partner, who has never failed to track down office supplies in remote western drugstores.

Finally, I dedicate this book to my extraordinary parents with all my love and gratitude. Their generous hearts and intellectual curiosity have always inspired my own. Ten years ago, my father's determination and my mother's industriousness helped transplant me to the Northern Cheyenne reservation, where I taught second grade and truly began this project. Later, they acted as tireless field research assistants, with my mother valiantly scrutinizing reels of microfilm and documents in archives throughout Montana and in Pierre, South Dakota, and my father accompanying me to the Indian

National Finals Rodeo in Saskatoon, Saskatchewan, Canada. Along the way, we collected files full of cherished memories, many of Indian rodeo cowboys and cowgirls, as well as many more of our very own.

While I am grateful for the abundant assistance I have received, the responsibility for the contents of this work remains my own.

# Abbreviations

AAIAA  All American Indian Activities Association

AIHF  American Indian Hall of Fame

AIM  American Indian Movement

AIRCA  All-Indian Rodeo Cowboy Association

BIA  Bureau of Indian Affairs

IECW  Indian Emergency Conservation Work

INFR  Indian National Finals Rodeo

IRA  Indian Reorganization Act

NRCA  National Rodeo Cowboys' Association

PRCA  Professional Rodeo Cowboys Association

SRCA  Sioux Rodeo Cowboys Association

WPA  Works Progress Administration

WPRA  Women's Professional Rodeo Association

RIDING BUFFALOES AND BRONCOS

# *Indians Still*

## SUMMER GATHERINGS STRENGTHEN TIES TO COMMUNITIES AND HORSES

W HETHER ON HORSEBACK COMPETING IN THE dust or in the grandstand cheering for family and tribal members at all-Indian rodeos, northern Plains Indians have endured.[1] More than a hundred years ago, few would have predicted it. Mainstream Americans, increasingly interested in resettling in the trans-Mississippi West, conveniently believed the message conveyed by artists, writers, missionaries, and politicians that Native peoples were inevitably doomed, an anachronistic culture and a "vanishing race."[2] By 1890, this prophecy seemed to be becoming a reality, as the United States government had confined all American Indians in the West to reservations via treaties and military conquests. Whether out of land hunger or out of genuine concern for American Indians, whom they viewed ambivalently as "noble" yet "savage" people, most observers agreed that Indians had but one choice left to them. The federal government, influenced by Christian reformers, became convinced that Native Americans, like the stream of newly arriving immigrants from southern and eastern Europe, must assimilate in order to survive. Indian Office officials viewed the segregated reservation environment as the ideal testing ground for their ambitious social experiment, an experiment aimed at transforming Indians into white men. On reservations, Bureau of Indian Affairs officials thoroughly expected American Indians to dissolve their communal bonds, forsake their tribal identities, and then as individuals enter into larger American society.[3]

Yet the northern Plains Indians that are the focus of this book—the Crows, the Northern Cheyennes, and the Lakotas on the Pine Ridge, Rosebud, and Cheyenne River Sioux reservations—did not assimilate. Rather, they found new ways to remain essentially Indian, as they realized that they could "be like white men and not be white men."[4] Remarkably, through this process of selective adaptation, they managed to reinforce their tribal affiliations and even forge pan-Indian ones via the very instruments of control used by a consciously hegemonic white culture. After all, they were no strangers to change. They had been adapting to their environment—experimenting with new methods of hunting, farming, and trading—since long before Europeans arrived.[5] By taking advantage of those innovations that would contribute to their community stability, they had vastly improved their economic lives while promoting cultural cohesion. Horses, and later cattle, for instance, allowed them to demonstrate Plains Indian virtues such as bravery, generosity in gift giving, and respect for the natural world.[6]

As they made the transition to reservation life, northern Plains Indians once again sought to incorporate certain European introductions. Cattle ranching, tribal fairs, and above all rodeo resonated with their own cultural priorities of being with family and community members, in the outdoors, and on horseback.[7] By competing in or attending government-sanctioned rodeos, northern Plains Indians resisted assimilation by reinforcing their ties to one another and to their horses. In doing so, they built on a long-standing tradition of meeting as tribes in the summer months and displaying their skills on horseback. By the late twentieth century, they had made rodeo into a Native tradition.

## PRE-RESERVATION COMMUNITY GATHERINGS

Before 1890, northern Plains Indians had developed ways to safeguard their close ties to one another—ties that they would later call upon when their identity was under siege. Through their buffalo hunting bands and seasonal gatherings, Crows, Northern Cheyennes, and Lakotas had fostered intratribal allegiances in order to withstand the vagaries of hunting, intertribal raids, and warfare associated with pre-reservation life. In *The Crow Indians*, anthropologist Robert Lowie describes the necessity of collaboration in a world in which

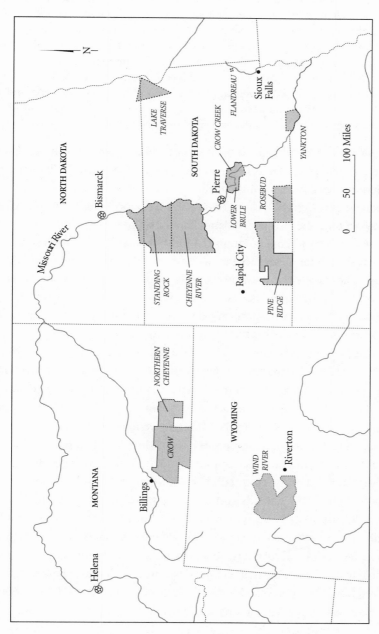

*Map of the reservations of the northern Plains.*

the single human being is a mere worm at the mercy of the elements. A man may be a champion marksman, but when there is no game to shoot he falls back on the pemmican his wife has stored against that very emergency; and even in the chase he is most efficient when he hunts in company. His robes and leggings are the work of his wives and kinsmen; his very arrows are not his own making but the handiwork of a skilled craftsman. If he seeks renown, what are his chances as a lonely raider? . . . Crisis lowered on every side, and it meant everything to be able to face life not alone but with a comrade, shielded by one's family and clan, in the bosom of one's club.[8]

For these reasons, during much of the winter and fall most northern Plains Indians remained with their bands and relied on them as their tribal groups scattered in order to hunt buffalo more efficiently. These bands were well ordered and cohesive. Each elected a chief, who decided with the help of clan headmen (if the tribe recognized clan relations) when to pitch and move their camp.[9] As each band embarked on the hunt, it was a "festive occasion," in which scouts rode far in advance to warn of enemies; police guarded the flanks; chiefs and old men led; and various families followed "with their horses, dogs and household possessions, the women dressed in their finest apparel."[10]

Recalling these processions, historian Frederick Hoxie used the parade as the central metaphor for his history of the Crows, who moved "forward in the world by arranging themselves into a coherent unit and proceeding together."[11] The Crows' worldview, in particular, has been predicated on inter- dependence and reciprocity, and nowhere has this been illustrated more clearly than in their term for clan, ashammaléaxia, which means "as driftwood lodges." As branches cluster together along a riverbank, Crow clan members have clung together for mutual support in good times and in turbulent ones.[12] Within their tribe, the Crows organized themselves into two major divisions, the River Crows and the Mountain Crows, which were further subdivided into politically distinct bands composed of members of thirteen clans.[13] These clans were matrilineal, with the children born or adopted into a family all taking their mother's clan name.[14] Other northern Plains Indians, includ- ing the Cheyennes and Dakotas, abandoned their rigid clan systems as too inflexible to accommodate their eighteenth-century migratory buffalo hunt- ing lifestyle. Yet the Crows, who preceded these groups onto the northern Great Plains by several generations, managed to maintain theirs.[15]

Like the Crows, the Northern Cheyennes and Lakotas also placed a premium on group solidarity, which they nurtured at annual summer rendezvous. In the warmer months, they would reunite at these gatherings for communal hunting and ceremonies. In a very real way, these meetings fortified tribal solidarity and well-being. Chiefs met to discuss strategies for surviving the upcoming year, and many in attendance participated in rituals and games designed to protect and celebrate their people. It was then that tribal, rather than band-level institutions entered into full play. When they convened, the Northern Cheyennes' governing body, the Council of Forty-four, as well as its six warrior societies represented each band in decision making.[16] The Dakota Sioux recognized a "general community relationship" but viewed themselves as the Dakota Confederacy and referred to themselves as the "Seven Council Fires."[17] They were divided into three broad divisions—the Teton, Yankton-Yanktonai, and Santee—which were further divided into tribes and finally bands. The Lakotas, also known as the Tetons, formed the western vanguard of the Dakota Confederacy.[18] In addition to political discussions, pre-reservation celebrations included ceremonies, singing, dancing, giveaways, praise songs, and feasting of relatives.[19] One of the most important ceremonies held at these seasonal gatherings was the Sun Dance. In *Cheyenne Memories*, John Stands in Timber, "one of the last Cheyennes to hear the tribal story from those who lived it," reveals the significance of the Sun Dance by situating its emergence in the time of the Northern Cheyennes' own origin story of the Great Race, when the relationships between humans and animals were established. Other historians would agree that the Northern Cheyennes were a probable center for the spread of the Sun Dance, bringing it with them onto the Great Plains around 1800. Shortly thereafter, it became an integral part of Plains Indian annual gatherings, as recalled by Stands in Timber.

> The Sun Dance was the greatest religious ceremony of the Plains . . . held every summer, when the grass was up and game plentiful and the people came together in one big camp for worship and social life after they had been scattered out during the winter. The bands all gathered at some chosen place and camped in a big circle, which opened toward the east. It was a time of fun and visiting . . . and it was a time of blessing, for the Sun Dance helped everyone in the tribe whether or not they took part in it.[20]

The Sun Dance served important functions for both the Cheyennes, whose Sun Dance focused on renewal of the earth, and the Crows, who held the Sun Dance to "seek vengeance for slain kinsmen." By 1881, the Indian Bureau was pressuring Plains Indians to desist from engaging in the all-important Sun Dance. While it is likely that Northern Cheyennes and others continued to

practice the Sun Dance secretly, they were not able to revive it as a public ceremony until the Indian New Deal period (the subject of chapter 3) beginning
in 1934.[21]

In pre-reservation times, summer gatherings were also times of pure rev-
elry, in which feasts, songs, and dances were held for occasions such as the
return of a successful war party. During such celebrations, the scout who had
first glimpsed the enemy was also the first to partake of his preferred food.
His wife was the next to partake, and then everyone feasted on stewed berries
and other foods. This was followed by the performance of "lodge-striking," a
ceremony in which singers beat drums and sang victory songs and men fired
guns, while others struck the tepees of the captains of the raid. Following that,
the men began to sing,

> Recently I went away,
> I have returned,
>    kiss me.

Dancing ensued in the center of camp, while the members of the returning
warriors' clans sang praise songs in their honor. The honorees reciprocated
by giving valuable gifts to the singers. These festivities often lasted a full day
and night, and "the noise was such that horses got frightened and ran away."[22]

Crow tribal historian Joseph Medicine Crow recorded that "during periods
of respite from the demands of hunting and warfare," Plains Indian women
and men also enjoyed "games for every age, and athletic sports and events for
all."[23] In his ethnography, Robert Lowie attends specifically to the social lives
of Crow women. He observes that "socially, the women enjoyed a good deal
of freedom. . . . To offset their domestic work, women could indulge in a variety of amusements, such as ball and dice games, sometimes among themselves, sometimes in the company of their husbands or lovers."[24] Wagering
accompanied most of these contests. Both men and women participated, each
gender separately, in a hiding, or hand, game, in which players concealed a
bone, elk tooth, or shell in an unknown hand. This game was considered the
gambling game par excellence. In it, each "club" sat in several rows on opposite sides of the tepee, with the wages of victory—including robes, beadwork,
and warbonnets—laid down as stakes. This guessing game involved ample
crowd participation, as those watching attempted to distract opponents and
cheered on teammates. Women, in particular, also participated vigorously in
dice casting, in which they wagered dresses, elk teeth, and quilts. Both genders

took part in gambling associated with athletic games like mock hunting and hoop throwing. In hoop throwing, competitors threw darts at a rolling hoop. They also took part in shinny, or ball striking, in which each team tried to drive a ball to the opposite goal which was marked by blankets that the champions would win.[25] Shinny was sometimes played on horseback, which made it even more appealing to Crows, Northern Cheyennes, and Lakotas, who integrated the horse into every aspect of their lives.

## INDIANS AND HORSES

Since their arrival in North America, horses have acted as enduring symbols of both power and promise within many western Native cultures, which begins to explain the origins and importance of rodeo within them.[26] After the Spanish introduced horses to North America in the mid-sixteenth century, American Indians in the West began to incorporate them into their social lives and economies in important ways. Diffusing northward from Spanish settlements in the Southwest, horses had become common among tribes north of the Missouri river by 1772.[27] Anthropologist Loretta Fowler, relying in part on the findings of John C. Ewers, describes the manifold societal transformations that horses brought about within northern Plains Indian buffalo hunting societies. As certain tribal members acquired more horses than others, new leaders emerged, who demonstrated their generosity by sharing food and horses with their more "horse poor followers." By ensuring a more stable food supply, horses afforded hunters more frequent reprieves, which they used for reunions and ceremonies. By transporting cumbersome "ritual regalia, clothing and large tipi covers," horses allowed the ceremonies to become more elaborate. And by transporting the convalescent between campgrounds, it is likely horses caused mortality rates among the very young and very old to fall.[28] There can be no doubt that northern Plains Indians welcomed horses as a boon.

Long before horses appeared in the northern Great Plains, many Indians had been expecting them. Prophets like the Northern Cheyenne holy man Sweet Medicine had eagerly predicted the coming of an animal "with a shaggy neck and a tail almost touching the ground. Its hoofs are round. This animal will carry you on his back and help you in many ways. Those far hills that seem only a blue vision in the distance take many days to reach now, but with this animal you can get there in a short time, so fear not."[29] Just as anticipated, horses quickly became a source of power. With the horse, Plains Indians could more effectively hunt buffalo, wage war, trade, and enlarge their own horse herds by raiding other tribes. On horseback, they could travel greater distances and command more territory, expanding their hunting grounds along with the ability to chase and hunt with more alacrity.[30] Plains Indians also employed riderless horses as runners, which pursued and guided herds of buffalo toward hunters waiting atop fresh mounts.[31]

American Indians explained this cultural augmentation with stories declaring that they had always had horses, thereby underscoring the extent to which horses had become ingrained in their existence.[32] Native accounts explained the origins of the horse: horses were obtained through a tribal person or persons' "heroic quest" or as a gift from the gods or the holy people. From this belief, and the fact that horses had replaced dogs in many tasks, the Lakotas named the horse *sunka wakan*, or holy dog.[33] Historians explain the Plains Indians' reverence for the horse by pointing to their belief that the Great Power endowed all animals with powers not given to humans.[34] According to one Crow elder, humans "must obtain spiritual power from animal emissaries and revealers." It follows that "many Crow medicine men attributed their gift powers to the horse," and "were blessed with the strength, stamina, speed and agility of the horse."[35] One Crow Indian, Magdeline Medicine Horse, archivist at Little Big Horn College and Archives, echoed this enduring belief, stating that the horse had always been her family's medicine.[36] To the southwest, others shared this view that horses lent power. Navajo rock art dating back to the seventeenth century in northern New Mexico and Arizona, for example, includes images of "Navajo cowboys and horses pictured alone, and . . . imbued with the spirit of the horses and the gods."[37]

Over time, this deep respect led American Indians of the West to develop unique relationships with horses and often to consider them as *kolas*, or "warrior brothers." GaWaNi Pony Boy, a Cherokee horseman and writer, described this relationship, saying, "Most important, the war pony was *kola*: a friend with whom you could face many enemies. The word *kola* is not normally used to describe animals but is reserved for human brother-warriors. In using *kola* as a descriptor of their relationship to their horses, Native American warriors acknowledged their horses' equal status as brother-warriors."[38] Pony Boy drew on the wisdom of elders from various tribes and observed that the Native rider attempted to recreate the roles played in a horse's natural herd by behaving as a leader, *itancan*, to his horse follower, *waunca*. Their partnership was improved most dramatically as the rider learned to listen and communicate more effectively with his horse. A Lakota story illustrates the union that a human rider could achieve with his horse. In the story, scouts Walking Crow and his nephew Laughing Beaver chased a reluctant sun all the way from the west to the east, and in the three years that they spent with their horses in the darkness they fused with their horses. When the scouts reappeared, each sat upon his pony's back with no legs of his own. Big Tree, a Lakota medicine man explained: "They and their ponies had become one."[39] As Indian identity became more closely bound to horses, so too did Indian family names, which could be given by an older relative or elder to reflect status or ideals. By the late twentieth century, family names that included horses could identify not only a person but also his or her Indian nation. Historian Peter Iverson observed that "if you meet a Riding In, you assume he or she is Pawnee. A Medicine Horse is likely Crow, a Whirlwind Horse probably Lakota (Sioux). Other names are used more widely. One meets White Horses (or White-horses) in Cheyenne, Kiowa or Navajo country."[40]

As horses became part of Native identities, they also became partners in activities that presaged the modern rodeo. One finds the earliest antecedents of North American rodeo in the pre-reservation equestrian activities of Indians of the Southwest. Historians such as Mary Lou LeCompte and Richard W. Slatta have emphasized that in the Americas, "many cowboy cultures evolved from a blending of the Spanish heritage of the conquistadors and pre-existing Indian cultures."[41] The Pueblo people along the Rio Grande were among the first Indians to acquire Spanish horses and cattle from the Coronado party in 1540. They were also among the first Indian cowboys trained at any of the twenty-five Spanish missions established along the Rio Grande Valley between 1598 and 1632.[42] The Pueblos had ranching experience as early as the late sixteenth century, more than a century before that of the Indians who ranched at missions established by Junipero Serra along the California coast and that of the Indian vaqueros of south Texas.[43]

The Pueblos integrated horses into their post-contact ceremonial lives through ritual games that resembled the rodeo in form and cultural function. From the Spanish, Indian cowboys inherited games such as *pialar*, which means to lasso an animal by the legs, and *correr el gallo*, the "chicken race," or "rooster pull."[44] The Pueblos transformed Santiago, the patron saint of Spain and guardian of all horsemen and soldiers, into an ally of Pueblo people and a defender against their oppressors. They paid tribute to Santiago in many

ways, most often through ritual dances using a hobbyhorse to represent Santiago, and through ritual games. The Pueblo ritual game known as the rooster pull was developed in the late 1600s and early 1700s to honor Santiago,
who was believed to have killed a rooster; by playing the game, the Indians
ensured the fecundity and good luck of all Indian people. In the most common form of the rooster pull, prevalent among the Pueblos and the Navajos
from the 1600s to the 1960s, participants buried the rooster or chicken in the
sand, allowing only its neck and head to be exposed. The horsemen then galloped, one by one, from about seventy yards away, bareback or leaning out of
saddle, and attempted to wrench the unfortunate chicken from the ground
without falling off the horse. The others chased the rider who succeeded, and
then all struggled to steal the bird. Thus, in the case of the rooster pull, we
have not only an indication of the Pueblos' adaptation of Spanish religious
heroes like Santiago into their own religions but also an anticipation of Indian
rodeo in both form and function. In form, the rooster pull required the same
types of skill needed for rough stock rodeo events in which the rider must
stay on the bronco or bull while holding on with only one hand. In function,
the rooster pull was similar to the later Indian involvement in rodeo, as it
restored the domain of Indian men whose status had been disrupted by the
Spanish.[45] The connection between Indian rodeo and the rooster pull is also
evident in linguistics. The Navajo word for rodeo, *naa'ahooha,i* also translates
as "chicken pull."[46]

Horse races were also significant in the development of rodeo among
Native groups in the Southwest and northern Great Plains. They became
Navajo community events in which "each group placed wagers. Items wagered
included buckskins, saddlebags, blankets and bundles."[47] Similarly, Indians of
the Great Plains relished a variety of opportunities to display their developing
equestrian skills—skills that in some ways anticipated their involvement in
rodeo. Following the eighteenth-century appearance of the horse on the
Great Plains, Plains Indians became superlative horsemen through hunting,
intertribal warfare, raiding, and horse races. Frank Gilbert Roe's now classic
commentary on the "buffalo Indian's" horsemanship sounds very much like
a rodeo announcer's description of a bareback bronc competition:

> Rapidly, the Indian became an excellent horseman. . . . The fighting native
> needed both hands to shoot his bow and arrow, and as a result he became a
> marvelous rider. Actions such as dropping on the far side of a galloping horse
> and shooting under the neck at an enemy, mounting and dismounting at a

dead run, and picking up a fallen comrade were all feats. When it is considered that the Indians accomplished these feats without any saddles and without holding the reins, guiding the horse entirely with the knees, the extraordinary skill of the Indian riders can be appreciated.[48]

The Crows of the northern Great Plains were widely recognized for their equestrian talents. An observer in 1834 described a Crow camp along the south basin of the Yellowstone that was filled with four hundred tepees and nine to ten thousand horses. According to all accounts, the Crows were accomplished horsemen, throwing "themselves from side to side during battle."[49] The Sioux winter count of 1871, which records the year when Crow on horseback stole their horses, also testifies to the Crows' formidable equestrian skills.[50]

Native horsemen on the Great Plains developed other rodeo skills by competing in bucking bronco and horse racing competitions. Plains Indians prided themselves on their fine racehorses and often came together to match their animals' endurance and speed. Such contests were waged within private warrior societies, with other native groups, and with white traders.[51] Apparently they did quite well in these races, as is seen in Colonel Richard Irving Dodge's begrudging account of a horse race that took place in 1846, in which "the officer's Kentucky mare was beaten by a 'miserable sheep of a pony,' on which his contemptuous Comanche jockey rode backward, beckoning his American rival with 'hideous grimaces' to come on a little faster!"[52] The Crows were no exception to a fondness for horse racing, as they reveled in betting on horse races, often wagering blankets, saddles, and other horses. Places such as Hoskin and McGirl's Trading Post, located on the present site of Huntley, Montana, were prime locations for horse races between the Indians and traders. One such race took place in 1879 between Plenty Coups on his buckskin and a cowboy from Bozeman on a horse with the luckless name of Snail.[53] Crows competed not only with Anglos but also with other Indians, as tribal historians remind us. Crow band leader Medicine Tail told his grandchildren of pre-reservation competitions that took place on the flats at Spear Siding, where they would camp out and race horses.[54] Other tribes would sometimes challenge Crow horsemen to a horse race or to ride a wild horse. Crow oral historian Laurence Flatlip recalls, "at one time if there was a person that challenged the whole Crow tribe if they could ride their wild horse and tame it that they would pay him. A man could even earn an achievement, and under the category of achievements are coups, deeds and honors."[55] A modern Crow cowboy explained that in the old days, the Crows enjoyed this sport so much that "they used to go out in the middle of a field ..., and they [would] put a bronc saddle on a horse and just compete by themselves. Before then, we didn't have cattle, we didn't have calves, so we started off with bronc riding and horse racing."[56]

## ASSIMILATION

Those who were enthusiastic about the Indian's potential to assimilate in 1880 failed to recognize the resiliency of northern Plains Indian cultures. For centuries, these Indians had maintained their ties within their tribes through common rituals such as summer gatherings and through symbols of strength and hope for the future such as the horse. They had been willing to adapt to meet the changing demands of their environments rather than relinquish their cultures. Seemingly unaware of these cultural defenses, the federal government optimistically adopted assimilation as its official policy toward the Indians by 1880. Assimilation was a paradoxical policy that intended to temporarily segregate Indians on reservations, where they would be urged to forsake their Indian identities and dissolve their tribal affiliations. Once the anticipated metamorphosis was complete, they could enter into mainstream society as Americanized individuals.[57] This transformation was to be accomplished through a three-pronged process of Christianization and education, land allotment, and citizenship to remake Indians into replicas of white men and women. Indian reformers were heavily influenced by Christian humanitarianism. Various reform groups met each autumn at the Lake Mohonk Conference in New York and claimed to be the "conscience of the American people on the Indian question." They readily acknowledged the Christian motivation behind their work. Herbert Welsh, a leader of the Indian Rights Association, the most influential organization lobbying for legislative reform of Indian policy since its inception in 1882, spoke for many when he avowed that the Indian needed to be "taught to labor, to live in civilized ways and to serve God."[58] To this end, the Indian Bureau, under the auspices of the Department of the Interior, established Courts of Indian Offenses in the 1880s that outlawed "old heathenish dances," like the Sun Dance. Secretary of the Interior Henry M. Teller asserted that such outmoded and barbaric rituals were "a great hindrance to the civilization of the

Indians."[59] To expedite the "civilization" process, reformers at Lake Mohonk and elsewhere agreed that Indians needed to be educated. For most, education was synonymous with Christianization.[60] Boarding schools, modeled upon Captain Richard Henry Pratt's Carlisle Indian Industrial School in Pennsylvania, became one of the principal means to administer both Christianization and education. To cure Indians of their identities, the Indian Bureau removed Native children from their homes for five years or more at a time and sent them to off-reservation boarding schools, where their hair was cut and they were forbidden to speak their language. On reservations, federal policy reformers such as Merrill Gates attempted to teach Indians to be less communal. Concluding that Indians had to become "more intelligently selfish," the bureau attempted to break up tribal land holdings through the General Allotment Act of 1887.[61] This act, also known as the Dawes Severalty Act, provided for the allotment of 160-acre parcels of land to each Indian head of household and the eventual lease and sale of vast tracts of "surplus" tribal lands.

The Indian Bureau continued to make these paternalistic assaults on Indian cultures and lands with varying degrees of intensity throughout the late nineteenth and early twentieth centuries. They intensely implemented the policy of assimilation from 1880 to 1920, relaxed it in the 1920s, abandoned it from 1934 to 1945, and resumed it in the form of "termination" until the 1960s. In formulating its policy of assimilation, the Indian Office had mistakenly assumed that it could erase Indian identity by simply altering Indian living conditions, hairstyles, languages, economies, and religious practices. They did not anticipate the resistance northern Plains Indians were prepared to offer in response. Despite these relentless attacks on their identity, Crows, Northern Cheyennes, and Lakotas did not assimilate. Rather they allowed for intense cultural change by adapting certain practices based on what their cultures and the Indian Commission would allow.[62] A similar cultural phenomenon occurred among the Gros Ventre, who engaged in "behavior that was symbolic of civilization to the federal officials," but that "the Gros Ventre themselves interpreted . . . as expressions of ideals that predated reservation settlement."[63] As seasoned traders of goods and elements of culture, first with other tribal groups and later with European Americans, American Indians of the West were skilled at discerning which imports to employ and which to reject. Even significant changes could not easily expunge their community and kinship bonds, and often reinforced them.

By 1890, northern Plains Indians had established tenacious bonds with others in their tribes and with the horses that had become a part of their way of life in the hundred years since they had acquired them. As assimilationist Indian Office officials attempted to dissolve tribal affiliations, they unknowingly provided forums that solidified these affiliations. As the Indian Bureau outlawed traditional Indian ceremonies and encouraged more suitable Anglo-American endeavors, Plains Indians applied their adaptive proficiency to the process of adopting certain government-sanctioned economic and social activities like cattle ranching and rodeo that resonated with their own established cultures. As summer gatherings had once done, rodeos fortified Indian relationships by providing a place for Crow, Northern Cheyenne, and Lakota communities to gather, to wager, and to compete on horseback. At the beginning of the twenty-first century, with more than two thousand Indian rodeo cowboys and cowgirls competing in an extensive all-Indian rodeo circuit and being cheered on by large crowds of Indian audiences, the Plains Indians have defied the pervasive predictions made a century earlier that they were on the verge of demographic and cultural extinction. Through rodeo and other cultural adaptations, they have remained Indians.

## CHAPTER ONE

# *Indians* and *Cowboys*

*1880–1920*

B Y 1890, ALL AMERICAN INDIANS IN THE WEST HAD either defiantly or voluntarily accepted life on reservations. Federal officials, influenced by Christian reformers, intended reservations to serve the paradoxical purpose of temporarily segregating Indians to prepare them for their ultimate integration into white society. On those reservations, Indians were supposed to relinquish their communal bonds and eventually enter into the larger American society as detribalized individuals.[1] This was the federal government's official assimilation policy from 1880 to 1934, a policy zealously carried out until 1920. During the four decades of intense implementation, northern Plains peoples were settled permanently on reservations and were encouraged to become farmers and cattle ranchers, even as they saw their lands allotted, sold, and leased. The Indians, however, did not give up their tribal identities; instead, they allowed for intense cultural change by adopting, and adapting to, selected practices based on what their cultures and the Indian Commission would permit.[2] Many Crow, Northern Cheyenne, and Lakota horsemen and -women effectively finessed the assimilationists by selecting only those activities that accentuated rather than dissolved their tribal ties. One of the ways northern Plains Indians sought this allowable middle ground was by becoming rodeo cowboys.

Because whites had made buffalo hunts impossible and had outlawed traditional Indian ceremonials, American Indians in the northern Great Plains and elsewhere sought government-sanctioned alternatives for providing for themselves and maintaining community. As a consequence, many northern

Plains Indians, drawing on an equestrian tradition dating back to the eighteenth century, selected cattle ranching and rodeo, both with origins in Hispanic and southwestern Indian cultures, as viable economic and social substitutes. Whenever Indian agents allowed them to choose between farming and cattle ranching, the Indians enthusiastically selected ranching. In addition to being more economically practical in the arid Great Plains, ranching was also a more culturally compatible substitute for buffalo hunting. As cattle ranchers, northern Plains Indians could work together rather than separately in the outdoors and on horseback, while maintaining their generosity by giving away cattle to family and tribal members.[3]

As the social counterpart to ranching, rodeo brought northern Plains Indians together in a setting much like their pre-reservation summer gatherings. At rodeos, spectators and contestants alike could enjoy the thrill of intense competition as well as the camaraderie, wagering, and giveaways that went along with it. As they made the transition to reservation life, many chose to participate in cattle ranching and to perform on horseback in local celebrations and county and state fairs, as well as tribal fairs, where they gained valuable experience in roping, riding, steer and calf wrestling, and performing that later served well those who went on to perform in Wild West shows and circuses. These skills became part of a cultural amalgam from which a rodeo culture developed. Plains Indian involvement in organized rodeos thus began with an acceptance of cattle ranching and an involvement in shows, both on and off the reservation.[4]

Indian Office commissioners and agents were ambivalent about their Indian charges' participation in cattle ranching and rodeo. Directed by a federal assimilationist policy in full force, Indian agents clearly preferred that American Indians dissolve their tribal ties and become independent yeoman farmers in the Jeffersonian tradition. Some agents encouraged Native ranching as an activity of acculturation, or at least they did so until white settlers became interested in northern Great Plains tribal grazing lands. Because the agents had no legal recourse to prevent Indian travel, and because they hoped that Indian participation in the horticultural competitions of off-reservation county fairs might inspire Indian agricultural efforts, some even tolerated the shows, although the events lured the northern Plain Indians away from their crops and newly assigned allotments.

By introducing a new event, the Indian industrial fair, Indian officials unintentionally provided Indians with one of their principal rodeo arenas and tribal meeting grounds. Indian Agent S. G. Reynolds inaugurated the first Indian fair on the Crow reservation in 1904 in an attempt to stem the disconcerting flow of off-reservation summer traffic while promoting his assimilationist agenda. By 1920, northern Plains Indians on the Crow, Northern Cheyenne, Pine Ridge, Rosebud, and Cheyenne River Sioux reservations in Montana and South Dakota had transformed these industrial fairs into Indian reunions. Indian participants focused less on the display of pumpkins, pigs, and pies that Indian officials expected and far more on equestrian competitions, which included horse races and rodeos. These contests provided opportunities for Plains Indian communities in transition to gather; to wager; to give away horses, cattle, and other gifts; to reaffirm the status of individual horsemen; and to retain certain elements of their own equestrian heritage.[5] These adaptations also allowed them to fashion an identity quite different from that which the federal authorities had sought to impose upon them. Anthropologists have described this convenient cross-cultural miscommunication, which Plains Indians used repeatedly to their advantage. Loretta Fowler explains that in the agents' view, "'progressive activities'—such as a ranching economy, an agricultural fair, allotment of reservation lands, and fluency in English—suggested a commitment to assimilation," but to Indians, "such activities offered the means to perpetuate cultural traditions and behavioral ideals."[6]

## INDIAN COWBOYS

As northern Plains Indians adapted to reservation life, horses remained an enduring symbol of power and hope. Native equestrian activities formed the roots from which northern Plains Indian cowboy and rodeo culture grew. In the closing decades of the nineteenth century, American Indians in the West realized their choices were narrowing. Because of this, the Crows chose to live at government-regulated Indian agencies, unlike the Northern Cheyennes and Lakotas who were forced to do so. The Crows began their new lives along the banks of the Little Bighorn River in 1884. For decades, the Crows (also known as the Absarokee) had resisted the territorial expansion of both non-Indians—by signing a "treaty of friendship" with the United States in 1825—and their Indian adversaries, by fighting the powerful Lakotas and the Northern Cheyennes to the east, the Blackfeet to the north, and the Arapahos to the south. Ultimately, disease and the destruction of the buffalo debilitated the Crows, making them vulnerable to their enemies and leading to their acceptance of reservation life.[7] Confined to reservations, the Crows, like their neighbors the Northern Cheyennes in southeastern Montana and the Lakotas in western South Dakota, defied Indian agents and "reformers" bent on their assimilation. From the economic options presented to them, all of which focused on agriculture, northern Plains Indian horsemen engaged most keenly in cattle ranching, which they recognized as both group and horse oriented.

In the 1830s and early 1840s, the Crows, led by Chief Long Hair, reached the height of their power, possessing more horses than any other tribe on the upper Missouri River.[8] But disaster hit in the 1840s and 1850s, as massive smallpox and cholera epidemics swept the northern Great Plains.[9] As the Crows weakened, so too did their capacity to defend their land. At its greatest extent, spanning vast areas of Wyoming, Montana, and parts of North and South Dakota, the Crows' beloved country began to slip away with the first Fort Laramie treaty, signed in 1851, which surrendered the Crow lands east of the Powder River.[10] The second Fort Laramie treaty, in 1868, further diminished Crow territory by reducing the tribe's holdings from 38 million to 8 million acres.[11] The result of this precipitous decline in Crow Indian numbers, strength, and land was that the tribe had little choice but to report to the first Crow Agency in 1870. Five years later the Crows moved to the second agency site.[12] These agencies acted primarily as autumn mountain trading and ration stations, as most Crows continued to follow buffalo and other game during the rest of the year.[13]

Because the great northern bison herd had virtually disappeared by the late nineteenth century, the Crows began to petition the federal government for cattle as an alternative food supply. With raids from neighboring Plains peoples continuing, a contingent of Crow leaders expressed a willingness to relocate to a permanent and protected settlement, one that would provide their people with adequate sustenance. In 1883–84, the Crow subsisted for fifty-two weeks on rations meant to last only seventeen weeks. Pleading the Crows' case to a Senate investigating committee led by Henry Dawes, Chief Iron Bull asserted that "all the buffalo and elk and deer are gone, and we have so little to eat that our children are starving. We want the Great Father to give us cattle, and we want cows that will have young ones, and we will put them at the foot of the mountains and along the creeks, and by the springs."[14] By the spring of 1884, the Indian Bureau had granted Iron Bull's request and had moved the Crow Agency headquarters permanently to the banks of the Little Bighorn River. When cattle were brought to the Crow reservation, the Crows

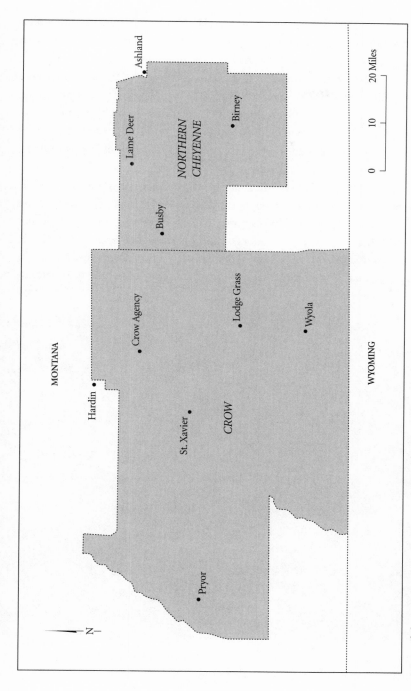

*Map of the Crow and Northern Cheyenne reservations.*

were expecting them. They were aware of Plenty Coups' 1857 vision in which
he foresaw the replacement of the buffalo by "spotted buffalo," or non-Indian
cattle. They also understood the message within Plenty Coups' revelation. If
each Crow cooperated with the non-Indians and accepted these "strange animals . . . after the Battle of the Four Winds he [would] still [hold] his home,
his country . . . and [know] there was safety for himself and his family."[15]

Out of desperation, many Crows sought, like Iron Bull, to become ranchers on their newly defined reservation. The Crows, like other Plains Indians,
soon realized that ranching was not only economically but also culturally
compatible with their way of life. It allowed for contact with one another, for
working with horses, and for being outdoors—and it was permitted by the
Bureau of Indian Affairs.[16] In response to the Crows' requests, the BIA distributed cattle to Crow band leaders within weeks of their arrival at the Little
Bighorn in 1884. From the 1880s on, the Crows remained actively involved in
both individual and communal ranching. Between 1898 and 1905, Indian

*Crow Indian cowboys on Crow reservation (Montana), circa 1890.*
Montana Historical Society, Helena (Photo #955-819).

*Crow Indian cowboys roping at the ranch on Crow reservation (Montana), circa 1890.*
Montana Historical Society, Helena (Photo #955-786).

agents reported that the Crows possessed approximately 4,000 tribally owned cattle. The Crows' ranching operations endured despite the competition presented by non-Indian stockmen on the reservation, who frequently rented the Crows' most productive grazing lands within the reservation boundaries.[17] To augment Crow cattle herds in 1914, the Indian Office purchased 7,000 two-year-old heifers, 2,000 yearling steers, and 550 bulls.[18] A year later, the *Oglala Light: For the Education and Civilization of the Sioux Indian* (a periodical published by the U.S. Indian School, Pine Ridge, South Dakota, to promote federal Indian policies) touted Crow cattle ranching efforts as "among the many accomplishments of the Indian Bureau during the last fiscal year." The article bragged that since the previous June, "the Crows had maintained 350 bulls in their tribal herd, with almost no losses during the winter. . . . The Crows own one of the finest white face herds in America."[19] The following year, Crow cattlemen shipped fifty-one carloads of cattle from their tribal herd to Omaha and Chicago to be sold at market. According to an *Oglala Light* reporter, "The stock business is handled by the Indians themselves. The annual roundup is

*Crow Indian police on horseback, 1892.*
Montana Historical Society, Helena (Photo #955-785).

conducted by the Indians, under the supervision, it is true, of the government agency officials." Commissioner of Indian Affairs Cato Sells supervised the sale and explained that the Crows had also cut and stacked seven thousand tons of hay to winter their herds.[20] So when the Canadian Pacific Railway screeched into southern Alberta in 1883 and allowed cattle ranching to become financially viable for the Indians surrounding Calgary, many Scarcee and Blood Indians eagerly took up cattle ranching to become cowboys both economically and culturally.[21]

Indian agents like Crow Superintendent Henry J. Armstrong preferred that Indians become individual farmers rather than communal cattle ranchers. Farming was more in line with assimilationist goals because it was essentially an independent enterprise that could be undertaken on relatively small plots of land. By contrast, cattle ranching necessitated that ranchers work in groups and on large tracts of land. While Indians were particularly attracted to these features, federal officials were not. Paternalistic Indian agents believed that Indians and whites alike would benefit from farming. They reasoned that as

*Canadian Indian cowboys on Bridges Ranch at Bull Head Lake (Alberta),
1906.*
Glenbow Museum, Art Gallery, Library, and Archives, Calgary (Photo #NA-5192-5).

Indians became farmers they would not only surrender their anachronistic
cultures—which only served to impede their becoming "civilized,"—but they
would also surrender a large portion of excess tribal lands, which white farmers and stockmen could cultivate. Following this logic, the federal government
designed the Dawes Severalty Act, or General Allotment Act, of 1887 to detribalize American Indians through individual land ownership. Modeled on the
Homestead Act of 1862, it authorized the president to allot 160 acres of reservation lands to each head of household. All remaining "surplus lands," that is,
tribal lands not allotted to Indians, could be sold or leased to non-Indians.
Eventually Indians were allowed, and even encouraged, to lease their allotted
lands to non-Indians.

By dismantling tribal land bases through the sale and lease of reservation
lands, the Dawes Act undermined, but did not end, northern Plains Indian
cattle ranching efforts. Officials began surveying Crow reservation lands in

the 1890s so land allotments could be distributed. By 1896, Crow families occupied 509 separate farms throughout the reservation.[22] As more non-Indians began to settle in Montana in the early decades of the twentieth century, the Bureau of Indian Affairs applied increased pressure to each Crow male head of household to select a 160-acre plot of land on which he and his family could cultivate crops, raise cattle, and perhaps establish a garden and a home.[23] Not all northern Plains Indians became yeoman farmers as a result of the Dawes act, but they did lose vast tracts of their tribal lands. This was certainly true for the Crows, whose collectively owned tribal lands were reduced from 3.4 million acres to less than 2 million acres between 1890 and 1920. In 1904 alone, 1.1 million acres were sold to non-Indians. By 1920, non-Indian stockmen had claimed virtually all of the tribe's remaining unallotted lands under BIA-approved leases.[24]

Indian agents also encouraged individuals to lease or sell their land, with the result that individually owned tracts of land were also passing out of Indian ownership. Frederick Hoxie explains the actions of Indian Office officials by observing a shift in the federal assimilationist policy. According to Hoxie, after 1890 Indian agents had become less interested in preparing Indians for full-fledged membership in mainstream American society and had become more convinced that Indians should remain society's dependents, operating as laborers on the periphery of the economy.[25] Accordingly, Commissioner Francis E. Luepp's 1908 report states that "employment has been obtained for Indians on ranches, farms and railroads. . . . Such steady employment as wage earners . . . outside of the reservation not only brings the Indians monetary returns . . . but also develops self reliance."[26] Indian officials, motivated by this belief and the enduring desire to make the Indians into independent individuals, convinced tribal members to lease or sell their lands and divert tribal funds to "community expenses," including those of education and irrigation. On the Crow reservation as elsewhere, Crow tribal lands were "being turned into cash. Rather than being a proving ground for tribal members or a testing ground for tribal entrepreneurs, Crow country was generating dollars for individual survival."[27] As the Crows leased their grazing

◄ *Scarcee Indian boys,* left to right: *Anthony Dodging Horse, George Big Plume, Frank One Spot, Pat Dodging Horse; circa 1912.*
Photo by Brewer Studio. Glenbow Museum, Art Gallery, Library, and Archives, Calgary (Photo #NA-4951-1).

lands to non-Indian stockmen, their own cattle ranching efforts suffered. By 1922, the tribal herd was nearly gone. During this period, some Crows managed to acquire individually owned herds, which they grazed on their small ranches.[28]

Lakota cattle ranching efforts on the Pine Ridge and Cheyenne River Sioux reservations followed a similar pattern. In the aftermath of the Sioux Agreement of 1889, the Great Sioux reservation was diminished, and six reservations were created. Historian Herbert T. Hoover states that "the Sioux Agreement of 2 March 1889 reduced the reservation by 9,274,668.7 acres, leaving to the Teton and Yanktonai tribes only 12,681,911 acres within the boundaries of the Cheyenne River, Crow Creek, Lower Brule, Pine Ridge, Rosebud, and Standing Rock reservations."[29] Following their permanent settlement on the Pine Ridge reservation and the tragedy of Wounded Knee in 1890, Oglala Lakotas adopted stock raising as a more sensible alternative to farming. Initially, Agent Charles G. Penney pushed for cattle ranching on a tribally owned land base. The Pine Ridge Sioux cattle herd grew from 19,000 head in 1901 to 31,000 in 1902. For the first time, in 1907, the Indian Department issued cattle to the tribe as a whole. More than 6,000 head of cattle and 160 bulls were delivered.[30] Lakota cattle interests declined throughout the 1910s, however. One reason for the decline was that Oglala Lakotas had made efforts to limit the size of the non-Indian herds in the early part of the decade. As one observer explained in 1905, "A few years ago, as a result of the complaint of some Indians, an order issued by the Department [imposed] a tax of one dollar a head on all individual herds greater than one hundred. This was on account of the large holding of squaw men (white men married to Indian women) and mixed bloods. The full-bloods soon found that the order affected their cattle as well, and since then their herds have decreased."[31] Another reason for the decline was that in response to pressure from local ranchers, federal agents continued to approve the leasing of reservation grazing lands. By 1917, outside companies run by H. A. Dawson, Will S. Hughes, John Glover, and others had taken control of the lands. John Glover, foreman of the Quarter 71 outfit of the Newcastle Land and Livestock Company, eventually acquired 500,000 acres of lease land at Pine Ridge. In 1920, Glover Ranch leased in Porcupine Creek, the center of Pine Ridge.[32] Even as their tribal cattle raising

◄ *Chief Big Belly and Jack Waters, Scarcee Indians, 1919.*
Glenbow Museum, Art Gallery, Library, and Archives, Calgary (Photo #NA-4951-6).

efforts waned, many Lakotas remained active as cowboys working on non-Indian ranches on their own reservation lands.

After 1889, the various bands of Lakotas that settled on the Cheyenne River Sioux reservation forged a new collective identity as Cheyenne River Sioux. For many this new identity came to include a sense of themselves as cowboys. Originally, existing bands settled together, but allotment in 1900 forced the Lakota population to disperse across the reservation. Consequently, the Blackfeet, Sans Arc, Minneconjou, and Two Kettles bands of Lakota that had settled on the reservation came to consider themselves as part of something new, the Cheyenne River Sioux Tribe. Like other northern Plains peoples, the Cheyenne River Sioux participated in certain government-sponsored pursuits such as cattle ranching, which served the interests of the group. In the 1890s, the Indian Office stationed white district farmers in each district to monitor farming and cattle ranching. Initially the Lakotas were successful, selling 500,000 pounds of their cattle to the agency for rations in 1890, and double that amount in 1899. But the 60 percent rise in the non-Indian population in South Dakota over the next ten years, combined with the initiation of allotment in 1900, opened the reservation and its grazing lands to outsiders. By this time, many Lakotas had already begun to forge a new Indian identity as both Cheyenne River Sioux and cattle ranchers, because they chose to keep working as cowboys on both remaining tribal and recently sold non-Indian ranches.[33]

## NORTHERN PLAINS INDIANS IN WILD WEST SHOWS, FAIRS, AND RODEOS

As cattle ranchers, Crows and Lakotas learned skills that became part of the cultural mixture from which a rodeo culture developed. Like many Plains Indians, they adopted cattle ranching and rodeo in the final decades of the nineteenth century, yet Indian Bureau officials treated Plains Indian participation in ranching and rodeo with ambivalence. Native stock raising was initially supported but later subtly discouraged, as white cattlemen increasingly populated the Plains. Likewise, rodeos were both tolerated and scorned by bureau officials. Indian agents supported rodeos in the hopes that they would distract American Indians from antiquated and heathenish ceremonial gatherings like the Sun Dance, while they perpetuated the more appropriate image of Indians as cattle ranchers making productive use of the land. But

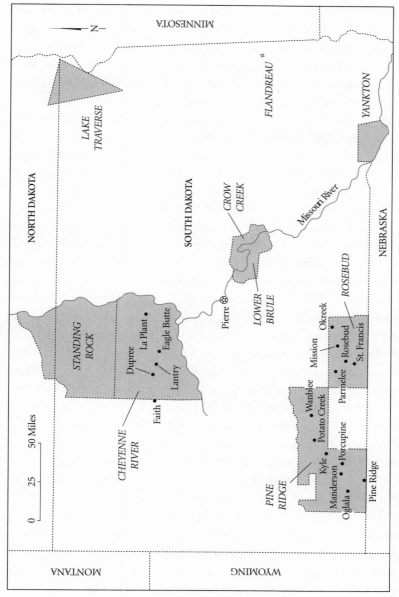

*Map of the Pine Ridge, Rosebud, and Cheyenne River reservations.*

the Indian Bureau bristled at the notion of Indians neglecting their reservation homesteads and crops for prolonged periods of time to perform in successive rodeos that took place at Wild West shows and state and county fairs throughout the summer months. Despite their disapproval, most commissioners of Indian affairs and Indian agents allowed Indian travel in accordance with the Standing Bear decision of 1879, which gave all peaceable Indians the right to come and go from their reservations as they so desired.[34]

Many northern Plains Indian cowboys first performed alongside white cowboys in Wild West shows, professional rodeos, local celebrations, and county and state fairs. Rodeo activities first appeared on agency cattle ranches as ways for Indian cowboys to amuse themselves, just as non-Indian cowboys had joined in cowboy sports to pass the time on cattle drives.[35] It was not until July 4, 1882, when William F. Cody brought cowboy games to the stage in his Wild West show that city folks got their first glimpse of the rodeo.[36] As anthropologist Elizabeth Atwood Lawrence explains, rodeo is both a sports contest and a performance. The origins of the sport lie in earlier cowboy competitions on the range, and the performance element of rodeo can be attributed to Buffalo Bill Cody's Wild West Show. Cody's historic reenactments—such as "Cowboy Fun" (which included steer wrestling, roping, riding bucking broncos, a Pony Express ride, horsemanship demonstrations, buffalo hunts, and "Custer's Last Stand")—were all precursors of modern rodeo activities.[37] Many who participated in these Wild West rodeo shows were white cowboys seasonally out of work, yet they could not have staged these scenes without their counterparts, the Indian horsemen. The program for Buffalo Bill's 1883 Wild West Show records that Pawnee, Wichita, and Sioux Indians took part in the show's premier performance a year earlier.[38] Cody eventually employed more northern than southern Plains Indian horsemen, as the former were nationally renowned as prototypical buffalo hunters and warriors.[39]

In Wild West shows, the Indians performed in ways that conformed to the cultural assumptions of white audiences, namely that Indians were a colorful feature of the fading landscape of the Old West. For the "show Indians" like the Lakotas, the shows let them claim their cultural independence by offering opportunities to travel, wear traditional clothing, ride horses, and defeat Custer night after night.[40] Either way, reformers and Indian officials viewed Wild West shows as denigrating activities that perpetuated the image of savage Indians. In October 1890 Commissioner Thomas Jefferson Morgan issued a ban on Indian employment. He advised Indian agents to "impress upon the

Indians the importance of remaining at home . . . establishing comfortable homes, cultivating farms, building houses, and acquiring thrifty, industrious habits."[41] Abiding by this policy, in 1902 the U.S. Indian agent at Crow Agency, Samuel G. Reynolds, advised another agent, W. H. Smead, that "the Department objects to Indians leaving the reservation for show purposes." Reynolds suggested that Smead could make arrangements with the Crow performers, White Swan and Curley, to petition the Indian Office directly.[42] Morgan's successor, Commissioner William A. Jones, continued to oppose Indians appearing in Wild West shows, but like Morgan he was powerless to stop them. Francis Luepp, commissioner of Indian affairs from 1905 to 1909, maintained the assimilationist posture but was more pragmatic, admonishing Indian agents to exercise some paternalism and require employers to leave cash deposits. Still, Indian Office employees complained that participation in Wild West shows "breeds laziness. . . . They ought to be doing something instead of making an exhibition of themselves."[43]

Despite the grumbling of Indian Bureau officials, the years 1900–1917 marked the heyday of Wild West shows.[44] Plains Indians remained eager to perform. Many viewed these tours as opportunities to dress in traditional clothing, leave their reservations, see the world, and make money.[45] When a troop returned in 1909 from a summer spent performing at Earl's Court in London, the *Oglala Light* noted that "all Indians have reported that they had a very pleasant trip, and that the exhibition was successful from a financial standpoint."[46] Attitudes toward the shows had changed so much that by the time Cato Sells became commissioner of Indian affairs in 1913, he assumed Indians would be employed by Wild West shows.[47] More Oglala Lakotas from Pine Ridge traveled with Cody's Wild West Show than Indians from any other group. Audiences throughout America and Europe were intrigued by the Lakotas' exploits in the Powder River war of the late 1860s and the Battle of Little Bighorn in 1876, and flocked to Wild West shows to see these battles reenacted.[48] In 1911, 230 Oglalas joined five different shows in five different corners of the world in what one observer termed "the Wild West exodus."[49] Lakota showmen also traveled with The American Wild West Show in Brussels in 1910; Bud Atkin's Circus and Wild West Show in 1912; Young Buffalo Bill's Wild West Show in 1914; Miller Brother's 101 Ranch Wild West Show in 1911, 1912, 1915, and 1916; Robinson's Famous Shows in 1915; and Sells-Floto Circus in 1916.[50] The death of Buffalo Bill Cody in 1917 and the entry of the United States into World War I in the same year marked the decline of Wild

West shows and Indian involvement in them.[51] Those remaining Wild West shows shifted their emphasis from historical tableaux to rodeo features. Shows such as Texicole-Charley's Troupe of Wild West Performers and the Sells-Floto Circus "wanted Indians who could perform as fancy ropers and bronco riders."[52]

Before 1920, northern Plains Indians were also making some notable appearances in professional rodeos. As Kristine Fredrikson observes in *American Rodeo: From Buffalo Bill to Big Business*, in the first few decades of the twentieth century, rodeo began to divorce itself from the "circus and carnival elements of the touring wild-west shows, where the cowboys' roping and riding exhibitions had been only one small part of many and varied acts by military drill teams, Bedouins and Cossacks, snake swallowers, and the like."[53] Although the Rodeo Association of America, the nation's first rodeo association, was not established until January 1929, many Indian cowboys were competing alongside white cowboys in increasingly professional rodeos.[54] George Defender was an accomplished Lakota bronc rider whose riding triumphs led him to be described as "a cowboy who straddled the hurricane deck of many an outlaw without pulling leather." When he was sixteen years old and working for the DZ Cattle Company on the Standing Rock reservation, he began to gain fame. He won "first money" at the Miles City Roundup in 1914 and went on to compete in "all the big time events—Calgary to Madison Square Garden. Most agree that he was the greatest rider of all time."[55] Defender's contemporary David Blue Thunder was another wildly successful Lakota bronc rider.[56]

At the turn of the century, two of the most noteworthy rodeo cowboys in the northern Great Plains and Canada were Indians. Jackson Sundown and Tom Three Persons, both legendary Indian rodeo cowboys, won their early fame in non-Indian rodeos. Sundown, a Nez Percé, grew up competing in area rodeos in the early 1900s. Of his most memorable bull rides, one took place in 1912, at Grangeville Border Days, and the other in 1916, when he earned the world bronc riding championship in Lewiston, Idaho.[57] Likewise, Tom Three Persons, from the Cardston Blood Reserve in Alberta, won the World's Bronc Riding Title on September 5, 1912, in the Calgary Stampede's first year.[58] He bucked his way to legendary cowboy status by taming the notorious Cyclone. The yarn told by old-timers claims that the outlaw bronco Cyclone "had bucked off nearly 2,000 cowboys and had never been ridden. That is, until Three Persons stayed on him that day."[59] At that moment, the six-foot-two-inch Blood Indian, wearing a bright scarf and red angora chaps, "rode into a niche in the hearts of westerners who will remember him as long as cattle graze in the foothills and cowboys ride after them."[60] On that final day of the 1912 Calgary Stampede, Indian spectators "galloped their ponies . . . chanting and whooping loudly."[61] Tom Three Persons proved to them that rodeo was not just for non-Indian cowboys and that they too could successfully compete in any rodeo event they chose to enter. In effect, he inspired the Indians of Alberta, Canada, to develop their skills as rodeo cowboys and eventually to organize their own rodeos.[62]

Cheyenne Frontier Days, the "Daddy of 'Em All" that began in 1897 in Cheyenne, Wyoming, was another early rodeo in which American Indians were a major presence. Shoshone and Arapaho Indians from the Wind River Reservation in Wyoming and Lakotas from Pine Ridge and the Lower Brule Sioux reservations in South Dakota appeared in the grand entry parade and danced "at each rodeo and night arena show, at the chuck wagon breakfasts . . . and early in the evenings in downtown Cheyenne."[63] They also took part in regularly scheduled horse racing events such as the Indian pony race, which first appeared in 1900 and which was still on the program in 1938.[64] Further evidence of Plains Indians participating in Cheyenne Frontier Days is the captions of photographs in the September 6, 1905, edition of the *Wyoming Tribune*, which read "Sioux Chief: Stunts with the 'Rope'" and "A Sioux Warrior . . . Holding a Steer."[65] In 1910, Frank Goings and thirty Lakotas from Pine Ridge "with a carload of horses, left on August 20th for Cheyenne, Wyoming. They appear, as an attraction, at the Frontier Day Celebration."[66] It is likely that they rodeoed in addition to dancing and parading. A year later, experienced Oglala Lakotas traveled beyond the Great Plains to compete in The Cowboy Tournament in Denver, Colorado.[67]

As rodeos became more popular in the 1920s, Native participation in them also increased. Lakota and Crow communities regularly attended off-reservation county and state fairs, as well as reservation celebrations of U.S. government–approved national holidays. Fair associations realized it was profitable to feature Indians.[68] After 1910 Indian agents supported the opportunity for Indian farmers and stock growers to exhibit their agricultural prowess yet continued to scoff at the travel it involved. Plains Indians valued these new events as opportunities to gather and compete in rodeos and horse races with their own communities and with non-Indian contestants. On their reservations, they transformed government-sanctioned celebrations, staged in honor

*Tom Three Persons with admiring child at first Calgary Stampede, 1912.*
Glenbow Museum, Art Gallery, Library, and Archives, Calgary (Photo #NA-1137).

*Four old-timers, left to right: Roy McMakin, George Defender, Turkey Track Bill, and Fred Forman at the McLaughlin, South Dakota, Indian Fair, 1928.*

State Historical Society of North Dakota (Fiske 4286).

*Jackson Sundown, champion rider, at Lewiston Roundup.*
Montana Historical Society, Helena (Photo #PAC78-72 f32).

*Jackson Sundown on bucking horse.*
Montana Historical Society, Helena (Photo #PAC78-72 f32).

of American national holidays, into reunions. It is ironic that the Lakotas, who decades earlier had fought and lost battles for their own freedom, would celebrate America's Independence Day. But they utilized these celebrations— as they had the Wild West shows, rodeos, and county and state fairs—as valuable occasions for camaraderie and equestrian competition. For example, in 1897, a bronc ride concluded a six-day Fourth of July celebration on the Rosebud reservation.[69] Similarly, in 1905, a Fourth of July celebration took place near Pine Ridge.[70] Four years later, Lakota cowboys from the Wakpamni, White Clay, Wounded Knee, and Porcupine Districts celebrated Independence Day.[71]

On the Cheyenne River Sioux reservation, Indian cowboys competed annually on the Fourth of July against the non-Indian cowboys of the towns of Faith and Dupree, South Dakota. In 1910, Indians from Cherry Creek, Thunder Butte, Standing Rock, and Pine Ridge attended an Independence

*California Roundup, San Jose. Jackson Sundown in center.*
Montana Historical Society, Helena (Photo #PAC78-72 f32).

Day celebration in Dupree. There, Blue Arm's horse won the horse race. On the Fourth, a group of Indians, many of them cowboys themselves, and some two hundred cowboys enacted a sham battle. The Lakotas came "in spite of the stand the agent took against Dupree, and the bad men of Dupree, as he calls them."[72] One hundred Sioux warriors also performed as dancers in the Fourth of July celebration in Faith in 1910, where "Bronco Busting, Horse Racing and Ropeing [*sic*] Contests" were part of the day's events.[73] Lakotas from the Cheyenne River Sioux reservation also took part in an "Eagle Butte Fete," where "visitors found a broncho busting exhibition in full swing. Old time cattle men in the crowd of spectators said they never saw a better performance."[74] Dupree's Fourth of July celebration once again attracted crowds of homesteaders and Indians in 1911. After bareback riding and roping contests, One Horn and Iron Hawk raced against Peter First Eagle and Chase-an-Eagle to kill and dress the steers. William Ewing and John Iron Hawk won the

"Indian horse race."[75] In 1916, the Cheyenne River Sioux Indians hosted a Fourth of July celebration at the Thunder Butte Substation that was attended by non-Indians and Indians from various reservations. Horse racing, bronco riding, and roping were the main attractions, but the rope-pulling between the Indians and the whites was also memorable.[76] "Broncho riding" and fancy rope twirling were also a part of a 1919 Dupree homecoming celebration for veterans of World War I.[77] Then in 1920, the Preharvest Day Celebration in Dupree promised a "bucking broncho contest" and a "tug-of-war: Indian vs. White Men."[78] Indian agents approved of such friendly rivalries, in which Indians appeared to be forging relationships with the surrounding white community. They hoped that such contact would encourage Indians to emulate non-Indians and abandon their Indian identities.

As long as they were allowed to get together and compete, northern Plains Indians continued to participate in settings that local non-Indians and Indian agents viewed as innocuous. Likewise, the Crows seized opportunities to gather for horse races and rodeos at summer celebrations and fairs in the Montana towns of Hardin, Billings, Miles City, Bridger, Forsyth, and Powell and in the Wyoming towns of Sheridan and Cody.[79] Paternalistic Indian agents approved of such events only if they believed that Indians, by competing principally in agricultural contests, would be projecting the image of peoples in the process of rapid acculturation. If they feared that Indians would behave otherwise—by appearing exclusively in parades, tepee encampments, and horse races—they objected. Indians were forced to justify their social activities to their agents. In 1898, E. H. Becker, the Indian agent at Crow Agency, wanted to send a large delegation of Crow Indians living on Pryor and Little Bighorn to the Billings Fair, which he also referred to as "your annual race meet at Billings." But he feared that "if I permitted a large number of Indians to go to Billings next week . . . making a general exhibition of themselves . . . the Commissioner would get me up on the carpet."[80] Originally, S. J. Reynolds was amenable to sending Plenty Coups, Bell Rock, and other Crows from Pryor to the Billings Fair in 1902 to "have a good time."[81] Even on the first year of the Crow Fair, Reynolds wrote Van Hoose at Pryor, saying, "The people of Billings count on the Indians as making the attractions for their fair and I presume it will be best to arrange to let your people go over. I do not see how they can attend that fair and have time to get over to this one."[82] But by 1906 Agent Reynolds was discouraging travel to fairs. His clerk denied a request in his stead, stating, "The Crows would have a fair of their own this year and . . . if the Indians went to Bridger-Forsyth-Sheridan-Billings . . . they would not have time to look after harvesting, threshing, haying . . . and he would not allow them to go to any of the fairs."[83] Like the Lakotas, the Crows were invited to non-Indian Fourth of July celebrations. In 1907, Reynolds refused C. J. Burt's request to have the Crows participate in the latter's Belfry, Montana, event. Reynolds responded: "They will suitably observe the day at home and be there for work on the fifth, we hope."[84] A year later Crows were given permission to attend Sheridan, Wyoming's, Fourth of July festivities involving rodeo. In 1909, however, Reynolds again denied permission, reiterating his earlier sentiment that "it means no crops and a world of damage to them" in that travel "upsets . . . a program of work."[85]

After 1910, however, Crow and Lakota Indian agents began to recognize the benefits of county and state fairs. By 1915, the Indian Office was encouraging the presence of Indians at county fairs. Commissioner of Indian Affairs Cato Sells believed the fairs offered certain advantages over exclusively Indian fairs, which he correctly observed reinforced a distinctive Indian identity "from a racial standpoint—rather than their community of interests with the whites.'"[86] The entire Crow nation was invited to the 1913 Big Horn County Fair in Hardin, a town that borders the reservation. A large group of Crows attended the fair, which "showed up the possibilities of Big Horn County in an agricultural way." Crow horsemen and -women—including Sam Horn, Clark Utterbull, Yellow Brow, Ties His Knee, and Little Owl—placed near the top in horse races and bucking bronco contests.[87] Organizers of local county fairs and rodeos encouraged the Crows' presence: Plains Indians donning headdresses and riding buffaloes served as tourist attractions.[88] At the Miles City Roundup in 1915, Sampson Bird-in-Ground was the first Crow to ride a buffalo. Nevertheless, many Indian agents remained skeptical about the benefits of Indians attending off-reservation county fairs. For example, the acting superintendent of the Cheyenne River Sioux reservation disapproved of Lakotas traveling to the county fair in Faith, "especially in view of the fact that there is always more or less liquor sold to Indians on occasions of this kind at this town."[89]

Lakotas entered the South Dakota State Fair in Huron, South Dakota, for the first time in 1915. Commissioner Sells appreciated that the Indians would be exhibiting "Indian agricultural products rather than the Indians themselves."[90] From 1918 to 1921, Crows, including Max Big Man, Arnold Costa, and Barney Old Coyote continued to attend state fairs in Helena and

*Crow Indian riding buffalo at Miles City Roundup, 1915.*
Montana Historical Society, Helena (Photo #PAC84-1).

Billings.[91] These state fairs often included "the riding of bucking steers and the skillful roping of ferocious outlaw horses."[92]

## CROW, LAKOTA, AND
## CANADIAN INDIAN FAIRS AND RODEOS

During the period when Indians were actively participating in off-reservation events, the Indian Office attempted to develop Indian industrial fairs as a substitute for county and state fairs. In so doing, they unwittingly provided a forum for Indians to maintain and foster intratribal and intertribal ties to one another and to the horse-oriented life they loved, particularly at the rodeo.[93] The Indian Office also established 4-H clubs, Farm Clubs, Farmer's Institutes, and Five-Year Agricultural Plans.[94] Many of these 4-H clubs would form the membership basis for rodeo associations. Commissioner of Indian Affairs

*Jim Wade riding a wild buffalo, Central South Dakota Roundup, 1928.*
State Historical Society of North Dakota (Fiske 4268).

Francis Luepp and others envisioned tribal fairs as a means to foster agricultural competition and enthusiasm among the Indians, while keeping them
close to home. The commissioner's report in 1905 explained: "As a further
incentive, it would be well to arrange district fairs, and give prizes for the neat-
est and best kept homes, for the best crops: for poultry, stock, etc."[95] The tribal
fair movement spread after 1904. Crow Fair, the first Indian fair, was held in
1904; the Navajo fair was second in 1909.[96] By 1911, fairs were held on fourteen
reservations, and by 1917 fifty-eight were active.[97]

By 1914 Indian agents had become concerned that Indians might use these
industrial fairs to celebrate their Indian identity. To prevent this, Cato Sells,
who was commissioner of Indian affairs in 1914, attempted to control the
fairs' content and administration. He issued an order to eliminate dancing,
horse racing, and sham battles. He also dictated that large reservations should
hold their fairs during the same week to halt the practice of Indians visiting
one fair after another while neglecting their crops and livestock. Fairs were
also to be financed locally through ticket sales at the gate and grandstands,
through concessions sales, and through cash donations given by local non-
Indian communities.[98] It was too late to halt this trend on the Crow reservation, where the Crows remade Crow Fair into a tribal celebration almost
immediately. S. G. Reynolds, Crow superintendent from 1902 to 1910, proposed the Crow Fair in 1904 to promote Crow Indian agriculture, livestock
raising, and homemaking endeavors. In his words, he expected the Crow
industrial fair "to help elevate and encourage the Indians in industrial
work."[99] Reynolds hoped to encourage "emulation, friendly rivalry and competition," among the Crows by granting "attractive ribbon badges . . . with the
word 'Exhibitor' on them."[100]

Although there were no industrial exhibits that first year, in future years
agents covered the reservation with premium lists. In succeeding years,
exhibits were "astonishing in number and quality."[101] The ethnocentrism of
the events was glaringly apparent, as Crows were rewarded for complying
with the assimilationist agenda. Blue ribbons and monetary prizes were given
for "District making best display of farm products," "Biggest pumpkin," "Best
work team," "Indian making best display of pigs," "Indian woman having nicest
kept teepee," and "Indian woman having the best meal and table cooked and
set for four."[102] As the fair grew, so too did its grounds, from its beginnings as
a large tent on forty acres of reserved land at the agency, a mile from Little
Bighorn Battlefield, to a complex five years later that included an agricultural

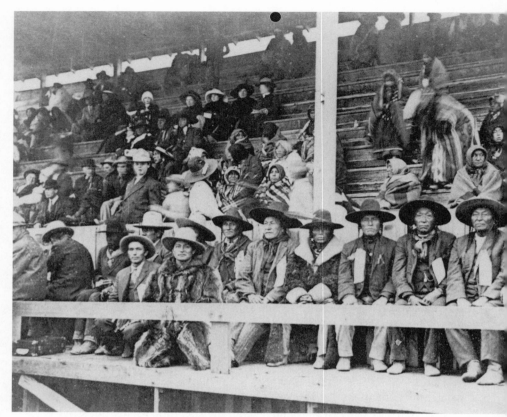

*Crow Fair Indian Rodeo, early 1900s.* Left to right beginning with the man who is wearing a fur coat and kneeling in the front row: *Jim Hill, unidentified, Jim Big Shoulder, Medicine Crow Sits Down Spotted, Bird Hat, Packs The Hat, unidentified.* Second woman left of pole: *Mrs. Iron Horse.*
Photo collection of Dennis L. Sanders. Hardin Photo Service, Hardin, Montana (Photo #898).

hall for farming and industrial exhibits, a barn for livestock and poultry, another barn for horses, a grandstand seating eight hundred people, and a half-mile racetrack for horse racing.[103] For the celebration to continue with the rodeo events and horse races they liked, the Crows had recognized that they also had to show ostensible interest in setting tables for four and parading their pigs and pumpkins.

In line with the Indian Bureau's objective to "civilize" Indians, Reynolds wanted the fair to provide the Crows with business as well as agricultural

*Rodeo grandstand, possibly Crow Fair, early 1900s.*
Montana Historical Society, Helena (Photo #PAC84-1).

experience. At the end of each fair, the Indian Fair Association for the next year was organized, and officers were elected by all the Crows, while the members of each district selected a district committee of three members.[104] The Crows did manage the fair, "selling tickets, collecting license privileges, paying bills and premiums, fixing grounds, keeping up buildings, arranging exhibits, awarding prizes, running refreshment stands and lunch counters."[105] In 1912, Reynolds mysteriously declared that "the Indians are quite successful in the management of the program, but we have found it necessary to have a representative of the Office take charge of the finances."[106] Reynolds believed the greatest accomplishments of the Crow Fair were the discontinuance of rations and the decrease in "wandering" off the reservation.[107] After all, Reynolds had intended the Crow Fair to give the Crows "the opportunity of coming together and enjoying themselves, thus taking the place of those detrimental gatherings . . . [such as] the habit of going in body to the adjoining towns whenever there happened to be a fair, circus, Fourth of July celebration, or other public gathering."[108]

Most importantly, as Reynolds declared, the Crow Fair was "by and for the Crow Indians. It is their week—the only time that they come together in a general body."[109] This type of reunion tapped into an established Crow tradition of communal gatherings dating back to pre-reservation and early agency days, when, as Crow oral historian Laurence Flatlip asserted, antecedents to the Crow Fair had taken place. He explained, "When my great grandmother was alive and her mother was still there [in Butte, Montana], some of the times that the gathering was there, these different bands would come together. That's what Crow Fair is about. Sometimes they would gather and when my great grandmother was about three or four years old they taught her the stories that she knows of the gathering being at Three Forks or Bozeman."[110] Another Crow, Eloise White Bear Pease, born in 1918, told a similar story of a rendezvous of Mountain and River Crow and Kicked-in-their-Bellies that took place at the black rocks at the mouth of a canyon upstream of the Yellowstone River. She explained that the Crows met there to see new grandchildren and young people who got married during the year. Her two uncles, Joseph and Tyrone Ten Bear, told her of a similar meeting that took place in the fall when the Crow finished hunting at Three Forks. Eloise White Bear Pease related that the Crow were then forced to split apart into small groups as many people began to contract smallpox.[111] Gatherings of Crows— such as those in Butte, Three Forks, and Bozeman—included "horse racing, the riding of broncs, arrow flying, bows and arrows, and family reunions."[112] Thus Flatlip maintains that "those are the original Crow Fair. The only difference is it wasn't called Crow Fair. It was a Crow gathering, but it is still considered what we now call Crow Fair. It was still that. The only thing they added was the word fair."[113]

The Indian Bureau had changed the name but not the essence of these summer gatherings. To many Crows, affixing the English word *fair* to an essentially Indian gathering seemed a logical step in a series of adaptations and inclusions, among them horses, cattle, rodeos, and now Indian "fairs." Under the leadership of Plenty Coups, Medicine Crow, Curley, and others, the Crows transformed Crow Fair into a vehicle for maintaining unity by reinventing and reestablishing a common culture centered on horsemanship at a time when numbers of people, extent of their land, and amount of contact with one another were all declining.[114] Between 1880 and 1920, the Crow population reached its nadir. Infectious diseases had decimated Crow Indians, especially young adult women, who died in disproportionate numbers, either of tuberculosis or in childbirth. To compound this loss of numbers was the further forfeiture of territory to the federal government in 1882, 1890, and 1904.[115] During this transitional period, the Crows dispersed throughout the reservation and settled either along Pryor Creek or near the Little Bighorn or Bighorn Valleys. These areas became the three major divisions of the Crow reservation. The reservation was further subdivided into six districts: Loyola, Lodge Grass, Reno, Black Lodge, Bighorn, and Pryor. As the Crows scattered and settled according to former buffalo hunting band status and clan membership, and as their land base and population diminished, the prospect of a communal gathering became attractive to them. Responding to this need, the Crows enthusiastically attended Crow Fair, which successfully united all of the districts with the exception of Pryor and Lodge Grass, which held their 1911 and 1912 fairs separately.[116]

The Crows wasted no time adding horse races and "riding bucking broncs," along with parades, dances, and giveaways, to their Crow Fair program.[117] Since the first Crow Fair in 1904, the agricultural exhibits had been the intended centerpieces of the fair, but as early as 1912 Superintendent W. W. Scott complained that "the intense interest taken by the Indians in their horse racing and dances . . . overshadows that of the agricultural exhibits."[118] The inclusion of racetrack and rodeo events made Crow Fair an increasingly popular and significant presence on the reservation. The rodeo provided an opportunity for competitors to test their skills as equestrians and cowboys on "nothing but stock owned by the Indians."[119] For Crow spectators, it afforded an opportunity to gather and wager. According to Thomas Bull over Hill, a Crow who was eighty-six years old when interviewed in 1987, "Crow Fair came with a rodeo. In the beginning, there were no chutes; the riders would mount the rodeo animals right in front of the judge's stand."[120] A local writer corroborated this statement when describing the 1905 Crow Fair. She recalled that "the relay races were particularly enjoyable, and the crowd went wild over the bucking bronc riding."[121] The 1907 Crow Indian Fair Program listed events such as "riding bucking broncs, free for all," "two mile pony race, Indian stock," and "two mile relay race, cowboys, by districts." The monetary prizes for these events ranged from five dollars for winning the bucking bronc ride to fifteen dollars for winning the district relay races.[122] By 1908 the Northern Cheyennes, the Crows' rivals in pre-reservation days, were their featured guests and participated in the horse racing.[123]

As Crows cultivated such intertribal affiliations, they also encouraged a non-Indian presence, which pleased their Indian agents and ensured the fair's continuance. The Crows were aware that they needed the approval of the Indian Office and the ticket receipts of local whites to maintain their gathering. As public interest grew in 1909, a large crowd from Billings, including seven hundred students, was entertained by a sham battle put on by Crow horsemen.[124] Max Big Man, seasoned by state fair experience, impressed the crowds at the 1913 Crow Fair, as he "gave an exhibit of fancy rope whirling." The last race of the afternoon that year was the "two mile relay race in which the riders changed horses each half mile, the rider roping and saddling his own horse." Elmer Takes Wrinkle won money, while James Big Shoulder and Alfonsus Child came in second and third.[125] An advertisement for the 1915 Crow Fair boasted, "Every afternoon there will be races of every description and the Indians will ride bucking bronchos and perform various feats of horsemanship and roping."[126] A reporter for the *Hardin Tribune* observed that some two thousand spectators attended Crow Fair in 1917, many of whom enjoyed the "rough riding" events.[127] The 1918 Thirteenth Annual Crow Fair Program and Premium List included a "bucking contest" and a "two mile relay race, change horse in corral" on the schedule for Friday afternoon. Prizes ranged from five dollars to twenty-five dollars for these events.[128] What made the rodeo at Crow Fair more thrilling was unique events performed up to the 1930s. The events included contests such as goat (instead of calf) roping in which Milton Yellow Mule and Clifford Singer were successful and the difficult feat of Roman riding—riding atop four horses, straddling the inside two—expertly performed by Sam Horn of Lodge Grass and Francis Leforge of Wyola.[129] In later decades, Crows participated in these events less frequently, but in the early years, they helped establish Crow Fair's rodeo as a distinctive event that appealed to both Indians and whites.

Following Tom Three Persons's phenomenal bronc ride at the first Calgary Stampede in 1912, all-Indian rodeos were often included in Canadian Indian fairs. Most of these Canadian Indian rodeos were organized in small towns like Lethbridge, Cardston, Gleichen, Fort Macleod, and Glenwood. As Glen Mikkelson relates, "A few were just country picnics combined with rodeo events. They served the function of community gatherings where people could socialize, make business deals, and catch up on the latest gossip."[130]

Like Crow Fair, Banff Indian Days was introduced by whites but was transformed by Canadian Indians into an Indian event. Banff Indian Days began in 1889 as a form of entertainment for guests at the Banff Springs Hotel when the Canadian Pacific Railway line through the Rockies was, as the story goes, knocked out by a torrential downpour. The original participants were Morley Stoney Indians. In a couple of years, Stoney from the North Saskatchewan River, Kootenay from the Columbia Valley, and Scarcee from near Calgary joined Banff Indian Days, and the grounds were moved to the flats near Minnehappa, the waterfall near Banff at the foot of the Cascade Mountains. Eventually added to the program—then consisting of horse races, foot races, tug-of-war, dancing, singing, and parades—was an Indian rodeo.[131] Because Banff Indian Days was created as a tourist attraction, coordinators resisted the incorporation of Indian cowboy events as not "authentically Indian," but the new generation of Canadian Indian cowboys insisted, and a rodeo was included.[132] The rodeo took place separately on the Indian grounds outside Banff. It was "a small but complete rodeo: bareback and saddle bronc bucking, brahma bull riding, barrel racing, calf roping, steer decoration, wild cow milking, and a wild horse race."[133] The insistence of these Canadian cowboys that a rodeo be held in conjunction with Banff Indian Days reveals how cowboy culture had become a part of their Indian identities and how rodeo had become associated with community events.

Similarly, on the Cheyenne River Sioux and Pine Ridge reservations, Lakota cowboys included rodeo and race meets in their reservation-wide fairs. In 1911, Pine Ridge Superintendent John R. Brennan suggested that a reservation-wide

*Indian saddle bronc rider at Banff Indian Days Rodeo, Banff, Alberta, 1941.*

fair replace the numerous previously staged district fairs. Realizing the central place of equestrian contests in these fairs, he offered to build a larger race-track to accommodate all those involved in the tribal fair.[134] A letter to district farmers justified this shift from district to reservation fair, claiming that "these small fairs are a detriment. . . . Held all through the month of September and to the middle of October, the Indian, with his roving disposition, has no trouble following each fair start to finish."[135] The first Indian fair was held at Cherry Creek and was attended by four thousand Indians and two hundred whites. Accordingly, the four districts of the Cheyenne River Sioux reservation met at Goose Creek and decided to hold their second annual fair at Dupree. The *Dupree Leader*, a local newspaper, estimated that ten thousand Indians would be in attendance at the 1912 fair from all four Lakota reservations.[136] Like Crow Fair, "the entire management is left to the Indians, as to the program." As a result, in September 1912 the Lakotas put on the Cheyenne River Indian Farm and Stock Fair in Dupree; the events included horse racing, bronco riding, and roping.[137] Likewise, on the Pine Ridge reservation, both the 1917 and 1919 Pine Ridge Fair schedules listed a barrel roping contest and "a cowboy race by riding bronchos."[138] As one reporter from the *Dupree Leader* noted, the Lakotas at Cheyenne River had included "horse races, broncho busting, roping and all phases of western ranch life which they have adopted."[139] The reporter did not recognize the ethnic origins of these rodeo events, but he did see that the fair was becoming an important community celebration on the Cheyenne River Sioux reservation, where Lakotas could meet and enjoy the "western ranch life" that southwestern Native and Hispanic peoples had helped originate and that they now enjoyed as rodeo cowboys.[140]

By the close of the decade, northern Plains Indians valued their Indian fairs and rodeos as family and tribal celebrations. On the Cheyenne River Sioux reservation in 1915, Indian parents petitioned the Indian Office to allow them to take their children to attend the fair and rodeo before sending the children off to their boarding schools. Jack Bull Eagle, Save Eagle Chasing, Fish Guts, and Ed Swan wrote their Indian agent in 1915 to request that the dates of their fair be changed to a time "before we take our children to school as they will be away from us a long time, and we wish to have them celebrate this day with us before we separate from them."[141] Contrary to the goals of the Indian Office, these Indian fairs were not dissolving tribal ties but reinforcing them.

## RESTRUCTURING INDIAN IDENTITY

Over four decades, from 1880 to 1920, Plains Indians began to forge new identities based on their restricted environments and their enduring commitments to their communities and their horses. In an assimilationist era when it was thought Indians of the West should be detribalized, the federal Great Father stripped his Indian wards of their lands and livelihoods through official support of concentration, allotment, and finally, leasing. In promoting civilization and Christianization programs, the Indian Office subjected northern Plains Indians to federal control of their children's educations, their religions, and their cultural ceremonies. Despite these assaults on their culture, the Plains Indians remained Indian. They did so because they refused to remain static or to simply accommodate the wishes of the Indian Department. Instead they sought new ways of maintaining connections across tribal groups, as summer gatherings had once done, by selectively participating in activities condoned (at times begrudgingly) by the Indian Office, including cattle ranching, Wild West shows, professional rodeos, local celebrations, county and state fairs, and tribal fairs.[142] Participating in these events was a logical step in a series of northern Plains Indian cultural adaptations and inclusions from which their rodeo culture developed. By performing in ways that conformed to non-Indian cultural assumptions and aspirations, northern Plains Indians effectively resisted assimilation under the vigilant supervision of the Indian Bureau.

CHAPTER TWO

# The Growth of Rodeo as a Crow and Lakota National Pastime

*1920–1933*

B Y 1920, MOST CROWS AND LAKOTAS WERE PRODUCTS OF reservation life, through which they had reinvented their identity rather than relinquish it. Even as they became United States citizens via the Citizenship Act of 1924, they did not assimilate. Rather, the tribes remained culturally as nations within a nation.[1] The lessons American Indians had learned from their government school educations and agricultural training were mirror images of those the Bureau of Indian Affairs had intended them to learn. Just as young students solidified their tribal, and eventually intertribal, affiliations at boarding schools designed to detribalize them, northern Plains Indians on reservations converted the federal government's agenda of promoting agriculture into their own agenda of serving the social needs of their communities. Through their widespread acceptance of cattle ranching and their consistent participation in rodeos at county and state fairs and Indian industrial fairs, northern Plains Indians drew on their equestrian heritage to maintain tribal connections and to forge a new pan-Indian identity.

In the two decades following World War I, northern Plains Indians reaped the unintended cultural benefits of an intensified federal leasing policy. Indian agents encouraged Indians to lease their allotments, thus benefiting individual Indians and westering whites economically while further dissolving tribal bonds. The unexpected result was that many Plains Indians experienced greater freedom of cultural expression from the steady flow of leasing dollars into their reservations, coupled with the subtle relaxation of the assimilationist policies of the Bureau of Indian Affairs.[2] They were also enjoying greater liberties as a result of their newly conferred dual citizenship.

Crows, Northern Cheyennes, and Lakotas seized this opportunity to alter the character of their reservation gatherings. They replaced their government-sponsored Indian industrial fairs, designed to transform them into yeoman farmers, with Indian-organized rodeos such as the Crows' Indian fair and rodeo and the Lakotas' annual Pine Ridge rodeo. They also initiated Fourth of July rodeos in Lodge Grass, Wyola, and St. Xavier on the Crow reservation. Entirely responsible for the organization, funding, and management of these events, they dropped the industrial contests from their programs and featured rodeos and horse races exclusively. Given their relative freedom in the interwar years, they continued to come together as communities rather than becoming isolated as individuals. Voting with their feet, they demonstrated that rodeos had become the favored forum for tribal and intertribal reunions and contests.

## FEDERAL ATTITUDES TOWARD INDIAN GATHERINGS

Throughout the 1920s, Indian Agents continued to disapprove of frequent Indian travel but lacked the authority or gumption to stop it. Repeatedly, Indian commissioners and agents made feeble attempts to prevent Indians from abandoning their farms and ranches and traveling to the greener pastures provided by on- and off-reservation fairs and rodeos. They continued to disapprove of Indians frequently congregating only for the purposes of socializing and competing; such activities were impediments to the stated goals of assimilation. Indian agents felt that as a consequence of attending such fairs and rodeos, Indians were neglecting their fieldwork, emptying their pockets, and tarnishing their public image by appearing more as sideshow attractions than as the assimilated farmers the agents aspired for them to be. Crow Superintendent Calvin Asbury typified this apprehensive attitude of Indian officials. He strongly believed that if the Indian Office allowed Indians to "attend rodeos, Fourth of July celebrations, and County fairs at Sheridan, Miles City, Big Timber, Forsyth, Billings, Cody, and sundry other places besides the race meets and fandangos the Indians have themselves . . . we had better discharge our Farmers and establish issue stations."[3]

Realizing that they could not bring a decisive halt to Indian comings and goings, Indian agents attempted to limit Indians' presence at such occasions. They attempted to convince both the managers of rodeos and fairs and the Indians themselves that such events denigrated Indians. Crow Indian Agent Asbury was one such agent who repeatedly expressed his disapproval to other Indian officials, fair promoters, and the Indians themselves. Asbury suspected that managers of off-reservation county and state fairs—the Billings and Sheridan fair directors being named as particular culprits—were not prompted "by any special love of the Indian, but by a keen regard for the money that he spends freely at such times."[4] In response to an invitation from the Midland Empire Fair in Billings requesting the Crow Indians' presence, Asbury insisted that "such a camp is always a disreputable place. . . . It shows them at their very worst."[5] Similarly, he recommended that Crow Indians not accept an invitation to compete in the Cody Stampede on July 4, 1925, maintaining that his principal objective was to persuade "the Indians to farm and to stay home and to avoid unnecessary assemblage."[6] Asbury's repeated protestations reveal not only his decade-long frustration but also the opportunities that Plains Indians were creating and seizing to gather together, especially at rodeos and fairs.

As long as Plains Indians were showcasing their agricultural skills at county, state, and tribal fairs, Bureau of Indian Affairs officials reluctantly approved. As in the previous decade, Indian agents supported Plains Indians who attended off-reservation fairs, ostensibly to show off their agricultural talents. Fearing that the sporadically held Crow Indian Fair had "become a thing of the past," Indian agents such as Asbury conceded that there might be some benefit to Indian participation in county and state fairs because "we are reaching a much larger audience there than in a separate fair."[7] While castigating Crows who appeared in rodeos, race meets, encampments, and dances, Superintendent Asbury admitted the advantages of Indians exhibiting their produce and livestock at fairs in Hardin, Billings, and Sheridan. He believed that such displays would "help to remove the somewhat ancient but persistent idea that the Indians do nothing but run races and dance, as the feather feature of the Indian has been shown much more often than the agricultural activities."[8] In 1927, Cheyenne River Sioux Superintendent William O. Roberts echoed Asbury's qualified endorsement. He informed the president of the Faith, South Dakota, fair and rodeo association that "the Indian Department is agreeable to the matter of Indians participating in County fairs in a competitive effort and to observe the quality and production in white communities. Our restrictions in matters of this kind hinge on the economic condition of the individual Indian. You, of course, know that there are Indians who will be gone a week before fair and stay a week after, thus injuring himself through long absence from his garden and poultry."[9]

Indian agents were often disappointed with the lack of enthusiasm Plains Indians showed for the agricultural contests that they were admonished to enter. In 1926, Asbury optimistically sent the commissioner of Indian affairs booklets that listed the names of the Crow agricultural contest prizewinners at both the Big Horn County Fair in Hardin and the Midland Empire Fair in Billings. He was pleased to report that "considerable attention has been given by the Indian women, to the canning and preserving of wild fruits, of which there was a large crop this year."[10] A couple of years later, Mrs. B. C. Keough, the Indian Office's representative at the Midland Empire Fair, shared Asbury's confidence that it would be a "good idea" for Indians to compete with the whites in the various departments, and "this year it might be well to try."[11] While a number of Crows attended the Midland Empire Fair, "Montana's Greatest Exhibition," in 1928, both Asbury and Keough were disappointed that the Crows who managed the agricultural exhibits had "neglected Billings."[12] The Crows in attendance were more actively involved in the "Monster Rodeo" and the "Running Races for Indian Horses and Indian Relay Race" that were also on the Midland Empire Fair's program that year.[13] To prevent such a showing at another fair, Asbury directed two of the district farmers who were charged by the BIA with assisting and promoting farming among reservation Indians to go to the Fourth Annual Big Horn County Fair and to bring a display.[14] Clark J. Nation, the Crow Indian entrusted with overseeing the Crows' industrial displays at a later Midland Empire Fair, warned Agent Asbury that their efforts that year would be mediocre at best, explaining, "I will do my best, but I really think our exhibits will look 'pretty tough.'"[15] This was presumably a consequence of the Crows' apathy toward the exhibits and the fact that, like most western farmers, they were suffering from drought in the late 1920s. Northern Plains Indians were clearly not attending these county and state fairs for the opportunity to display agricultural exhibits; most came to mingle and to compete at the rodeo. By regularly attending such events in large numbers, Plains Indians demonstrated that they perceived of themselves not as being exploited but as fortunate to have occasions to assemble, to rodeo, to

*Superintendent W. O. Roberts addressing Indians at Cheyenne River Rodeo, 1920s.*
State Historical Society of North Dakota (Fiske 439).

race horses, and often to wear traditional regalia in reenactments, entry parades, and dances.

Equipped with United States citizenship, leasing dollars, and the support of an emerging cadre of Indian-policy reformers, Plains Indians rendered all official Indian Department protestations irrelevant. They determined that they would socialize and compete wherever and whenever they pleased. Charles Burke learned of his powerlessness to restrain Indian social activities as he began his tenure as commissioner of Indian affairs in the early 1920s. Burke attempted to carry on the assimilationist policies of his predecessors by issuing a circular prohibiting dances that involved "frequent or prolonged periods of celebration which brings the Indians together from remote points to the neglect of their crops, livestock, and home interest."[16] While Burke's "dance order" would have been applauded by politicians and the general public alike in the late nineteenth and early twentieth centuries, the 1920s marked a changing American cultural climate in which women and American Indians had been enfranchised for the first time. The Roaring Twenties also produced a new breed of Indian-policy reformers like John Collier, who railed against attacks on Indian cultures.[17] Such criticism prevented Bureau of Indian Affairs officials from strictly imposing rigorously assimilationist edicts like Burke's "dance order." Commissioner Burke in turn passed along this lesson to his Indian agents. In 1925, Commissioner Burke reminded Superintendent Asbury that, despite their opposition, the Bureau of Indian Affairs had no real authority to prevent Indians from attending such gatherings, as all Indians had become citizens according to the Indian Citizenship Act of 1924.[18] Similarly, in 1926 Burke responded to a large number of requests for Indian appearances by saying, "Apparently you do not realize that Indians are as free as other citizens to go and come from their homes and reservations as they see fit."[19]

Heeding Commissioner Burke's admonishment, Agency superintendents reticently passed along all requests for Indian appearances to the Indians themselves. When E. Pat Kelly of Livingston, Montana, invited the Crows to the Livingston roundup, Superintendent Asbury grudgingly responded, "We are not favorable to such participation during farming season. You might be able to negotiate direct with the Indians making your own contract and agreement with them."[20] Asbury's successor as Crow superintendent, James H. Hyde, also reluctantly allowed the Crows to make their own social arrangements. When members of both the local chamber of commerce and the American Legion committee asked "Indians to come and help celebrate . . .

sports, music, [and] dance" at the Community Picnic at L. R. McLean Ranch, Hyde reminded Mr. L. Stith that "this office does not look with favor on delegations such as is suggested in your letter . . . although if the Indians are contracted directly and decide to go on parties of this nature no action is taken by this office to prohibit them."[21] As helpless agents removed themselves from Plains Indians' social lives in the latter half of the decade, Crows, Northern Cheyennes, and Lakotas took advantage of the opportunity to enjoy rodeos in a variety of settings throughout the summer and early fall months. They competed frequently in non-Indian rodeos, on and off their reservations, while transforming their Fourth of July celebrations and Indian industrial fairs into widely attended reservation rodeos and community events.

## PLAINS INDIANS IN NON-INDIAN RODEOS

For ten years, Crows, Northern Cheyennes, and Lakotas spent much of their summers competing and visiting among themselves and with other Indians at non-Indian-hosted rodeos. To them, these events began to feel like intratribal and intertribal reunions, where they could socialize and also gain valuable experience competing in and watching rodeos. As rodeos became an increasingly popular pastime for all westerners, Plains Indians found a growing number of non-Indian rodeos both off their reservations and at ranches leased or owned by whites on their reservations in which they could take part. The hosts frequently invited their Plains Indian neighbors to compete in the rodeo arena, undoubtedly because the Indians were tourist attractions as well as competitors. Many Crows, Northern Cheyennes, and Lakotas invariably accepted.

For the Crows such opportunities seemed endless. In August 1922, Bill Orser of Pryor Agency put on a Wild West show where a "horse or steer was coming out of the chute every minute with someone sitting on the middle of him." Orser, a non-Indian tenant of the Crow reservation, erected his rodeo grounds—with grandstand, chute, corrals, and racetrack—outside the town of Pryor. He planned another rodeo to be held on Labor Day of that same year.[22] The following year, the shopmen of the Burlington shops at Sheridan, Wyoming, held a Labor Day picnic at Crow Agency's fairground and featured "Indian riding, roping, races, etc." as part of the day's events.[23] The "Lone Wolf" dude ranch on East Pryor Creek also held a dance and rodeo in August 1928, at which a large Crow encampment performed Indian dances and presumably participated in the "bucking, roping and wild cow milking."[24]

Crows and Northern Cheyennes also found ample opportunities to rodeo at the Big Horn County Fair in the reservation border town of Hardin, Montana. The county fair had not occurred regularly during World War I, so organizers were determined to make its comeback a widely attended event. They capitalized on the Indian presence not for the "feather feature" that Asbury had claimed, but for the ability of Indian cowboys and cowgirls to raise the level of competition in the rodeo arena. Repeatedly, journalists covering the Big Horn County Fair declared that the talented Crow and Northern Cheyenne equestrians who competed annually in the rodeo made it a better contest. An enthusiastic reporter for the *Hardin Herald* reported in 1925 that "one of the best attractions of the entire fair" was an "Indian rodeo," in which "a large number of Indians, with their strings of race horses and bucking bronchos took part."[25] A year later, a reporter avowed that "a western rodeo is not complete unless real Indians take part in it." And take part they did. Between five hundred and six hundred Crow Indians traveled to the Big Horn County Fair Rodeo in early September that year.[26] The rodeo was acclaimed to be the "Best of All. . . . This is due largely to the fact that the Crow and Cheyenne Indians, constituting the larger number of the rodeo performers, reside close to the fair grounds."[27]

Crow rodeo competitors recognized that their participation benefited them as much as it did the Big Horn County Fair promoters. It was at the Big Horn County Fair that members of developing Crow rodeo families found a venue where they could consistently compete against strong adversaries using good stock. Members of the Not Afraid, Holds Enemy, Big Lake, and Pickett families, who had been involved in rodeos since the turn of the century, began to have their accomplishments documented yearly in print in local newspapers. For example, at the 1928 Big Horn County Fair, the Crows' rodeo events were said to have been "pulled off with the precision of clockwork," and a number of Crows placed in the open rodeo, including Lee Not Afraid in bareback riding.[28] In the fall of 1929, the rodeo at the Big Horn County Fair was said to be "the best rodeo of any county fair so far this year in either Montana or Wyoming." Crow cowboys Al Holds Enemy, Jim Big Lake, and Joe Pickett made a showing there alongside famous professional non-Indian Montana rodeo cowboys, including Turk and Bill Greenough.[29]

Northern Cheyenne equestrians in Montana and Cheyenne River Sioux in South Dakota also attended and competed often in non-Indian rodeos. In August 1928, one thousand Northern Cheyennes, many of whom were involved in cattle ranching, camped on the bank of the Tongue River during the three-day rodeo celebration in Ashland, a town bordering their reservation. They were so eager to get together that most arrived by wagon and team a week before the rodeo began.[30] On another occasion, Northern Cheyenne ranchers not only attended in significant numbers but also provided rodeo stock— "ten big white-faced steers from the Cheyenne Indian reservation"—for the Fourth of July celebration in nearby Lee, Montana. The heartiness of the Cheyenne-raised stock made the rodeo action "strenuous enough to entertain the most seasoned spectator and at the same time make things interesting for the experienced cowboy."[31] In South Dakota, as government agents cringed helplessly, sizable contingents of Cheyenne River Sioux cowboys, cowgirls, and spectators made their way to the variety of rodeos off their reservation. Many traveled to the border town of Faith to participate in the Faith Fair and Rodeo. The fair and rodeo organizers clearly recognized the appeal of Indian rodeo contestants and offered "four free beeves" (sides of beef) to the Indians who attended.[32] There, Lakotas competed in rodeo events such as bronc riding, goat roping, and wild horse racing.[33]

As rodeos replaced reenactments as featured acts at Wild West shows, shows such as Texicole-Charley's Troupe of Wild West Performers and the Sells-Floto Circus "wanted Indians who could perform as fancy ropers and bronco riders."[34] Joe Yellowhead of Cheyenne River was one of those who answered the call, working for the Miller Brothers 101 Wild West Show in the late 1920s. Yellowhead rode both broncs and buffaloes, recalling that his employers had him "paint up as a Indian with the war bonnet." He preferred riding the show's tame buffalo over busting broncs, which he recalled as "too tough—just like riding a big barrel you know."[35]

While Bureau of Indian Affairs officials may have grudgingly accepted Indian participation in county and state agricultural fairs, they possessed strong misgivings about Indian competition in often-distant Wild West shows and professional rodeos. In 1927, five Lakotas who had been touring with the King Brothers Rodeo Circus were stranded near Detroit when a sheriff seized the delinquent show's property.[36] Showing little sympathy for their request for transportation home, Cheyenne River Superintendent Roberts informed Commissioner Burke that Archie Did Not Go Home, Black Man, Felix Dog Arm, and Mr. and Mrs. George Hunter had "left the reservation strictly on their own responsibility." Roberts continued, "It is also very reasonable to assume that the Indians were fully acquainted with the advisability of arranging contracts through the office.... When [an Indian] takes matters into his own hands in this respect, it seems to me advisable to permit him to reap the rewards of such a contract if he has been successful, and to make other arrangements if his judgement was in error."[37] Despite agents' displeasure, Plains Indians continued to travel to these non-Indian rodeos. Meanwhile, Crows, Northern Cheyennes, and Lakotas were staging rodeos closer to home on their own reservations.

## DECLARING CULTURAL INDEPENDENCE:
## FOURTH OF JULY RESERVATION RODEOS

Although the Crows held the Crow Fair and Rodeo sporadically throughout the 1920s, they, like their Northern Cheyenne and Lakota counterparts, were consistently gathering at district rodeos. The Crows asserted their cultural independence as proud members of two nations by holding district rodeos on the Fourth of July in St. Xavier, Lodge Grass, and Wyola on the Crow reservation. They were building on a tradition of celebrating government-sanctioned holidays begun by their predecessors in the late nineteenth century when traditional Indian gatherings had been outlawed. Roughly two decades later, Plains Indians had transformed these Fourth of July rodeos into significant intratribal community celebrations.

Following World War I, the Crows successfully wrested control of these events from disappointed Indian agents who would rather have seen Indians farming than gathering as Indian nations to celebrate an American national holiday. Crow Superintendent Asbury expressed this sentiment clearly: "I suppose there is no such luck as our having it [the Fourth of July] go by without a gathering. . . . This office has not been handling these gatherings. . . . [They are] entirely in the hands of the Indian committee."[38] Likewise, R. C. Halgate, a district farmer assigned to the Crow reservation, attempted to undermine the Crows' proposed district rodeo in Pryor in 1926. Halgate scornfully reminded Crow rodeo organizers Luke Rock and Simon Bull Tail that "your 'rodeo' last year was a failure. . . . You came into debt . . . and the quality of the show was so poor that it was a laughing stock." He posed the common complaint of the Bureau of Indian Affairs that all of the time Plains Indians spent traveling to these gatherings could be better spent on their farms. Halgate argued: "If you put on a 'Rodeo' you will begin now to get ready and no more work will be done till it is over. By that time it will be time to go to the Custer Battle Field re-union, from there you will go to the July 4th celebration at Wyola or Big Horn and we will see but little of you until after the Billings Fair this fall." Only reluctantly did Halgate cede the decision to the Crows. Condescendingly, he admonished them that "now you are men and not children and we have no notion of compelling you by force to abandon the idea but we hope . . . you will elect to have no 'rodeo' this year and if you have one it will be no more than two days."[39]

Despite such impotent protests from Indian Office officials, the Crows' efforts to organize and attend Fourth of July rodeos continued unabated. On the Crow reservation, the St. Xavier rodeo became one of the most popular Independence Day rodeos. In 1921, the Crows announced that the St. Xavier rodeo would be organized entirely "under the auspices of the Big Horn District of the Crow Indians." The St. Xavier celebration included "horse bucking contests, steer bulldogging, roping contests, etc."[40] The number of Crows who attended these rodeo celebrations attested to the attractiveness of these home-grown social and sporting events. In 1922, St. Xavier again hosted a Fourth of July rodeo where "half of the Crow tribe" attended "the big doings," which included "races, bucking exhibitions and events of an interesting nature in that line." It was so important for Crows to meet and compete at the St. Xavier rodeo that Indians who celebrated the Fourth elsewhere "hurried themselves to St. Xavier the very next day."[41] They came for the camaraderie and to enjoy a rodeo that boasted "all the twists and turns of a wild west rodeo."[42] Crows were holding Fourth of July rodeos across the reservation in 1928, not only in St. Xavier but also in Wolf Community and in Lodge Grass, where "over five thousand people collected at the rodeo grounds."[43] The Crow reservation district of Wyola also offered "horse races, bull dogging and all rodeo events" to commemorate Independence Day in 1930.[44] By 1931, Crows in Lodge Grass had appointed a rodeo committee—which included respected Crow cowboys and community members James Blaine, Sam Horn, and Richard Cummins— to be responsible for what had become an annual event.[45] By the end of the decade, the Crows had transformed these Fourth of July celebrations into Indian rodeos that paid an appropriate tribute to the Crows' complex identities as Indians, as cowboys, and as citizens of two nations.

## FROM INDIAN INDUSTRIAL FAIR TO CROW FAIR RODEO

The Crow tribe demonstrated its resurgent cultural independence, community values, and increasingly pan-Indian sensibility through the shift that they engineered in the content and frequency of Crow Fair during the 1920s. With their tribal herd virtually gone by 1922 and most of their irrigated farming and ranching lands leased but providing a steady income, the Crows experienced cultural resurgence despite dwindling economic power.[46] Attending and competing in fairs and rodeos both on and off the Crow reservation, Crows had asserted their preference for horse racing and rodeo over industrial contests. This was nowhere more apparent than at the Crow Fair.

In 1919, the Crow Fair was suspended due to drought, and in the following decade the Crow Indian industrial fair, as Reynolds had envisioned it at the turn of the century, occurred only sporadically. The Crow community's transformation of the Crow Fair, viewed in the context of their frequent participation in a variety of rodeos, reveals their burgeoning cultural autonomy. The Crows held Crow Fair in 1920, but Crow Superintendent Calvin Asbury objected to it once again in 1921 out of concern for their crops. He warned district farmers that "they have had race meets recently at Crow Agency, Black Lodge, Big Horn and probably elsewhere. . . . I feel there will be real suffering as the crops have been poor. . . . I do not think we should encourage any further race meets or Fairs this year."[47]

The Crows' insistence on organizing and holding the 1922 Crow Fair and Rodeo revealed their desire to continue the annual gathering, although they also wanted to alter its content, just as they had done in their district fairs. Crow leaders such as Plenty Coups were eager to revive the Crow Fair as a reservation-wide gathering. In a letter to Superintendent Asbury, Plenty Coups expressed the desire of the members of his district (Pryor) to attend a reinstated reservation fair.[48] Plenty Coups received Asbury's support. Asbury hoped to resurrect the Indian industrial fair as the Indians' main tribal event. Seeing no other recourse to limit persistent Indian travel to countless district fairs and rodeos on the reservation, Asbury agreed to resuscitate the annual reservation-wide Indian industrial fair. Like his counterparts in the early 1900s, he hoped the tribal fair would encourage the Crows' interest in industrial pursuits and would substitute for the multitude of events deemed less appropriate. Asbury presented his case to the commissioner of Indian affairs. In his letter to the commissioner, Asbury indicated the extent to which the Crows had already changed the character of their district fairs. Asbury acknowledged that these district fairs had become essentially race meets and rodeos, even though the Indian Office had hoped to limit such events that brought the Crows together and took them away from their individual homesteads. He explained, "I would rather encourage the Fair here at the Agency and . . . give them some assistance in the way of premiums, than . . . have several little district fairs, or rather race meets, on other parts of the reservation."[49] At the end of the decade, Superintendent Asbury made a similar attempt. In a patronizing tone, Asbury granted that "Indians, like children, must have some play time." For this reason, he urged the commissioner of Indian affairs to reinstate a "Reservation Fair."[50] But the Crows never again held the type of Crow industrial fair focused primarily on agricultural and industrial displays and contests that Indian agents favored.

Intermittently, the Crows were remaking the industrial fair meant to detribalize them into an intratribal and intertribal event by attracting crowds of Crows and Northern Cheyennes to their featured rodeo. Having obtained official approval and some funding for their fair, the Crows planned the 1922 Crow Fair as an event that would reunite Crows residing in various districts of the reservation with one another and with their reservation neighbors and former rivals, the Northern Cheyenne. The Crows made their fair and rodeo open to all and proclaimed that there would be "Nobody Barred." "Hundreds of whites" eagerly attended, but the reported two thousand Crows and Northern Cheyennes who participated as audience members and competitors in the fair and rodeo vastly outnumbered them.[51]

To appease the Indian Office, the Crows included some agricultural exhibits in the Crow Fair's revival, but they clearly emphasized the rodeo events. Superintendent Asbury must have been pleased to read in the local newspaper, the *Hardin Herald*, that the agricultural exhibits were a "revelation to those . . . not familiar with the productivity of the Crow reservation."[52] But surely he was disappointed that the premiums he suggested for "best bread, cakes and pies, best butter, best sow and spring brood, best milk cow, best team of mares, best spring colt and best brood mare" went unclaimed.[53] The Crows also expressed their enthusiasm for the rodeo as the fair's main attraction by posting advertisements in the *Hardin Herald* that promised "Roping, Riding, Bucking Contests, Indian Dances . . . Catch 'em Cowboy . . . Some of the wildest and hardest buckers in this section of Montana will be there."[54]

As Superintendent Asbury became less vigilant about monitoring the Crows' social lives during the 1920s, the Crows continued the trend of transferring Crow Fair's emphasis from agricultural exhibits to primarily all-Indian rodeo events. In 1923, the Crows organized their own fair, unbeknownst to Superintendent Asbury, who thought they had "given it up."[55] The 1923 Crow

Fair advertisements proclaimed it to be "the largest and best Indian Fair ever," with "Races, Roping, Bucking Contests, Indian Dances."[56] Although many Crows continued to participate eagerly in Crow Fair's rodeo, at least one dissenting Crow Indian named Shiek wrote the superintendent a year later, claiming that "a number of Indians from Lodge Grass, Reno and Black Lodge . . . decided they want to make a real fair of it—more exhibits and not so much wild west stuff."[57] Despite this request, no such Crow industrial fair occurred—then or ever again.

Instead, Crow organizers staged a memorable Crow Fair rodeo. Fifty-five years later, Crow Indian Thomas Bull over Hill recalled having competed in the rodeo at Crow Fair in 1924. He mused, "I rode saddle bronc on a famous bucking horse named Hamburger. . . . Hamburger was a famous bucking horse brought in from Billings Fair, that no cowboy could stay on, to test the Indian riders."[58] Thomas Bull over Hill passed that test and proved his skill as a Crow Indian horseman to his Indian and non-Indian challengers and audience. In 1925, the Crow superintendent recognized the transformation in Crow Fair's content and also revealed the degree to which the Crows had assumed control of it. In response to an inquiry regarding Crow Fair he explained, "It is true the Indians have sometimes had a fair, which was more of a race meet or a rodeo than it was a Fair, but I know of no plans for such a fair this fall."[59] Yet the Crows held Crow Fair again that fall. They advertised it as "their annual race meet and rodeo," and the program consisted of three days of horse races and bucking bronc contests. Although the Crows chose to hold the Crow Fair rodeo in the reservation border town of Hardin, Montana, it was easily accessible to the Indians of Pryor and upper Big Horn districts, and they proclaimed it to be an all-Indian rodeo.[60]

Marking the semicentennial anniversary of the Battle of the Little Bighorn in 1926, the Crow Fair and Rodeo brought Crows, Lakotas, Northern Cheyennes, and non-Indians together to celebrate an event that had once bitterly divided them, as many Crows had aligned themselves as scouts for the U.S. Army against their Lakota and Northern Cheyenne adversaries. In addition to the rodeo events, the attending Plains Indians staged a reenactment of the legendary battle. The rodeo events paused on June 25, 1926, for those in attendance, northern Plains Indians and whites, to recognize the achievements of all Little Bighorn veterans through a reenactment of the battle. The Seventh Cavalry retraced Custer's steps down the south side of the ridge. A contingent of Northern Cheyennes and Lakotas, a hundred of whom had fought in the actual battle, advanced toward the Custer monument from the north side of the battlefield. Afterward, the Crow Indian rodeo continued, with Indian and non-Indian cowboys competing.[61] By reenacting the battle, the Indians remembered and honored their role in the resistance to reservation life and showed that they continued to see themselves as Indian freedom fighters who were determined to win the ongoing battle for their cultural identity.

Reenactments of the Battle of the Little Bighorn had originated with Buffalo Bill Cody's Wild West Show and had become a mainstay in that show. Although Wild West show Indian battle reenactments had diminished in popularity following World War I, Indian and white participants and audiences in Montana still valued this particular battle reenactment as part of their local history. For Northern Plains Indians, including the Northern Cheyennes and Lakotas who fought in 1876 to resist their forcible confinement to reservations, the "last stand" remained a symbol of their greatest and last victory. Those among them who had toured with the various Wild West shows or had themselves been present at the Battle of the Little Bighorn relished the opportunity to once again rout Custer's Seventh Cavalry. For the Crows, the rodeo and battle reenactment allowed them to commemorate the efforts of members of their tribe who had scouted and fought alongside Custer against their Plains Indian foes. Local whites and government officials also supported the intertribal event, which they viewed as an entertaining tribute to the cavalrymen martyred at the Little Bighorn. Many "dudes" from Birney, Montana, and elsewhere attended and competed in the open rodeo.[62] Superintendent Asbury showed his support, tepid though it was, for the celebration by allowing the Crows to withdraw money from their tribal coffers to construct new rodeo grounds with parking for four thousand cars on a flat near Crow Agency in preparation for the event.[63]

The semicentennial anniversary Crow Fair and Rodeo revealed that Crows were becoming adept promoters of both intertribal solidarity and non-Indian tourism. Northern Plains Indians realized that they could advocate pan-Indianism as long as it was packaged as tourism. Crows, Northern Cheyennes, and Lakotas used the anniversary not only to honor their shared past but also to reconsider the nature of northern Plains Indian relationships in the future. The semicentennial celebration afforded them a government-sanctioned opportunity to demonstrate that in the reservation era, northern Plains Indians were allies—enemies no longer. They were engaged in a common struggle to retain their languages, religions, and tribal affiliations in an era when many were intent on detribalizing and assimilating them. The Crows elected Robert Yellowtail as chairperson of the Crow Rodeo Committee. In the decade to follow, Yellowtail would become superintendent of Crow reservation. He would also be instrumental in promoting Crow Fair and Rodeo as an intertribal event, ostensibly to attract local ticket buying by non-Indian audiences but also to foster Native strength through unity.

This trend toward pan-Indianism was already evident in 1926 as Crow organizers accentuated the intertribal character of the rodeo. In their public announcement before the fair, they declared that for the three days before and after the ceremony "the Crow Indians will gather with other Indian nations at Crow Agency for a picturesque tribal festival and the largest rodeo ever staged by Indians."[64] Notably, the Crow Fair and Rodeo and Little Bighorn reenactment had begun with White Man Runs Him, one of Custer's noted scouts, who "smoked the peace pipe with his former enemy, the Sioux." The Crows had successfully staged an event that demonstrated their pride in their pre-reservation warriors as well as their willingness to ally with other Plains Indians in future battles. They knew this would be allowed only in a setting that also honored and welcomed Anglo American Little Bighorn veterans, audience members, and rodeo participants.[65]

In this government-sanctioned setting, the Crows were free not only to rodeo but also to enjoy traditional Indian dancing and singing, which were otherwise outlawed. Government agents made exceptions in the case of Indian fairs. Thomas Bull over Hill's first memory of the singing and dancing that constantly filled the air at Crow Fair dated back to 1907. He fondly remembered that when he was six years old, "the districts each set up big long tents and the people danced in their own district tent. Districts competed against each other by how many dancers and singers they had under each tent."[66] By the 1920s, the districts were dancing and camping together. John Bull Tail recalled a Crow Fair during that time when "people would pitch up tepees and tents, and at night they would build a big fire and have a big dance. They didn't have contests, they just danced and danced because they enjoyed dancing. They called it war dancing. They would dance until about midnight and after that the people would have door way singing [singers visiting and serenading occupants of tents and tepees] until dawn."[67]

Due to their preoccupation with their district rodeos and horse races, which were wholly unsupervised by their agent, the Crows, however, had virtually abandoned Crow Fair by 1930. In 1929, Asbury reported that "we have not had any regular Crow fair for several years . . . and we know nothing at present of any arrangements for a separate Crow fair this year."[68] In a letter to the Sheridan Commercial Club, Asbury described the lack of Crow interest in reviving the Crow industrial fair. As proof, he reported an exchange between Mrs. B. C. Keough, the "field matron" responsible for encouraging Crow agricultural endeavors, and an unnamed Crow. When Keough suggested the possibility of holding a midwinter industrial fair at Crow Agency, the Crow responded, "What about the horse races?"[69] In a letter to Superintendent Asbury, Keough lamented the Crows' obvious preference for the rodeos, which they staged, over the agricultural contests, which were her bailiwick. She wrote that "the Crows have not had a regular Crow Agricultural Fair for several years. They did have fairs for quite a while but they rather degenerated into nothing but a rodeo and race meet."[70]

In 1931, the Crows resurrected Crow Fair and asserted that the fair was their own creation by dropping the word "fair" and advertising it simply as "Crow Rodeo," using it to advance not only their social but also their political well-being, while Commissioner of Indian Affairs Charles J. Rhoads watched with concern. Just as the Crows had previously honored their pre-reservation and World War I warriors at the Crow Fair, they used the 1931 event to honor a person who was fighting for their legal rights—their tribal attorney, Charles J. Kappler, who was visiting from Washington, D.C.[71] Having fought numerous battles to prevent the further alienation of Crow lands, culminating in the Crow Act of 1920, the Crows were beginning to recognize the importance that legal battles to protect tribal resources would assume as the twentieth century progressed. This may explain why approximately fifteen hundred Crow Indians were present for the adoption ceremony of their tribal attorney, Kappler, who had endeared himself to the tribe through his service.[72]

The reemergence of the Crow Fair and Rodeo as simply the "Crow Rodeo" in 1931 inspired renewed concern from Commissioner of Indian Affairs C. J. Rhoads. In a letter to the new Crow superintendent, Hyde, Rhoads disdainfully described the Crow Rodeo program, which he felt was sorely lacking in industrial contests. Instead, Crow Rodeo's program attracted predominantly Crow and Northern Cheyenne crowds who were eager to watch and participate in the horse racing, bronco riding, and relay races. The Indian and non-Indian guests and contestants also gathered to watch a "big pow-wow" in which Crow dancers performed the War Dance, Owl Step ("the equivalent to the pale faces' one-step,") Scalp Dance, Medicine Pipe Dance, and Victory

Dance. Rhoads explained that the Crows ended their celebration by inviting their guests to partake in a big feast, which had been a mainstay at northern Plains Indian reunions since pre-reservation times.[73] Thus, in this reincarnation of the Crow industrial fair as the Crow Rodeo in 1931, an event which paid tribute to their tribal attorney and offered a feast and performances of previously outlawed "Indian dances," the Crows revealed the priorities of a community that was overtly becoming politically and culturally aware.

## PINE RIDGE SIOUX RODEO: A LAKOTA EVENT

Oglala Lakota men and women from the Pine Ridge reservation also took advantage of their relative cultural independence in the 1920s by remaking their tribal fair into the Pine Ridge Sioux Rodeo. During the 1920s and early 1930s, the Pine Ridge Sioux Rodeo became an important community celebration, generating outside attention for the reservation and involving Indians at every level, from managing to competing to attending as spectators.

Pine Ridge Sioux Agent John R. Brennan had instituted a reservation-wide Pine Ridge fair in response to a growing number of Indian fairs, originally organized on a district-by-district basis, which he found to be as distracting as off-reservation events. In 1912, he urged reservation residents to "get together and agree to discontinue the district fairs and . . . hold but one fair on the Reservation each year."[74] The editor of the *Oglala Light* concurred. "These small fairs are a detriment in a way to more and better farming," the editor wrote, "and also, as these fairs are held all through the month of September and (this year) to the middle of October, the Indian, with his roving disposition, has no trouble in following each fair from its start to its finish."[75] Two years later, the government instituted a single reservation-wide fair with the stated purpose of "encouraging the people of the Pine Ridge reservation to grow more and better crops and to improve the quality of their cattle and increase their herds."[76] The annual reservation-wide fair, which the Indians themselves helped to organize and manage under the agent's direction, also provided an opportunity for Indians to compete in their own rodeos. The Pine Ridge Indian Fair schedules for 1917 and 1919, for example, listed rodeo events such as a barrel roping contest and "a cowboy race by riding bronchos."[77]

In addition, many Lakotas had more freedom to attend such gatherings. Following the turn of the century, federal agents, who had initially supported tribal ranching efforts, bowed to pressure from non-Indian ranchers and approved the leasing of individual reservation allotments to outsiders. By 1917, large non-Indian companies dominated reservation grazing lands. On Pine Ridge, for example, John Glover, foreman of the Quarter Circle 71 outfit of the Newcastle Land and Livestock Company, acquired five hundred thousand acres of leased land at the center of the reservation.[78] Taking advantage of a meager but steady income from such lease payments, many Lakotas spent part of their time during the 1920s traveling to summer fairs and rodeos.

By the mid-1920s, Indian agents had become dissatisfied with the reservation-wide fairs, the focus of which had shifted from agricultural displays to equestrian contests. This sentiment led to the Indian agent's cancellation of the annual Pine Ridge Indian Fair in 1925 in favor of "local industrial exhibits [to] be held in the various districts."[79] Two years later, forty-six Lakota men petitioned Commissioner Burke for the resumption of the Pine Ridge fair, which they said had "been an incalculable value to the Indians from the aspect of advertising and demonstrating the industry and farming produce of the Indians, to the outside communities from which vast numbers of white people attend the celebration."[80] Although officials maintained that the district agricultural displays should meet this need, many Lakotas did not find the local exhibits socially gratifying.

Subsequently, a group of Pine Ridge men took action to bring rodeo back, illustrating the extent to which the Lakotas had embraced rodeo and incorporated it into their lives. In 1928, the Oglala Lakotas themselves formed the Pine Ridge Sioux Rodeo Association to offer reservation Indians an opportunity to gather and compete as cowboys and community members in an activity that formed part of their heritage. On the Pine Ridge reservation, all eight districts—Oglala, Allen, Kyle, Manderson, Porcupine, Wakpamni, Red Shirt Table, and Wanblee—were represented at the rodeo. Similarly, on the Cheyenne River reservation, an Indian-organized reservation-wide fair and rodeo was held that united the Promise, White Horse, Eagle Butte, Cherry Creek, and Thunder Butte districts.[81]

The new Pine Ridge superintendent, James H. McGregor, expressed fear that the annual rodeo "would take many away from their homes and have them camped here for a week, when they would need to be at work on their farms and gardens."[82] Still, he and other Indian Office officials tolerated the rodeo in hopes that it would slow the trend of Indians leaving to participate in off-reservation shows, fairs, and rodeos. The officials also expressed optimism that the rodeo would indirectly promote animal husbandry by glorifying the skills of cattlemen.[83]

In the absence of either government interference or assistance, the Pine Ridge Rodeo Association took full responsibility for public relations, financial affairs, facilities construction, policing, and staging. At an organizational meeting on February 6, 1928, in the Pine Ridge Young Men's Christian Association (YMCA) building, the group elected five officers: Hermus Merrival, president; Charles Yellow Boy, vice president; James La Pointe, corresponding secretary; Frank G. Wilson, recording secretary; and Godard Cottier, treasurer. A three-member board of directors consisted of Philip Romero, John Colhoff, and Ben Janis. Another seventeen Lakota men signed on as members.[84] The association set forth its objectives early on. Through its annual reservation-wide rodeo, the group intended to generate outside attention, raise revenue, and promote Lakota pride and camaraderie. According to its organizers, the rodeo's primary aim was to "put Pine Ridge on the map. Let the people know where it is; let them know what kind of country it is; show them the wonderful farmlands [and] natural resources."[85]

During its decade-long existence, the Pine Ridge Rodeo Association publicized itself to large non-Indian audiences. Newspaper advertisements, feature articles, and word-of-mouth accounts inspired numerous inquiries from throughout South Dakota and from as far away as Rochester, New York.[86] In 1929, Francis Case, then editor of the *Hot Springs Evening Star* and a future United States senator from South Dakota, contacted association president Hermus Merrival to request "a write-up of the Rodeo and perhaps some paid advertising."[87] Reporters for area newspapers wrote glowingly of their rodeo experiences. A Rushville, Nebraska, newspaper deemed the 1931 "bucking contests, bull-dogging and calf roping contests . . . especially good," concluding, "People in this part of the country always look forward to the Pine Ridge Rodeo."[88] The publicity attracted an eclectic group of spectators. Captain A. E. King, commander of the Fourth Field Artillery regiment at Fort Robinson, Nebraska, arranged for 250 men to hike sixty-five miles to the 1929 rodeo in a training exercise that combined work and pleasure.[89]

Throughout the late 1920s and 1930s, the rodeo associations on the Pine Ridge reservation subsidized their events through ticket sales, concession sales, and fund-raising dances. Once the receipts were counted and expenses paid, the rodeos rarely made a profit, even when gate receipts were high, as at the 1927 Cheyenne River Sioux Rodeo when receipts were

$114 per day, a sizable profit for the time. Supplies, including posts, poles, lumber, and miscellaneous hardware were costly.[90] In 1933, Pine Ridge Rodeo Association secretary Frank Goings calculated that the organization's treasury was $15 in the red, due in part to unanticipated expenses. "All had authority to hire this man and that man," he complained. "One bill I didn't know was paid which I objected to was $8.00 given some cowboys who did-n't have any way of getting out of town."[91] Clearly, the demands of staging such an event sometimes strained the association's budget and tried the tem-pers of its members.

Although white cowboys were allowed to compete in the Pine Ridge Sioux Rodeo, the association consistently sought to employ Lakotas in as many rodeo-related jobs, from rodeo clowns to suppliers of beef, as possible. It also purchased beef for the event from Lakota cattle ranchers and charged non-Indian vendors a concession fee of five dollars per day to sell their wares, which ranged from nectar drinks to blankets and novelties. In addition, the association secured donations from local non-Indians; for example, Richard Talmadge of Rushville gave seventy-five dollars for the purchase of beef in 1928.[92] Dances, proposed at the first meeting of the rodeo association in 1928, provided the steadiest flow of revenue. An appointed committee attended the dances, held every Saturday night in the months leading up to the rodeo, to collect "voluntary gifts toward the good cause."[93] The dances proved to be profitable ventures, for the musical entertainers received just five dollars per night to perform.[94] By providing local whites with these country-and-western dances and with entertainment at their rodeo, the Pine Ridge rodeo commit-tee accrued the financial means necessary to ensure that Lakotas would also be able to gather as a tribe in a way that they enjoyed.

In addition to enriching the social environment of the reservation, the Pine Ridge Rodeo Association used its treasury to improve the reservation's built environment. At their second meeting on November 16, 1928, the direc-tors discussed work on the existing rodeo grounds, including the track and dance hall.[95] In 1929, they began building a bigger hall to accommodate the large crowds of rodeo-goers and evening revelers. The association predicted that the new dance hall would provide "a continual source of revenue," envi-sioning its use as a "town hall, community hall, a place for government offi-cials to meet Indians, a council hall, exhibit hall for the district fair and any number of things."[96] The United States government did, in fact, use the build-ing to house Emergency Conservation Workers on the reservation in 1933.

*Crow Creek rodeo clown on Crow Creek reservation (South Dakota), circa 1922.*
Cline Library, Special Collections and Archives, Northern Arizona University, Leo Crane Collection (Photo #658.854).

The association also built a sun shade, or dance pavilion, and maintained all of the structures well, reporting damage from vandalism only in 1932.[97]

With the funding and buildings in place, the Pine Ridge Rodeo Association was left with the tasks of staging and policing the annual event. The organization's bylaws required the group to arrange for patrolling the grounds and to "take care of all relief cases arising from attendance at the rodeo."[98] The directors also devised a set of Official Rules banning "liquor, rowdyism and quarreling."[99] In 1930, Superintendent Jermark reported one incident of illegal alcohol consumption to the commissioner of Indian affairs and expressed concern that rodeo "not infrequently attracts an undesirable element."[100] The following year, however, Pine Ridge Indian agent B. G. Courtright assessed the association's regulation positively: "So far as I can learn from the records and inquiry," he reported, "there have [sic] heretofore been no disorder or trouble in connection with policing the grounds and no unruly or objectionable element has been encouraged to enter the reservation on account of the Rodeo."[101]

The Pine Ridge Rodeo Association also determined the program and prizes for the event, which was usually held for three days during the first week of August. Most of each day was devoted to bronc riding, steer wrestling, and horse racing, but the program also featured activities such as battle reenactments, baseball games, parades, and traditional dances. Noticeably absent from the published program was the premium list for agricultural contests that had been a feature of government-sponsored Indian fairs.[102] Although non-Indians were invited to participate, the rodeo contestants were predominantly Lakotas, who relished the opportunity to display their skills as horsemen and to compete for such prizes as bridles and Navajo blankets. The estimated three thousand Lakotas who attended the 1931 Pine Ridge Rodeo attested to its popularity, and the *Shannon County News* declared the event "a genuine Sioux Rodeo."[103]

In 1933, Hermus Merrival resigned as rodeo association president to devote more time to farming, and the local American Legion chapter stepped in to assist with fund-raising and conducting the dances while sharing in the profits. The prospect of the American Legion, made up of whites, taking over their Lakota rodeo prompted dissent among association members. Tensions among rodeo association members climaxed in 1934 when the Legion requested use of the dance hall for its own July rodeo and then proposed that it take over management of the Pine Ridge Sioux Rodeo as well. Rodeo association secretary Frank Goings, with support from Superintendent McGregor, entreated the other members to accept the offer, but in the end the board refused to relinquish either the rodeo or the dance hall.[104] The Pine Ridge Rodeo Association continued to have management authority until the annual Pine Ridge Sioux Rodeo was replaced later in the decade with a reincarnation of the reservation-wide agricultural fair and rodeo.

## PLAINS INDIAN NATIONS AND NATIONAL PASTIMES

In the decade following World War I, rodeo had become an increasingly popular pastime for Anglos and for Native Americans, including Crows, Northern Cheyennes, and Lakotas. Northern Plains Indians experienced greater freedom of cultural expression as a result of their newly conferred dual citizenship status, subtle changes in BIA policies, and the steady flow of leasing dollars into their reservations.[105] In response, Crow, Northern Cheyenne, and Lakota men and women stepped up their excursions on and off their reservations to participate in rodeos at county, state, and tribal fairs and at Wild West shows. It was an era of transformations, in which Crows converted government-sanctioned Fourth of July celebrations into Indian rodeos where they could celebrate their complex identities as both Crows and Americans, cowboys and Indians. Similarly, Crows and Lakotas replaced their government-sponsored Indian fairs with Indian-organized rodeos such as the Lakotas' annual Pine Ridge rodeo and the Crow Indian rodeo. Through their actions, they demonstrated that rodeos, not the Indian industrial fairs meant to detribalize them, had become the preferred forum for tribal and intertribal reunions and contests. In the process, northern Plains Indians effectively transformed the very events designed to transform them while Indian agents stood by helplessly. They realized that they could not prevent Crow and Lakota citizens from celebrating as they pleased on or off their reservations.

The BIA's "salutary neglect" of the 1920s gave way to increased federal attention to Indian affairs in the mid to late 1930s. In response to the 1928 publication of *The Problem of Indian Administration*, also known as the Meriam Report—which revealed the BIA's failure to provide Indians with adequate health care, education, and protection of tribal land bases—federal officials in the Hoover administration began to reorganize their bureaucracy and to reconsider their strident assimilationist approach to Indian policy. Franklin Roosevelt's newly appointed commissioner of Indian affairs in 1933, John

Collier, a longtime Indian reformer and advocate of cultural pluralism, intensified the efforts of his predecessors by pledging to grant Indians greater cultural, economic, and political autonomy.

For all the reformist rhetoric and goals espoused by Collier, the Bureau of Indian Affairs continued to behave like a well-meaning yet meddling parent. Their paternalism led them to replace the autonomous Pine Ridge Sioux Rodeo and Crow Fair and Rodeo, which they viewed as purely entertainment-oriented gatherings, with "educational" tribal fairs.[106] As Collier's agenda sought an Indian economic and cultural renaissance, the revived Indian fairs were meant to showcase Indian agriculture and, for the first time, Indian traditional culture. Emerging Lakota and Crow leaders like Crow Indian Superintendent Robert Yellowtail, who grew up cattle ranching and rodeoing on the reservation, realized that rodeo had become an integral part of their culture. The Indians would demonstrate that in the decades to come by making rodeo a centerpiece of their resurrected reservation-wide tribal fairs.

## CHAPTER THREE

# Rodeo and Renewed Cultural Life during the New Deal

*1933–1945*

J OHN COLLIER, FRANKLIN D. ROOSEVELT'S APPOINTEE AS commissioner of Indian affairs from 1933 to 1945, spearheaded the Indian New Deal, a policy that was indeed new in its intention to grant American Indians greater cultural, economic, and political autonomy. Collier, fresh from a fight to preserve Pueblo lands, was steadfast in his commitment to safeguard the right of tribes to maintain and augment their tribal land bases, as well as to save as much as possible of their traditional cultures and governments. When he attempted to implement these reforms through the Indian Reorganization Act (IRA), or Wheeler-Howard Bill of 1934, however, he met with mixed success.[1] A number of tribes, including the Crows, rejected the provisions of the IRA as they remained suspicious of the old bureaucracy and were reluctant to invite increased interference by that bureau into their tribal affairs. They recognized that even though the BIA had drastically shifted its policy away from assimilation to one that allowed Indians to be Indians, it still claimed the right to define what being Indian meant. In this respect, the Indian New Deal was as old as the aging organization that had conceived it. The exception to this was an Indian agent who actually was an Indian—Crow Superintendent Robert Yellowtail. Through his leadership, Yellowtail, who shared Collier's dedication to Indian economic and cultural revitalization, offered a glimpse into the potential of true Indian sovereignty. Through the revitalized Crow

Fair and Rodeo, Yellowtail proclaimed to a widespread Indian and non-Indian audience his unique vision of what traditional Crow and pan-Indian culture had become and was becoming.

Collier had arranged for the appointment of Yellowtail, an advocate of Crow rights, as the first Native American superintendent of his home agency, Crow Indian Agency. During his tenure in office, from 1934 to 1945, Yellowtail promoted European American tourism, using the revitalized Crow Fair and Rodeo as a vehicle to proclaim the Crows' modern national identity. Through aggressive advertising, Yellowtail aspired to transform Crow Fair and Rodeo into both a national institution and an informal Plains Indian conference, attracting non-Indian tourists and American Indian guests from throughout the United States. For their visitors, Yellowtail and the Crows managing the fair and rodeo made a conscious effort to stage an event that would display the Crows' successful adaptation of both traditional and newly acquired elements into their contemporary culture.

A similar pattern occurred in many Northern Plains communities where the still-powerful Indian agents replaced the independently organized rodeos of the 1920s with tribal fairs as their reservations' primary gatherings. Although white Indian agents on the Pine Ridge and Rosebud reservations resumed control of these tribal fairs, they were more sympathetic to Native culture than their predecessors. Thus, the Lakotas retained some voice in determining the content of their tribal fairs. They, like the Crows, included rodeo events alongside their adapted Indian dances and ceremonials for an expanding pan-Indian and non-Indian audience.

It was under Yellowtail's leadership on the Crow reservation where the most dramatic demonstration of what Indians could accomplish when they possessed cultural autonomy could be seen. The cultural content of the fair and rodeo was designed not as a white Indian agent perceived it but as the Indians saw it. The Crows chose to display their culture by featuring rodeo, which was staged on at least three of the event's five days. By featuring Indian buffalo riding throughout event, the rodeo further exemplified the Crows' successful integration of their past and present realities, as well as their desire to attract tourists. As it became a Plains Indian contest from 1934 to 1945, the Crow Fair and Rodeo presaged the future of rodeo as a pan-Indian event.

## ROBERT YELLOWTAIL'S VISION FOR A
## MODERN CROW NATION

Robert Yellowtail—Crow cattle rancher, politician, and rodeo aficionado—represented the experiences and values that had shaped the identities of many of those in the first generation to grow up on the reservation. Yellowtail and others like him became stalwart Indian advocates and found a political voice during the Great Depression as mainstream America and the federal government became more sympathetic to communities in distress. As superintendent of the Crow reservation, Yellowtail was able to promote the Crows' political, economic, and cultural agendas. Yellowtail's unprecedented appointment was made possible by the 1932 presidential election of Franklin Roosevelt. Roosevelt appointed Harold Ickes, a charter member of the Indian Defense Association, to the position of secretary of the interior. Ickes in turn named John Collier, one of the Indian Defense Association's reformist founders, as commissioner of Indian affairs. Through the Defense Association, Collier had "urged the government to protect native traditions and nurture the growth of Indian Community leadership."[2] Thus, it was not surprising that in May 1934, Collier took the unparalleled step of appointing the Crow Indian rancher Yellowtail as the first Native American superintendent of his home reservation.

Yellowtail was born in 1888 to Chief Yellowtail, a chief in the Lodge Grass district of the Crow reservation, and his mixed-blood wife, Lizzie Shane. He attended a federal boarding school in California, the Sherman Institute, where he acquired a proclivity for American history and law. In 1910, he returned to the Crow reservation and took up politics as well as ranching on his allotment south of Lodge Grass. His network of extended family, his legal knowledge, and his belief that the Crows should determine their own affairs made him "a favorite in councils and committee meetings."[3]

As Crow tribal historian Joseph Medicine Crow explains, "He [Yellowtail] served as counsel and interpreter for Crow chiefs such as Plenty Coups and Medicine Crow in their many negotiations with the government over attempts by Montana senators and congressmen to open the Crow reservation for Homesteading by whites. Yellowtail knew how to deal with whites."[4] By 1934, Yellowtail had cultivated relationships with many Crow elders, as well as with many more in his own generation of Indian and non-Indian politicians. Most Crows agreed that he was the ideal envoy for their twentieth-century Crow

*Crow Indian cowboy Robert Yellowtail, later superintendent of Crow reservation, and Blossom T. Neef, later Mrs. Calvin Sampson, 1907.*
Montana Historical Society, Helena (Photo #PAC 89-113).

nation. In 1934 when Collier arranged for Yellowtail's appointment to be voted on by the Crows in a general referendum, Yellowtail won in a "landslide."[5]

In his inaugural speech, Yellowtail attempted "to define a common Crow national identity that might legitimize his tenure in office and to set an agenda for the future."[6] He declared a "new deal has dawned for the American Indian." Yellowtail asserted his commitment to home rule, demanding Crow rights to self-government, independent economic development, and cultural and religious freedom.

> Today a new hope is flashed across the skies of a hitherto dark horizon.... We find ourselves gathered here today prepared to initiate a ... home rule program that we lost with the passing of the buffalo and the first treaty we concluded with the government, but which we have just recouped this day. A new era, a new hope and a new deal has dawned for the American Indian.

Yellowtail condemned the federal government's previous policies and treatment of Native peoples. He complained that "during this long autocratic rule, our constitutional rights and other liberties were trampled under foot," and he promised to institute a government that would defend those rights. He assured his Crow audience that he would represent them, stating, "This is your domain and therefore your business.... You should be heard at all times on any and all phases of its administration."[7]

The Crows spoke decisively on the issue of the Indian Reorganization Act. John Collier hoped to develop cultural pluralism and Indian self-sufficiency through this legislation by revamping Indian education, allowing for the creation of tribal governments, offering revolving loan funds for land purchase and economic development, and abolishing the land allotment provisions of the Dawes Severalty Act. As proof of his commitment to increased, if not complete, Indian sovereignty (the IRA required that tribal councils adopt a BIA-approved constitution), he allowed tribes to vote in a referendum to accept or reject the IRA. To his dismay, many Indian communities, including the Crows, reluctant to surrender any of their hard-won political autonomy, voted to reject it.

Asserting their commitment to home rule, every Crow district rejected the Indian Reorganization Act at their May 17, 1935, referendum, and only 112 votes (13 percent) out of 801 votes (an 80 percent turnout) were cast in favor of its acceptance.[8] Both Robert Yellowtail, by not actively promoting it until late in the process, and his political adversaries, who campaigned relentlessly against it, presented obstacles to ratification. Ultimately, the Crows rejected the Indian Reorganization Act because they saw it as infringing on their freedom and rights. Because it offered to restructure their government according to standards set in Washington, D.C., the act threatened to undermine the concept of Crow self-rule, which Yellowtail had so recently and so eloquently proposed in his inaugural address. Thus, the Crows' rejection of the Indian Reorganization Act in 1935 was another declaration of their renewed sense of "independence and nationhood."[9]

Like John Collier's IRA, Yellowtail's "new hope" for the Crow nation focused extensively on their tribal economic development. He reversed the policies of his predecessors, who were determined to make independent individuals of the Crows, by seeking an improvement in the tribe's income, both collective and individual. He urged the Crows to establish themselves as ranchers, farmers, and owners of potentially lucrative oil and mineral natural resources.[10] Yellowtail and the Crows worked strenuously to achieve these daunting economic goals. To do so, they had to overcome the consequences of past and present federal policies regarding Indian economic development. The General Allotment Act, which aimed to assimilate the Indians, had disastrously splintered their reservation grazing and farming lands. Most recently the Crows also were denied the economic assistance provided by the IRA because, by rejecting the act, they had disqualified themselves from borrowing money offered through the revolving fund it had established.

Yellowtail and the Crows were able to invigorate their tribal economy with the help of other New Deal relief programs that brought amenities and employment to the reservation. In a speech made before the National Emergency Council held in Billings, Montana, on April 10, 1936, Superintendent Yellowtail outlined the "good work that the expenditure of public funds from the U.S. Treasury through the PWA [Public Works Administration], WPA [Works Progress Administration], IECW [Indian Emergency Conservation Work] and other divisions of relief has accomplished."[11] He credited the WPA with providing approximately $6,000, which the Crows used to "extend relief during the long winter [they] just emerged from" to 150 families who were "rejects from the IECW on account of the rigid physical examination." He also reported that the IECW had spent $159,000 employing 240 Crows since its installation there. Crow ranchers and farmers in isolated communities throughout the reservation also benefited from the WPA's roads department, which had allocated $65,000 for the construction of roads. These roads allowed far-flung Crows to drive to town for supplies in all seasons. Yellowtail was pleased that the Crows had helped to replenish their reservation and their incomes with the sweat of their own brows. He reported that "twenty-six teams were employed from the Lodge Grass area," giving them "money with which to buy food." Yellowtail applauded the efficiency of the Crows' road builders, boasting that "the Crow Indian reservation is now building roads a good deal cheaper than any other state organization in the state of Montana. The lowest price under contract is around 27 cents per cubic yard while we have built better roads on the Crow reservation for 14 cents per cubic yard."[12]

Yellowtail was also dedicated to replenishing the environment and economy of the Crow reservation by reintroducing wildlife and by building up the numbers of domesticated livestock. As part of the effort to reintroduce wildlife, he restocked the Crow reservation with buffalo and elk. His many reasons for doing this included "the esthetic sense." "The Indians, who have depended on the buffalo for ages . . . naturally love the wildlife and on account of this custom we are most happy to have these animals in abundance around us now." In 1936 Yellowtail estimated, "We now have between three hundred and four hundred buffalo roaming the mountain areas of the Crow reservation and perhaps a thousand or more elk." Yellowtail's economic considerations for reintroducing wildlife to the Crow reservation included "building up a herd for a meat supply to take care of such depressed times as we have been going through the last few years."[13]

A rancher himself, Yellowtail was dedicated to revitalizing Crow cattle ranching. In order to combat the effects of allotment, which had deeply undermined tribal ranching efforts, he encouraged extended family groups to consolidate their allotments. He intended to develop the "economic-self sufficiency of the Crow Indians" by "grouping these allotments together in family units . . . which will allow large areas, depending on the size of the family group, . . . sufficient grazing lands to maintain cattle and horse herds to meet their economic support needs."[14] Impressively, a number of these Crow family ranching outfits made a go of it during the Great Depression—despite droughts, frosts, lack of irrigation, and plagues of insects. The *Crow Helper*, or *Absaroka kkuxce*, a Crow periodical published by the Bureau of Indian Affairs, encouraged these efforts by reporting several successes. Paul Williamson from Crow Agency was said to be "making a commendable start in the livestock business. He now has 13 head of good cattle in his possession." Likewise, "Robin Iron has been a good young stockman on this reservation for a number of years. He has 75 head of cattle." And "Mike Bull Chief and his son, Henry, are working out arrangements to go into livestock together. Henry now has 9 head of white-face cows and is expecting to get a number in addition."[15]

New Deal funds also helped to revive Crow tribal ranching. The storage of water on dry lands made possible by federal funds helped nourish 50,000 cattle and 100,000 sheep on the Crow reservation. While non-Indians who had bought or leased land on the reservation owned most of this stock, Yellowtail touted the fact that "the Indians themselves owned over 4,000 head of cattle," a number of sheep, and 3,000 horses that roamed the reservation. The Crow tribe earned an estimated income of $200,000 from the sale of these cattle and sheep. According to Yellowtail, the Crows were receiving "an average rate of $3.31 per head for the cattle, 64$^1/_2$ cents for the sheep and an average of 10$^1/_4$ cents per acre for the lands leased. It is safe to say that these funds made possible the enhancement of the industry of agriculture, the income from which goes to the pocketbook of every Crow."[16]

Crow cattle ranching nevertheless continued to be inhibited by the white ranchers who leased and often purchased "surplus" or inherited parcels of allotted reservation lands. Yellowtail complained that "one of the biggest problems at the Crow Reservation at this time, and which will increase as time goes on, is the ownership of Indian lands. At the present time the land is passing from an original status to an inherited status at the rate of from 17,000 to 51,000 acres per year." Inherited parcels of allotted lands, often small to begin with, were further subdivided into smaller entities. The heirs of the deceased often found it impossible to eke out a living out from these small parcels of land and were more likely to lease them to non-Indians. To prevent this, Yellowtail called for a method whereby living heirs or the tribe could purchase undivided heirship lands.[17] In 1936, Yellowtail feared that if this transfer of land from Indian to white hands went on unabated, the Crows would be forced to sell their shrinking natural resources rather than exploit them. He foresaw with consternation that "it will be plain to realize that our chief industry is the sale of grass to sheep and cattle raisers."

Unfortunately, the least successful of Yellowtail's programs was his daunting economic mission. He was unable to create an all-Indian agency staff, which could have lent force to his attempts to break up the power of the white tenants who leased the bulk of the Crows' land and to his attempts to gener-

*Superintendent Robert Yellowtail on horseback, Crow Fair, 1930s.*
Photo by Dennis L. Sanders. Hardin Photo Service, Hardin, Montana (Photo #813).

ate income from the exploitation of Crow minerals and oil.[18] His economic agenda would also have benefited from funds earmarked for tribal enterprises in the Indian Reorganization Act, which the Crows had rejected. Yet in their rejection of the IRA, which promised to end tribal land loss and encourage economic development, the Crows demonstrated that they were more determined to preserve their cultural and political freedoms than to achieve economic prosperity.[19] While Yellowtail had favored the adoption of the IRA, he sympathized with its opponents who clung to their sovereignty zealously. One historian concluded that for Yellowtail "freedom—the right to act in accord with a distinctive cultural agenda, as well as to organize politically—was the key to Crow survival."[20]

## CROW FAIR AND RODEO AS A TOURIST ATTRACTION AND "NATIONAL INSTITUTION"

Yellowtail restored the Crow tribal fair and rodeo as an annual reservation-wide event from 1934 to 1945. By heralding the Crows' complex national identity, which incorporated pre-reservation traditions and values into their contemporary lifestyles, the Crow Fair attracted non-Indian and Plains Indian guests alike. Yellowtail hoped these visitors would generate both the tourist dollars and political support necessary to advance the Crows' economic, political, and cultural agendas.

Crow Fair's daily opening parade celebrated the disparate cultural and political elements that had come to compose the Crows' contemporary identity. Yellowtail was fond of parades, as they were inspired by the pre-reservation processions of Crow bands setting out on buffalo hunts. He made sure that both his own inauguration celebration and every Crow Fair began with one. Following an order similar to Yellowtail's inaugural parade, Crow Fair and Rodeo's opening processions were led by the front rank of officials, including Superintendent Yellowtail and his predecessor, both on horseback and flanked by three Crows, who were often military veterans, in full regalia. In Yellowtail's inaugural parade, they were accompanied by the tribe's two attorneys and followed by the president and secretary of the Crow tribal council. Behind them rode the local Indian Office staff, members of the American Legion, a group of aging Crow scouts, and "row upon row of representatives from the tribe's clans, dancing societies, school groups and community organizations," many wearing beaded buckskin costumes and headdresses."[21] Such a procession symbolized the Crows' adaptation of their traditional cultural, religious, and economic practices to a new setting. The procession was led by politicians and military heroes who had protected and were protecting their independence, foremost as Crows but also as Americans.[22]

In remaking Crow Fair and Rodeo into a "national institution,"—increasingly staged for non-Indian as well as Indian visitors—plus remaking it into a "Plains Indian conference," Yellowtail became adept in what has become known as *cultural tourism*.[23] In *The Enduring Seminoles: From Alligator Wrestling to Ecotourism*, Patsy West explains that "cultural tourism—the sharing and displaying of certain highly visible aspects of their touristic experience—serves to reinforce a tribe's group identity."[24] At the Crow Fair and Rodeo, the Crows reaped substantial cultural, and marginal economic, benefits from this type of tourist enterprise. Yellowtail and the Crows who managed the fair participated in cultural tourism by showcasing aspects of modern Crow culture for their Indian and non-Indian guests, while in the process promoting Crow community cohesion. Yellowtail promised visitors that "activities and reenactments of old and new Indian life" would be presented at the Crow Fair.[25] In promoting the Crow Fair in a circular sent to neighboring towns and included in local newspapers, Yellowtail shared his own nuanced convictions regarding Crow identity, which championed the Crows' right to cultural independence. In so doing, he appealed to both Indians and non-Indians. For instance, he claimed that he "forswore the ways of his forefathers when he entered the white man's schools," yet he avowed the Indian's right to "dress, live and worship as he chooses," notwithstanding his degree of so-called civilization."[26] He wanted Crows and other Plains Indians to be able to demonstrate their complex twentieth-century identities in public.

Yellowtail declared Crow Fair and Rodeo to be a "Plains Indian conference." As such, it granted a forum for Crows and all Native peoples to gather and discuss relevant issues. As a pan-Indian event, Crow Fair and Rodeo's strength remained its role as a reunion, a time to gather, compete, and celebrate. In this regard, Indian dancing gained prominence, but the rodeo and racetrack events remained a central part of Crow Fair and Rodeo's attraction throughout the Indian New Deal. Usually, the last three days of the four- or five-day fair were dedicated to rodeo. Yellowtail was even able to directly link the rodeo to the Crows' past by including Indian buffalo riding as a featured event.

Yellowtail had political aims in making Crow Fair and Rodeo into a national event that was staged for both Indian and non-Indian visitors.[27] He did not want the Crow community to be isolated, and as a savvy politician, he realized that the Crows would benefit politically, economically, and socially by establishing good relations with non-Indian America. To this end, he invited both government officials and tourists to the Crow Fair and Rodeo. With citizenship established in 1924, Yellowtail began rallying Indians to become more involved in politics on the local, county, state, and national levels.[28] In a speech entitled "A Conscious Citizenship," the Crow superintendent encouraged Indian unity in voting for candidates "who are in fearless advocacy of their rights as persons within the meaning of the Constitution of the United States." He promised that "there will be better Government for the Indians of the United States when they insist upon a more decent respect for their rights

as humans and upon their civic and political rights as guaranteed by the existing federal and state laws." He insisted that Indians must educate themselves
about political machinations, predicting that "these results will come if, and
when, the Indians . . . inform themselves about how their matters are handled
by their government here and at Washington."[29] Having seized home rule in
his own community, Yellowtail used Crow Fair as a means of broadening
Crow political awareness and participation.

Yellowtail developed Crow Fair and Rodeo into a political forum where
local and state politicians could make their agendas known to the Crows. In
turn, the Crows used the fair as an opportunity to make an impression on
these politicians, who were perceived as people who could help protect Crow
civic and political rights. In 1934, George M. Bourquin of Butte, a Republican
nominee for the U.S. senate, and Democratic Congressman Roy E. Ayers, running for reelection, spoke at the fair.[30] A year later, the Crows extended an
invitation to Governor Frank H. Cooney, and in 1936, "the entire Montana
delegation in Congress" addressed the crowds at Crow Fair.[31] In 1937, Yellowtail took advantage of his prior relationship with the newly elected governor,
Ayers. He boasted to the manager of the Midland Empire Fair, "Governor
Ayers will be here to address the throngs that will be here and the big shots of
the Government Service at Washington will be here."[32] That year, Yellowtail
took advantage of his prior relationship with the new Governor Ayers. Yellowtail had submitted a "Crow Fair Improvement Project" proposal to the
WPA Director's Office, calling for the "building of grandstand, bleachers,
agricultural exhibit hall, building for the exhibit of livestock, and general
improvements of the fair grounds."[33] Not getting the results he wanted, Yellowtail directly petitioned Crow Fair's honored guest, Governor Ayers, for
assistance, asserting, "I want the benefit of your influence before Mr. Parker."[34]
The practice of including influential state and local politicians continued at
Crow Fair in 1938, when Congressman James Francis O'Connor, Senator
Burton K. Wheeler, and Governor Ayers participated in the events, and Superintendent Yellowtail delivered an address on the pursuit of tribal sovereignty
entitled "The Case of the Indians."[35] O'Connor (Chairperson of the Committee on Indian Affairs in the seventy-eighth Congress), Wheeler (one of the
framers of the Wheeler-Howard Bill), and Ayers returned in 1940 to attend
"Governor's Day," the third day of the fair, when they "were present to address
the Indians on any subject the Indians are interested in."[36] In his comments,
Ayers noted that Crow Fair was beneficial to the state of Montana because it

helped "sell Montana attractions to other states."[37] Ayers rode in the fair parade with "hundreds of Crows" and afterward feasted on "a fat young buffalo ... especially selected for Governor's day" at the buffalo barbecue.[38] Crow Fair and Rodeo had become an event where the Crows could forge and reaffirm ties with their non-Indian political allies.

Through aggressive advertising, Yellowtail developed Crow Fair and Rodeo as an attraction for both local tourists and those from the East Coast. His motives appeared to be mostly diplomatic and cultural. The Crow Fair rarely profited monetarily, but it did rely on its paying spectators to meet expenses. As a result of the publicity, an estimated two to three thousand people, both Indians and non-Indians, attended the 1935 Crow Fair. One reporter recognized the diversity, noting that there were "as many whites as Indians from all points of the compass."[39] The local non-Indian community was not as enthusiastic about Crow Fair as were easterners. Dude ranches proved a ready source for audiences. Yellowtail wrote the secretary of the Dude Ranchers' Association in 1936 to notify him that "I am reserving Crow Park ... where the dude ranchers and their guests may camp and enjoy a week of festivities with us. Kindly let me know after this information has been broadcast as to how much space we should reserve."[40] In 1938, the Dude Ranchers' Association sent Yellowtail a list of their members to contact regarding the Crow Fair.[41] Yellowtail also informed the secretary of the chamber of commerce in Bozeman, Montana, of the event.[42] The Billings Commercial Club distributed "ten thousand copies through various tour bureaus" of a schedule of summer events for the region, which included Crow Fair and Rodeo.[43] Yellowtail also turned to the merchants of Crow Agency and Hardin for monetary contributions to Crow Fair. He encouraged their support by reminding them that Crow Fair and Rodeo would attract "a tremendous crowd of men and women who will have money in their pockets to spend and we hope that you people will benefit materially from the show."[44] He also gave Indian Office employees the day off to attend the fair, urging them to "go to Crow Fair and spend your money."[45]

When notifying the *Sheridan Press* of the upcoming event in 1940, Yellowtail expressed disappointment in local non-Indian support for the Crow Fair.[46] In a 1939 letter to the sports editor of the *Billings Gazette*, Yellowtail stated plainly that Crow Fair relied financially on the gate receipts to pay its expenses, and "each year we get through by the skin of our teeth, so to speak." He went on to explain that "so far the Crow Fair has not been patronized by the people of Sheridan, Billings and Hardin."[47] Yellowtail reiterated these complaints in another letter in 1941:

> Billings people seldom come and if they come they remain for the free parade and then run off again. This year I do not think we will have the free parade on that account. . . . We are going to grab every nickel we can as the Fair is dependent on the matter of receipts. We will offer many attractive events for the visiting people, the local people being content to see the free parade and then run off.[48]

While local non-Indian communities were all too eager to have Indians attend and participate in their state and county fairs, they were not yet willing to participate in Indian fairs with equal enthusiasm. Such unwillingness of whites to reciprocate reflected the existing prejudice and tension in Indian-white relations surrounding the reservation.

Lacking widespread support from local communities, Crow Fair promoters strongly urged tourists from the East Coast to add Crow Fair to their itineraries. In 1937, a Department of Interior press release read, "Tourists to Grand Teton, Yellowstone, or Glacier National Parks will do well to include the Crow Fair in their itinerary."[49] A year later a circular marketing Crow Tribal Fair announced, "The Northwest Circuit has included it as part of their regular Montana Fair Circuit . . . as an attraction that tourists and people living in the East should see. Already requests from people living up and down the Atlantic seaboard are pouring in . . . as to the kind of show that will be staged here this year."[50] Yellowtail described some of the publicity Crow Fair was getting in 1937: "This year we are expecting an unusually large crowd as the Indian Office is advertising through its publicity bureau . . . up and down the Atlantic coast, the Northwest Airlines is also doing the same thing, the National Dude Ranchers' Association is directing their people to come here and the Burlington and Northern Pacific railways are also advertising through out their territory."[51] When Florence Lee White offered to feature Crow Fair in her series of articles on American Festivals for the *New York Times*, Yellowtail welcomed the publicity.[52] White's August 28, 1938, article, "Montana Pow Wow" reported, "The Indian powwow here . . . has become a national event unique in character, for it draws no fewer than thirty tribes of the plains Indians . . . extending from the Great Lakes to the Pacific."[53] Yellowtail also used other media to spread the word about Crow Fair, as in 1936 and 1938 when he expected "to have the Fox Movie Tone people from

Hollywood here to make pictures of this unique event to flash pictures on the screen all over the United States."[54] In 1941, Ruthrauff and Ryan, a New York City–based advertising company, volunteered to broadcast the Crow Fair nationwide. By that time, Yellowtail was pleased with mainstream America's response to Crow Fair and Rodeo: "People from New York City are arranging to attend this Fair, by train or airplane. People from dude ranches in Wyoming are anxiously waiting to come . . . and people representing large Eastern newspapers have written their intention on attending. We now have national interest in the event."[55]

## CROW FAIR AND RODEO AS A "PLAINS INDIAN CONFERENCE"

Yellowtail also encouraged Indian people to converge at Crow Fair and Rodeo to partake in intertribal camaraderie. Crow Fair became a place where tribal and intertribal meetings and celebrations took place. Yellowtail was persistent in his efforts to drum up Indian participation. He contacted Blackfeet tribal leaders such as Oscar Boy and Wades in the Water from Browning, Montana, in 1936, and Thomas Main of Hays, Montana, in 1938, to invite them to the festivities. In an effort to coax the Blackfeet to attend, Yellowtail explained that "we want Indians represented here from every reservation in the state." He professed that various Indian groups from Wyoming, Gros Ventres from North Dakota, "a large delegation from your country" (in northern Montana) and the "Cheyennes that are close by will all turn out so that we ought to have about five thousand Indians here." He hailed Crow Fair and Rodeo as a distinctively Indian celebration and described its program, stating, "The first day of the fair, Monday, is going to be set aside for dancing and tribal festivities. The second day will be the regular races and rodeo events, etc. On Sunday, the last day of the Fair will be set aside for the election of officers and then the 'giveaway,' during which tribal members distribute gifts to honor their tribal members, especially clan relatives, as they had done in prereservation days."[56] In 1937, Yellowtail announced that Crow Fair and Rodeo would include western Native Americans from "Calgary in Canada [on the north] to the Indians of Oklahoma on the South and by the Nez Perces on the West in Idaho to the Gros Ventre on the East in North Dakota."[57] The following year, Yellowtail submitted an article on the Crow Fair to the Indian Emergency Conservation

Corps–Indian Division's publication *Indians at Work*, because it was "the best possible way of letting Indians all over the country know of the Fair."[58]

Yellowtail envisioned Crow Fair as an intertribal political and cultural event—"a get-to-gether each year at which time the Indians are privileged to discuss any and all problems relative to Indian administration."[59] Because of the deliberate intermixing of Indian children in government boarding schools, American Indians were embracing a pan-Indian sensibility in growing numbers. That sensibility led to the development of a number of supratribal cultural and political trends in the first decades of the twentieth century. Among these was the rising popularity of intertribal powwows and the Native American church, as well as the development of political organizations such as the Society of American Indians (1911), the All Indian Pueblo Council (1919), the Grand Council Fire of American Indians (1923), the Indian Association of America (1932), and the Indian Confederation of America (1933). Collier offered federal support for the pan-Indian movement, which led to the formation of the National Congress of American Indians in 1944. As Yellowtail had hoped, Crow Fair and Rodeo furnished a forum for such organizations. For instance, in 1938 he happily reported that a pan-Indian meeting of Montana Indians was held during the week of Crow Fair.[60] A Crow "Tribal Council Gathering," for which Yellowtail asked the forester to kill one elk from the Crow reservation to feed the participants, also resumed during the Crow Fair that year.[61] The following year, Yellowtail notified a *Billings Gazette* reporter that a "special gathering of an Indian organization" was slated to meet just prior to Crow Fair.[62] He had arranged with Lawrence Two Axe to have the conference of the League of Nations of North American Indians, a unity movement begun within the Iroquois Confederacy, rescheduled so that it would directly precede Crow Fair.[63] Subsequently, the League did meet before Crow Fair to read, amend, and adopt their constitution and laws; to nominate and elect national officers, councils, and committees; and to discuss the "Treaties, Executive Orders, Proclamations, Indian bills pending in Congress, and other Legislation affecting all Indians."[64] Yellowtail also welcomed an Indian rights advocate from Idaho who wished to deliver a speech. He assured him that "all Indians are cordially invited to meet here during the Crow Fair or any other period" and as for his speech, "such utterances, if enlightening, are always welcomed by anybody who is interested in Indian affairs."[65] In 1940, Yellowtail sent a circular to reservation agency superintendents in Montana, Oklahoma, South Dakota, Minnesota, Colorado, North

Dakota, Wisconsin, Oregon, Idaho, Wyoming, Kansas, Nebraska, and Washington.[66] The result was that five thousand Indians gathered at Crow Fair campgrounds in "more than two hundred tepees" and a number of tents in 1940.[67]

The Crows proved to be generous hosts to their American Indian guests, offering them barbecued buffalo and elk meat harvested from the Crow reservation. In 1936 the Crows slaughtered ten buffalo, fifteen elk, and about thirty beeves, all donated by Indian and white lessees "in order to feed the immense crowds that will be here." (The buffalo and elk meat was shared only with guests and was never sold to outsiders for profit.)[68] In 1938 the Crows prepared fifteen buffalo and an equal number of elk for their Native American guests. On the first day of the celebration, "all visiting Indians were assisted to living quarters . . . and received their meat rations."[69] Still, traveling to a pan-Indian event was expensive, and Yellowtail continually warned his Native visitors to be prepared to pay their own gasoline expenses. In 1936 he cautioned Wades in the Water, saying, "I wish to suggest to your people, through you, that they bring sufficient money to pay for their gasoline expenses both ways. The

*Indian tepees, Crow Indian Fair, August 30, 1938.*
Montana Historical Society, Helena (Photo #955-884).

Crows will take care of the rest."[70] By "the rest," he meant that the Crows were prepared to "take care of everybody in the way of providing camping room" and "furnish buffalo and elk meat only." Yellowtail said he regretted that the Crows simply could not provide transportation expenses, "owing to the fact that we have a tremendous crowd to take care of."[71]

Non-Indians in attendance viewed this politically and culturally oriented Plains Indian conference with a mix of curiosity and Old West nostalgia. In 1936 a reporter waxed romantically about the Native American rendezvous. He anticipated that "the Crows are again to play host to all Indian tribes between Canada and Oklahoma. . . . With their guests they will smoke the peace pipe, [and] eat buffalo and elk steaks as they did years ago over the camp fire."[72] Another reporter proclaimed the Crow Fair and Rodeo as "the biggest Indian fair pageant in the United States." The daily parades included "the entire Crow tribe" accompanied by "visiting members of the Cheyennes, Bloods, Blackfeet, Sioux, Osage, and Gros Ventre tribes in their finest tribal apparel, a feature alone well worth going across the continent to see by people living in the east."[73] Another non-Indian witness, this one a bit mystified, described a Gros Ventre Indian's "medicine or peace pipe adoption ceremony," in which the Gros Ventre adopted several Crow Indians, as "full of ritual."[74]

Out of his desire to display modern adaptations of Plains Indian traditions, Yellowtail also expanded the place of Indian dancing at Crow Fair and Rodeo. By 1934, "Indian war dancing" was featured along with rodeo and horse racing events.[75] The 1935 Crow Indian Fair and Rodeo closed with a war dance, followed by "dancing in the pavilion for everybody."[76] Yellowtail had a new dance pavilion built for this purpose and used it as a lure to attract Plains Indian participants. Yellowtail assured members of the Blackfeet tribe visiting the 1936 Crow Fair and Rodeo that they would be able to "take part in the Indian dances." He was eager to tell them that "we are building a great shade. . . . We are selecting the best singers among the Crows to sing for the War dance, Owl dance and other dances so that we will be assured of good music in that regard."[77]

The imaginations of non-Indian visitors were captivated by these dances. One observer characterized the 1937 War and Owl Dances as "highly entertaining, very picturesque."[78] Another mused, "The area in which the dancers and singers hold forth, coupled with the dust and the moonlight, gives a fine impression as if time were turned back sixty or eighty years."[79] These dances, however, were not relics but developing parts of Native American life in the

*Crow Fair Parade Dance, 1935. Leading the Parade are Gardner John Half and Hugh Little Owl; Alex Medicine Horse is next to tepee.*
Photo collection of Dennis L. Sanders. Hardin Photo Service, Hardin, Montana. (Photo #875).

twentieth century, parts that would grow into a powwow movement. Already by 1938, the Crow Fair program declared it "The Plains Indian Pow-Wow, Pageant: The Crow Tribal Fair-Rodeo," while scheduling a "Grand Dance To The Tune of Tom-Toms" for the evening of the first day.[80]

## CROWS RIDING BUFFALOES AND BRONCOS

Yellowtail also used Crow Fair and Rodeo as a vehicle to present all elements of Crow culture to the public, including those that were inherited and those that were newly acquired. One of those elements that the Crows had adopted and made a part of their lives on the reservation was rodeo, an activity with Native, Hispanic, and Anglo American origins.

The rodeo, having virtually replaced the Crow industrial fair in the 1920s, continued to be a centerpiece of Yellowtail's revived Crow Fair and Rodeo. The 1934 *Hardin Tribune-Herald's* Crow Fair headline—"Four Big Days of Horse Racing, Steer Riding, Calf Roping, War Dancing, Etc."—confirmed that rodeo and horse races had become Crow Fair's main attraction, while "war dancing" was gaining prominence. Yellowtail, the Crow Fair and Rodeo board of directors, and rodeo managers realized this. They agreed to schedule more time for the rodeo and racetrack events than for any other activity. Tribal and intertribal ceremonies at the campground took place the first two days of the fair, while rodeo and racetrack events at the rodeo grounds dominated the final three days.[81] Yellowtail was dedicated to improving the quality of Crow Fair's rodeo. By 1938, the purses offered at the rodeo had become a bit more substantial, with $150 offered for a relay race and $300 offered for trick roping."[82] Improvements had also been made to the racetrack arena and grandstand, but the Crows were unable to afford a starting gate for the rodeo. Yellowtail resolved to do without: "I think we had better drop the matter. We will use the old time system of getting started as best we can."[83]

Crow Fair's rodeo featured mostly Indian contestants as well as much Indian-raised livestock. The Not Afraid family was one of the Crow providers of stock for the fair, offering their string of bucking horses for bronc riding.[84] Observers extolled the attributes of the rodeo at Crow Fair, saying that it had distinctive "Indian style, which is in no way involved with the present day trickery of jockeys. These races will be a best horse win affair."[85] A visitor to the 1934 Crow Fair and Rodeo reported, "The program each day was good, there being several horse races, calf-roping, steer riding, cow-milking contests, tug-of-war, foot racing, [and] trick roping."[86] In 1936, an advertisement for the Crow Fair's rodeo also praised the "Indian cow punchers" themselves, as well as the stock, both horses and buffalo, that would be used:

A rodeo conducted strictly by the Indians themselves is now in the making, an assurance that the public will be pleased. The famous wild horse herd of David Dawes, so wild that they are hard to corral, or even to come near them on the range, will be corralled by Indian cow punchers. . . . These horses challenge for ferocity and meanness anything now being used for those events at Cheyenne, Pendleton, and other leading Wild West shows of the country. Buffalo from

*Crow Indian cowboys in the 1930s.*
Photo collection of Dennis L. Sanders. Hardin Photo Service, Hardin, Montana
(Photo #9870).

the tribal herd will be used for the rodeo events. This will be one of the big features of the rodeo that will be a part of the show.[87]

To add to the uniqueness of their rodeo, Yellowtail and the Crow rodeo managers chose to showcase Indian buffalo riding. Even more than other rodeo events, it directly linked the rodeo to the Crows' past and present experiences as both buffalo hunters and ranchers. Yellowtail also intended to attract rodeo fans. He acknowledged that buffalo riding was "unique for those kinds of sports and draws a large throng locally."[88] One of Crow Fair and Rodeo's programs declared that each day's rodeo would begin with a "buffalo coming out of chute with a wild Indian on his back, wearing a war bonnet and with a tomahawk."[89] The Crows' own description of this event was written to attract non-Indian spectators, as it portrayed the stereotypical image of an American Indian wearing his warbonnet and bearing a tomahawk. Newspaper reporters fastened onto this image and promised that "naked Indians painted and wearing war bonnets hanging onto buffalo manes all turned loose at the same time and also a similar number of Brahma steers from another part of the field will electrify the crowds."[90]

In advertising Indian buffalo riding in that manner, Yellowtail and the Crow rodeo managers made a conscious decision to promote their event by indulging in stereotypes, yet they recognized that the skills involved in buffalo riding were those of experienced Indian rodeo cowboys. It was also worth it to them to create a forum where only Indians could compete in a rodeo event that was decidedly of their own making. They realized that most Indian riders would be unpainted and fully clad in cowboy boots and apparel, but they also knew that the crowds would not be disappointed. A spectator in 1937 confirmed that their confidence was not misplaced as he described the "Indian cow punchers . . . each dressed in cowhand style, astride his horse" as they prepared for the rodeo. "The afternoon rodeos," he continued, "in which mostly young Indians participated, were as exciting as any of those performances staged by white cowboys. There were calf roping, bronc busting and, most thrilling of all, buffalo riding events. . . . The show was replete with a rodeo clown and tack pony whose antics kept the crowd in laughter."[91] Buffalo riding became such a popular local attraction that a manufacturer contacted Yellowtail about reproducing the image of an Indian riding a buffalo on a plate as a souvenir.[92]

Crows and their Indian guests also savored the incorporation of the buffalo into Crow Fair and Rodeo. The Crows were able to show off their recently augmented buffalo herd, as both their feasts and rodeos utilized buffalo. On one occasion in 1938, Frank Takes Gun gathered seven or eight head of buffalo and herded them into the corral in the center of the Crow Fair racetrack arena "for rodeo purposes."[93] Yellowtail was proud of the fact that bull riders rode "buffalo from the wild herd on the Crow Reservation, instead of Brahma steers."[94] A "buffalo scramble from each of the six gates," with contestants struggling to stay astride wild buffaloes, was also a daily opening event.[95] In 1941 the three-day rodeo continued to feature buffalo riding, along with bronc riding and calf roping. For the occasion, the Crows rounded up some five hundred young buffalo, out of which they selected about forty head to be used in the buffalo riding and buffalo barbecue.[96] The buffalo roundup preceding Crow Fair had become an event in itself for those Crows involved in it.[97]

With the exception of Superintendent Yellowtail, Bureau of Indian Affairs officials remained dubious about the benefits of Indian rodeo. In 1941 William Zimmerman Jr., assistant commissioner of Indian affairs, rebuked the enthusiastic Yellowtail for insinuating that his Crow Fair and Rodeo had the full support of the Indian commissioner and the secretary of the interior. Collier himself reminded Yellowtail that he was indeed "interested in the fair or any activity which has as its objective the economic development and the social welfare of the Indians. . . . If, however, the impression is gained that the fair is mainly a rodeo and sports event," he admonished that neither he nor the secretary would wholeheartedly support it.[98] In response, Yellowtail minimized the rodeo's importance at Crow Fair. In an apologetic letter to the commissioner of Indian affairs in 1941, Yellowtail insisted that "the fair is not a rodeo or sportive event. That feature is placed at the end of the program and it perhaps will not fare so well."[99] Even in an era in which Bureau of Indian Affairs officials were determined to listen to the Native voice, they were unable to understand it. They failed to appreciate the fact that the Crows' rodeo contributed to the tribe's social welfare and economic development through its emphasis on Native riders and stock, including Indian-raised buffalo, horses, and cattle. With the exception of Indian buffalo-riding, Crow Fair's rodeo events remained open to whites during this period. By competing in the context of a Plains Indian conference, Crows and other Native cowboys also gained a new perspective. Many began to recognize the potential benefits of organizing and competing in a rodeo that was exclusively Indian. In this way, the revitalized Crow Fair and Rodeo of the Indian New Deal years anticipated the inception of the all-Indian rodeo circuit of the following decade.

In the agricultural displays as well as in the rodeo, the Crows demonstrated the skills that they had acquired as cattle ranchers. An observer in 1936 described the fair and rodeo as "a mixed agricultural and tribal show, . . . a well balanced show, . . . this grand display of the efforts of both the government and the Indians themselves." In this case, "the government and the Indians themselves" were one and the same. This meant that Superintendent Yellowtail lent his support to Bureau of Indian Affairs initiatives, including agricultural exhibits at tribal fairs. He did this out of duty but also because of his own commitment to cultivating the Crow tribe's economic self-sufficiency. In this regard, Yellowtail resembled his early-twentieth-century predecessor,

Superintendent S. G. Reynolds, who had initiated Crow Fair in 1904 to encourage and display the Crows' mastery of agricultural skills. While Yellowtail echoed Reynolds's agricultural mission, he emphasized ranching over farming, saying that "the Crow Fair was reestablished . . . to encourage the breeding of better livestock and to inspire the Indians to take more interest in their homes."[100] Accordingly, a 1936 Crow Fair and Rodeo announcement proclaimed the revival of Crow Fair and Rodeo as an agricultural fair.[101] Yellowtail's agricultural agenda provided yet another reason for him to invite a diverse Indian and non-Indian audience to the Crow Fair and Rodeo. Yellowtail viewed the fair and rodeo as a valuable "means of comparing notes with whites and Indians alike in the matter of raising beets, other kinds of crops and all breeds of horses, . . . cow management . . . and other activities of the 4-H boys . . . that go to make life worth while on the modern ranch and farm."[102]

To garner Crow support for the agricultural aspects of the fair and rodeo, Yellowtail advertised in Crow agricultural periodicals, including the *Crow Stockman and Farmer*.[103] He also looked to young Crow members of 4-H clubs to foster enthusiasm for these displays. As an advocate of Crow cattle ranching and horse breeding, Yellowtail enthusiastically included "a grand livestock parade" in the 1936 fair. It featured a "grand champion Belgian stallion recently imported from Canada, . . . pure bred registered and nonregistered now in the hands of individual Crow owners," and "registered Morgan stallions, mares and colts, thoroughbred horses, registered Hereford cows and their calves." Crow 4-H clubs and "Calf clubs" also staged exhibits.[104] Agricultural and home economics exhibits were also displayed at the 1938 Crow Fair, where the 4-H club boys had "their fat steers on display" and an "agricultural parade of livestock and farm products" marched before the grandstand.[105] These educational features of Crow Fair were further testaments to the Crows' ability to integrate what they saw as worthwhile additions into their cultures.

## ADAPTED RITUALS AND DANCES

Yellowtail and the Crows who managed Crow Fair and Rodeo intended to exhibit their culture as a composite of activities adapted from their past and present circumstances. For the first time, the Crows were capitalizing on what they had always felt Crow Fair to be—a re-creation of their previous summer gatherings and the contests, rituals, and dances that had taken place there. While non-Indians viewed these Indian cultural activities with an observer's keen interest, American Indians participated in these rituals as living and developing parts of their cultures. Both groups were attracted to the vital American Indian culture, particularly the Crow culture, on display at Crow Fair and Rodeo, and Yellowtail capitalized on this interest. In the process, the group identity of the Crows was being reaffirmed.

Yellowtail displayed many inherited and adapted Crow traditions to preserve them, to promote tourism, and to celebrate the complexity of Crow culture. The presence of anthropologists such as Robert Lowie, head of the Department of Anthropology at the University of California, on the Crow reservation during the 1930s heightened the Crows' awareness of their pre-reservation culture and impressed upon them the importance of documenting these traditions, lest they vanish.[106] This belief in imminent Indian doom had been a recurring theme in late-nineteenth- and early-twentieth-century art as typified in James Earle Fraser's sculpture *End of the Trail*, which portrayed a defeated Indian leaning forward on horseback, presumably taking a "bow to the modern world."[107] This sentiment had changed with the advent of the Indian New Deal, as American Indians like Yellowtail made it clear that they had neither vanished nor surrendered their Indian heritage and identity to the modern world but had successfully integrated the two.

Still, Yellowtail realized that the older generation, which had successfully guided the Crows' transition to reservation life, would soon die. He wanted to ensure that their customs would be recorded for posterity to adapt and continue. For this purpose, he enlisted Fox Film Company in 1936 and Eastman Kodak Company in 1938 to film the Crow Fair and Rodeo's activities.[108] In a letter to John Collier, Yellowtail stressed the cultural importance of preserving the "dress, customs, etc. of the Indians who will be assembled there" for the benefit of future generations of Crows: "I would like to have the matter recorded as the old people are dying and it is only a question of but a few years before these matters are entirely forgotten and it will be beyond the ability of the rising generation to reproduce them again."[109] To further document Crow heritage, "famous Throssel photographs of the Crows in 1900" were exhibited at the 1936 Crow Fair.[110] In a letter requesting that his daughter Joy be excused from school to attend Crow Fair, Yellowtail underlined the educational purpose of the fair. He explained to his daughter's principal that "the Crow Tribal Fair attempts to keep alive for the younger generation of Crows the strenuous life that our forefathers lived but a very few years before their birth."[111]

Yellowtail also wanted non-Indians to witness the Crows' evolving culture. In 1936, Yellowtail wrote the secretary of the Dude Ranchers' Association that "Indian tribal custom rituals of every description are going to be revived for the benefit of the general public, and along with it there will be the regular race, rodeo and fair events."[112] A year later Crow Fair was advertised as an Indian pageant that doubled as a Crow history lesson. A *Hardin Herald* reporter described it as "an Indian pageant depicting prereservation and modern life—giving the visitor scenes that greeted the eyes of Catlin, Lewis and Clark and others in 1806, . . . a parade depicting the mode of travel from the very early days . . . on up to the modern conveyances with all the trimmings."[113] In 1940, Yellowtail offered a similar definition of Crow Fair and Rodeo's cultural agenda: "The Crow Tribal Fair is in reality, an Indian Pageant, depicting in a very vivid fashion, the kind of life the Indians lived when Lewis and Clark came through this country, and mixing in with it, the customs they have adopted from the whites."[114]

To this end, Robert Yellowtail reintroduced traditional Indian ceremonies and dances, previously outlawed by the Courts of Indian Offenses established in the 1880s.[115] Yellowtail was aware of the anthropological research that had been undertaken on Crow ceremonials at the American Museum of Natural History. The scholarly work of contemporary anthropologists like Lowie influenced the Crows' rendering of their own pre-reservation cultural practices and testified to non-Indians their importance.[116] Yellowtail referred to recent scholarship as he advertised the types of rituals that Crows would demonstrate. He listed one day's cultural highlights, saying, "Immediately following this [Sun Dance] will be the Crow Medicine Pipe Ceremonial that has more ritual than Catholic churches and others. The Crow Buffalo Dance, or Adoption Ceremony, as discussed . . . by Dr. Robert H. Lowie . . . will follow."[117] The 1937 Adoption Dance lasted all afternoon and was described as "highly ceremonial."[118] Similarly, in 1938 the Crow Fair program touted that the "adoption ceremonials and dances of the Tobacco Society," which took place all morning of the second day, were "full of sacred ritual."[119] Yellowtail also suggested that the Peace Medicine Pipe Ceremonial would be "of particular interest to Anthropologists, whose works are devoted to that kind of study."[120]

Crow Fair's Peace Medicine Pipe Ceremonial was one of the re-creations of a pre-reservation ceremony. As tribal historians recount, the head chiefs of buffalo hunting bands would meet to discuss where each would camp the following year. They would open medicine bundles and offer a pipe to Acbadadea, maker of things above, so that he would deliver each of the bands safely to their destination. The chiefs would pray for protection from turbulent rivers, Indian adversaries, and any other dangers that might impede the journey of each band.[121] Similarly, at Crow Fair and Rodeo, a pipeholder rode at the head of the Parade Dance as part of the Peace Medicine Pipe Ceremonial. The Crow Fair and Rodeo program explained that the pipe was meant to placate "the Great Spirits who live around us, above us, below us and within us." No one was allowed to cross the path of the pipeholder.[122]

As a revived and modified aspect of Native culture, the Shoshone-Crow Sun Dance was naturally included at Crow Fair and Rodeo. The Bureau of Indian Affairs had prohibited Sun Dances, yet the Indians had kept them vital by holding them clandestinely. Breaking with their staunchly assimilationist predecessors, BIA officials like John Collier and Robert Yellowtail encouraged public revivals of formerly prohibited Native rituals such as the Sun Dance. By 1941, many Crows—including Thomas Yellowtail, Crow Medicine Man, and Sun Dance Chief—had embraced the reconstructed Shoshone-Crow Sun Dance.[123] The Sun Dance inaugurated the 1941 Crow Fair, and the participants continued their ritual for three days and nights without food or water.[124] After the Crows concluded their Sun Dance, they engaged in the other Indian ceremonial events, which were followed by the rodeo and race track events.[125] Superintendent Yellowtail was particularly interested in staging ceremonial activities for that year's proposed nationwide radio broadcast of the Crow Fair. Aggressively promoting the Crow Fair, Yellowtail declared that the Shoshone-Crow Sun Dance was being staged "for the benefit of the visiting public, primarily for the visitors from the Eastern or Atlantic sections."[126]

For the Crows, Northern Cheyennes, and Arapahos "participating as principals," the reintroduced Sun Dance was not a tourist attraction but a religious ritual.[127] In 1943, Yellowtail showed that he also recognized the Sun Dance's significance to the Crow people as a "religious prayer dance for the Crow soldiers in the armed forces of our country," who had enlisted for duty in World War II. At the request of Crow parents, Yellowtail wrote an army officer in Casper, Wyoming, where a number of Crow soldiers were training, to entreat him to grant furloughs to Crow sons in the armed forces. He hoped that they might be able to "arrive here on the morning of the twenty-ninth at the very latest, in order to take part in this dance as they have done in the past.... Their parents requested that we write you to seek approval of a furlough."[128]

## CULTURAL CELEBRATIONS: INDIAN PRINCESSES AND
## WARRIOR HOMECOMINGS

By showcasing many of their traditions as adapted, the Crows reinforced their own reconstructed national identity. One of these traditions was the reunion of various reservation districts at Crow Fair and Rodeo in an assembly that resembled the seasonal meetings of pre-reservation bands. In pre-reservation days, bands of Crows would come together to hold councils before and after separating into bands to hunt, usually in the spring and again in the fall. Similarly, in its early years, the Crow Fair was also held in autumn. This caused problems for Crows from all over the reservation who risked getting caught in September, October, or November snowstorms on their way to the fair.[129] By moving Crow Fair and Rodeo to the last week in August, Yellowtail ensured that members of all reservation districts would be able to meet when the changeable Montana climate was usually warm and dry.[130] Committees of Crows selected Crow Fair and Rodeo board members, rodeo managers, and a princess to represent them. The board consisted of members of the respective districts, who were elected by the tribal council. In 1938, Johnny Cummins was board president. In years to come, his family name would become increasingly associated with rodeo.[131] As rodeo had ascended to a prominent position in the fair event schedule, Crows also selected cowboys and cowgirls to be managers of the Crow Fair rodeo. In 1938, two Not Afraid brothers, whose family had long been involved in rodeo, served as co-managers of the rodeo.[132]

The Crows' addition of the princess title was another example of their willingness to incorporate a European import, a title of royalty, into their own tradition of honoring women. Women had long held an important and respected place in Crow society. From buffalo hunting times into the twentieth century, the Crows had retained their matrilineal clan system in which children born or adopted into a family all took their mother's clan.[133] In part, it was through the maintenance of the clan system that women had preserved their independence and stature in Crow society into the 1930s. In his 1935 ethnography, *The Crow Indians*, Robert Lowie described the contemporary roles of women in community work, entertainment, religion, and property ownership. He concluded, "Altogether Crow women had a secure place in the tribal life and a fair share in its compensations."[134] At Crow Fair, women filled a variety of roles by preparing themselves and their family members, as well as the beadwork regalia each wore in the daily grand entry processions and ceremonies. Likewise, they arranged agricultural exhibits. Their participation as rodeo contestants was limited until ladies' barrel racing became a regular event in the 1940s.

Although Crows publicly honored the contributions of women in give-aways and other ceremonials, they also chose to bestow the European title of princess. The selected princess would "thereafter lead the tribal parades each day . . . through the camp and the Agency streets."[135] *Princess* was an interesting choice of titles, as it adhered to one of the stereotypes that Europeans had imposed on Indian women from their earliest encounters. Drawing on Native writer Rayna Green's "The Pocahontas Perplex: The Image of Indian Women in American Culture," Angelika Maeser-Lemieux points out that "the Indian Queen was presented as a symbol of the Americas which . . . became divided into the figures of Princess and Squaw."[136] Although historians and anthropologists have soundly rejected both categories as Eurocentric and inaccurate, American Indians have taken advantage of this regal title to elevate certain women as exemplars of their national and pan-Indian identity. In *The Most Beautiful Girl in the World: Beauty Pageants and National Identity*, Sarah Banet-Weiser explains, "Beauty pageants construct a specific imagined community. . . . Pageants create a national field of shared symbols and practices that define ethnicity and femininity in terms of national identity."[137] In "Princess and the Pageantry: The Serious World of Indian Pageants," writer Kelly Crow suggests the American Indian woman's reasons for appropriating the princess title:

> Of course, the pageant itself began as a white man's game. . . . But just as Indians have always adapted to the white world, they have taken the beauty pageant and filtered it through their own cultural lens. Indian pageants are about identity and the need . . . to assert their existence and their ideals. So even though she is not native, the Indian princess has become a huge part of Native life, revealing how the modern woman sees the world and in turn how she wants to be seen. Pocahontas, she is not.[138]

In the 1930s, the Crows structured their princess pageant both to reflect their own identity and to attract tourists from mainstream America, who arrived with specific cultural expectations for women and Indians. Thus, the first Crow Fair princess pageants used criteria similar to those of the early Miss America Pageants (the pageant had been inaugurated in 1921). They focused on pageantry and poise. The 1938 Crow Fair program, entitled "The Plains Indian Pow-Wow, Pageant: The Crow Tribal Fair-Rodeo," accented its

*Mollie Pickett, first prize costume in Crow Indian Parade, Lodge Grass, Montana, July 4, 1928.*
Montana Historical Society, Helena (Photo #PAC 97-52.5).

*Evaline Shane at the Crow Indian Fair, August 30, 1938.*
Montana Historical Society, Helena (Photo #955-885).

*Parade of Crow Indian maidens, August 30, 1938.*
Montana Historical Society, Helena. (Photo #955-886).

glamour, stating, "Note: the above is in effect a beauty contest and all women including visiting Indian women are eligible to participate."[139] The Crows integrated their own cultural norms into the contest by having the young female contestants present themselves in traditional clothing and on horseback. The program described the contest as a "Parade in Camp Circle by Women," having "all of the [Crow] women in camp with the best of their finery in dress, mounted on their choice of horses. . . . Before or after the parade a committee will select the most beautiful maiden and four escorts." This practice evolved into a variety of additional contests that chose district princesses, Miss Crow Nation, Crow Fair Rodeo princess, and queen. These contests more clearly reflected Crow tribal values because only Crows were allowed to compete. To be a viable contestant, a Crow woman needed to possess not only popularity but also knowledge of Crow language and culture, academic achievement, and horsemanship—all judged to be important Crow qualities.

Under Yellowtail's supervision, Crow Fair and Rodeo also became known as *Um-ba sax-billia*, meaning "where they make noise."[140] It purposefully echoed elements of past Crow celebrations, which included singing, dancing, giveaways, praise songs, and feasting of clan uncles and aunts, all of which became part of Crow Fair and Rodeo.

Clan relationships were also solidified at Crow Fair and Rodeo through praise songs, name givings, feasting of clan aunts and uncles, and giveaways. One newspaper reporter described the daily opening procession as "hundreds of participants dressed in their finest beaded dresses and outfits [followed by] clan uncles singing praise songs as they ride their best horses behind the honored person."[141] In 1936, a tribal grand entry parade featured "all Crow school students including all college students, undergraduates, high school and other students representing universities all over the country" as a way of publicly honoring their academic accomplishments.[142] This "parade of students of every university of the Pacific Coast region, holding aloft placards denoting the university," was repeated in 1941.[143]

The parades at Crow Fair and Rodeo deliberately recalled elements of processions of migrating buffalo hunting bands. They were organized much the same as Yellowtail's inaugural parade, with Superintendent Robert Yellowtail leading the procession. The 1935 and 1936 Crow Fairs opened "with a spectacular parade by the entire Indian camp of several hundred" that included the "various clans composing the Crow tribe. These various clans will, within themselves, strive to show better dress, better horses, better lodges, and with all the clans participating in these parades a great show is assured to the public."[144] One spectator observed in 1937, "They proceeded in single file, hundreds of Indians, each dressed differently, in a most magnificent and impressive array reminiscent of former times."[145] Mothers and the female clan relatives of recently married men worked for months or years preparing the beadworked dress, moccasins, belt, leggings, and accessories worn by their daughters-in-law and displayed first at their weddings and later in Crow Fair parades. When a woman appeared in such finery, she was making a statement that her "relatives are skilled and dedicated enough to do the beading. And each time these people appear in their distinctive formal dress they remind themselves, each other and outsiders that they are Crow."[146]

Yellowtail also encouraged the practice of giveaways and feasts at the revitalized Crow Fair and Rodeo. In an attempt to eliminate what they called "barbarous acts," Yellowtail's predecessors in the Bureau of Indian Affairs had

discouraged public giveaways and feasts.[147] Still, the Crows had continued to
practice giveaways. Mae Takes Gun recollected Comes from South singing his
personal song, bringing two horses and two buggies to Crow Agency, and proclaiming, "I am giving these away in honor of my children and if they want to
put me in jail for doing this, they can go ahead. . . . It is my choice and will to
give these away."[148] Until 1934, Crow Fair and Rodeo had been the only time
of year when giveaways and feasts were condoned. Yellowtail celebrated this
fact and set aside "a 'giveaway' day [during] which all the Crows will participate in taking care of visiting friends, relatives and other Indians that are
here."[149] By 1940, the Crow Indian Fair and Rodeo Program cited the occur-
rence of giveaways, or "Specials," interspersed throughout the four days of
activities.[150] These cultural rituals held different meanings for non-Indian and

*1938 Crow Fair Parade. Left to right in front: John Smart Enemy and his wife,
Myrtle.*
Montana Historical Society, Helena (Photo #PAC 79-37).

Indian participants, but all would have agreed that they were witnesses to a vital culture, whether they recognized it as quaint or modern. Although the rituals were not always approved of by non-Indians, witnesses could still see that they performed an important function for a vital culture.

Just as the homecoming of warriors was celebrated in the past, it was honored with ceremony at Crow Fair. To honor the Crow veterans who survived either pre-reservation battles or World War I, the first day of Crow Fair in 1936 was designated "welcome day." The Crows celebrated their warriors with "Indian war dances, early morning war party battle, [and] victorious return ritual," which included "military dances and other ritualistic work."[151] Again in 1937, the Crows recognized a "victorious return to Crow camp" with the reenactment of war deeds. In the reenactments, a "Crow war party charges an enemy, depicting the 'striking of coup' and minor acts of war. . . . During the ritual, military honor is publicly bestowed and rendered as in tribal history."[152] In 1938, the first day of Crow Fair included a sham battle reenactment of the 1876 Little Bighorn Battle, followed by "a war parade of warriors on horseback through camp." Later that afternoon, Crow men participated in a parade similar to the one held for the selection of the Crow Fair and Rodeo princess. During the "parade in the camp circle by men," spectators watched "the entire male population of the Crow Tribe, mounting their best chargers and wearing their best native dress of beads and feathers." The event was further "animated with individual and group singing of war chants and praise songs—the women going in the center to begin the Shoshone dance."[153] The 1940 Crow Indian Fair and Rodeo Program also promised its audience that the Crows would depict a "War Party coming home victorious, followed by a joy dance. Praise for the warriors who had come home with coups and scalps," would be lavished "by squaws and men beating tom-toms and dancing."[154] This victorious war party celebration was strikingly similar to the one that Robert Lowie described in his 1935 book, *The Crow Indians*, which was based on interviews with elders beginning in 1907 and which recorded their recollections of pre-reservation Crow traditions.[155]

During World War II, many Crows participated in the war effort, and the Crow Fair and Rodeo was suspended for part of that time. During the war, however, Crows began to revive their long-dormant warrior societies, which in pre-reservation days had been "open to promising young stars guided by celebrated veterans and marked by distinctive regalia and rituals.[156] Crow veterans of World War I and World War II were inducted into these honored societies. Crow Indian soldiers who saw action included Private First Class Robert Half, who received a Purple Heart; Matthew Stops, who served aboard the *USS Alabama*, a ship that raided the Japanese mainland twice; Henry Old Coyote; Barney Old Coyote; and Daniel M. Dreamer.[157] In 1942, a public relations office released a photo of the latter two soldiers in training, "showing one with a machine gun while the other held an Indian bow and arrow."[158] Through both the ceremonies they performed at Crow Fair and the bravery Crow soldiers displayed in battle, the Crows had carried their military tradition into the twentieth century.

## RODEO AT PINE RIDGE AND ROSEBUD SIOUX TRIBAL FAIRS

Lakotas at Pine Ridge and Rosebud reservations also participated in ranching, rodeo, and their tribal fair during the Indian New Deal. Unlike the Crows, they did not receive a Native superintendent. Although Indian New Deal funds inspired a resurgence of Lakota ranching, the New Deal also marked the resumption of well-intentioned government interference in the Lakota's cultural lives.

On the Pine Ridge reservation, the resuscitated Pine Ridge Sioux Fair replaced the Pine Ridge Sioux Rodeo in 1939. At that time, Agricultural Extension Agent R. F. Coulter proclaimed, "Pine Ridge is reviving its fair after having had more than 10 years of rest. It seems that the fairs here gave way to a rodeo which was strictly entertainment, but the people are now anxious to get back to something more educational."[159] In 1941, Pine Ridge Superintendent W. O. Roberts underlined the fact that the fair was no longer exclusively a rodeo. He wrote, "The Pine Ridge Fair and Festival (not rodeo) is held annually at the Pine Ridge Indian Agency." Like Yellowtail, Roberts intended the revitalized Pine Ridge fair to encourage both Lakota traditional activities and modern political and agricultural efforts. Superintendent Roberts explained, "In addition to an opportunity for . . . reenacting old scenes, displaying native finery, [and] joining together in Indian music and ceremonials, the event offers opportunities for the leaders of the Tribe . . . to discuss matters of general interest. The Fair feature of the program is intended as a means of encouragement to Indian farmers and stockmen."[160] Although their opinions were solicited, Lakotas no longer had complete control over the content of their annual reservation-wide event.

The leadership roles had shifted from the all-Lakota Pine Ridge Rodeo Committee to Indian Office officials. Having reduced Lakota autonomy, BIA officials anticipated that, after some more training, the Indians could resume complete control. This was an ironic statement in light of the previous decade in which Oglala Lakotas had managed every aspect of the Pine Ridge Sioux Rodeo. Philip S. Byrnes, the non-Indian secretary of the fair and festival committee, expressed the hope that "when we build it up on a sound business basis, . . . we can say to the tribe, now this is a good proposition; take it over."[161]

Given the recent support of cultural pluralism by the Bureau of Indian Affairs, Lakotas were encouraged to display their culture. Of the Oglala Sioux Fair and Festival, Superintendent Roberts declared: "The program is largely managed by Indians. The schedule is prepared in accordance with the Indians' point of view on Native celebration."[162] For many, their culture had come to include ranching and rodeo, and they successfully integrated it into their revived tribal fair. In addition to the usual rodeo events that appeared in the Oglala Sioux Fair and Festival program, Oglala Lakotas also included events that accommodated both their affection for rodeo and their superintendent's proclivity for reviving all things Indian for the benefit of the Lakotas and their non-Indian guests. To this end, Oglalas included the colorful event "bronc riding in Indian costume."[163]

On the Rosebud reservation, Lakotas held rodeos to commemorate important events, ranging from the Indian Reorganization Act to road building and World War II. In 1935, the Parmelee Indians of Rosebud put on "a big reorganization celebration and rodeo." There, they combined discussions with Lakota politicians—such as one with Ben Reifel (Reifel was a Sioux Indian who served as an employee of the BIA and eventually as the Commissioner of Indian Affairs in the 1970's) about the Indian Reorganization Act—with rodeo.[164] Earlier that fall, the Ring Thunder Camp had held a "big Indian celebration" that included "cow riding and calf roping . . . and keg roping," along with "Indian dances."[165] In 1940, the Lakotas of Parmelee hosted a three-day celebration at Spotted Tail Park. As advertised, "The celebration this year takes the form of a rodeo and carnival celebrating the completion of the first oiled road on U.S. Highway No. 18 in Todd County."[166] The following year, Parmelee sponsored another celebration at Spotted Tail Park, which they touted as the Annual Spotted Tail celebration featuring both "Sioux Indian dances" and "a big rodeo."[167]

To encourage the Lakota soldiers serving in World War II, as well as their families, the Rosebud Sioux staged a number of rodeos. In 1942, they held a Victory Encouragement celebration at Spotted Tail Park. "Riding, roping and sports of all kinds" followed the "Victory Encouragement Native Worship ceremony and dance."[168] Another three-day rodeo was organized at Parmelee in 1944 "in honor of the boys who are serving in the armed forces."[169] In 1945, the Rosebud Sioux celebrated the end of World War II in Europe as the Parents of World War II organization staged a VE celebration and rodeo at the Rosebud Fairgrounds.[170]

Like the Crows and Pine Ridge Lakotas, the Rosebud Sioux incorporated rodeo into their renewed tribal fair. From 1933 to 1945, the Rosebud Fair's program accentuated its livestock and agricultural exhibits, yet rodeo remained. In 1936, the "WPA women workers from St. Francis, Mission, Parmelee, Rosebud and Okreek" were the main attraction at the Reservation Fair at Rosebud, where they exhibited their produce.[171] But subsequent Rosebud Sioux Fair programs listed rodeo as a featured event, staged on two of the fair's three days.[172] In 1940, Senior Rodeo Director Bob Waln of the Rosebud Sioux expanded the rodeo events at the Rosebud Fair. A complete rodeo was held, including "bronco riding, cow riding, calf roping and other rodeo events."[173] Thus, on the Rosebud Sioux reservation, Lakotas continued to enjoy rodeo as a favored form of community celebration, held to mark significant occasions of all kinds.

## A DECADE OF INDIAN CULTURAL REVIVALS

The Indian New Deal ended in 1945 with the resignation of both Commissioner of Indian Affairs John Collier and Crow Superintendent Robert Yellowtail. Yellowtail departed his office to fight what would ironically become known as the Yellowtail Dam.[174] Both men influenced the character of future community celebrations held on the Crow, Pine Ridge, and Rosebud reservations. John Collier had mandated a government-sponsored policy that aimed for an economic, political, and cultural renaissance among Native Americans. The tribal fair, with its emphasis on culture and agricultural endeavours, was the ideal forum with which to promote these goals. Consequently, Indian agents on the Crow, Pine Ridge, and Rosebud reservations replaced the reservation rodeos of the 1920s with tribal fairs as their annual reservation-wide gatherings. Indian agents, often enlisting the aid of Plains Indians, revived these tribal fairs to showcase modern Indian culture, a culture which featured rodeo as a central element by 1934.

Robert Yellowtail shared Collier's goals for the Crow reservation. As the first Native American superintendent to run his own reservation agency, he was given an unprecedented opportunity to implement these goals. In an era in which federal policy was aimed at reversing the effects of assimilation and celebrating cultural diversity, Superintendent Yellowtail seized the opportunity. In the process of marketing aspects of the Crows' modern culture to an Indian and non-Indian audience, Yellowtail reinforced the Crows' group identity. For his numerous guests, Yellowtail designed an eminently Crow tribal fair where modern Crow identity was showcased. By engaging in daily parades, religious and social dances, and adapted ceremonial rituals, as well as rodeos and agricultural exhibits, the Crow men, women, and children celebrated important aspects of their twentieth-century culture and reaffirmed their community and clan ties. By refashioning the Crow Fair and Rodeo into both an American national institution and a Plains Indian conference, Yellowtail also reminded the Crows and their visitors that the Crow nation was essentially bound to a broader American Indian community and American nation.

On the Pine Ridge and Rosebud reservations, Indian agents had usurped control of the annual reservation-wide gathering, which they determined should be a tribal fair. Within the context of an Indian agricultural fair, they encouraged the Lakotas to express themselves culturally. Given this opportunity and its constraints, Lakotas incorporated rodeo into their revived tribal fairs. They further confirmed that rodeo had assumed a meaningful role in their community cultures by staging rodeos to honor momentous events that affected their lives, events ranging in scale from the Indian Reorganization Act and World War II to the paving of a highway.

From 1933 to 1945, Crows and Lakotas remained active in rodeos on their reservations. As the Bureau of Indian Affairs encouraged a revival of Indian activities, Crows and Lakotas made it clear that rodeo had become integral to their cultures. When given the opportunity to determine the content of their tribal fairs such as the Oglala Sioux Fair, the Rosebud Sioux Fair, and the Crow Fair, Crows and Lakotas did not abandon the rodeo as a favored form of community celebration. Rather, they included rodeo events alongside their adapted Indian dances and ceremonials. Crow Fair's rodeo was the most widely attended by northern Plains Indians. In the revitalized Crow Fair and

Rodeo, American Indians found, for the first time since their confinement to reservations, a forum—accepted by the Indian Office, non-Indians, and Indians alike—where they could gather on a large scale and freely express their identities. The fact that rodeo remained a central part of Crow Fair and Rodeo during its evolution from 1934 to 1945 presaged its own increasingly important role as a pan-Indian event in decades to come.

## CHAPTER FOUR

# The Emergence of Rodeo Families and All-Indian Rodeos

## 1945–1970

FOLLOWING WORLD WAR II, MANY AMERICAN POLITICAL leaders began to feel that there was no place within a democratic nation for separate semi-sovereign Indian nations residing on communal reservations. Criticizing John Collier's Indian Reorganization Act for its alleged emphasis on collectivism, its increase in paternalism, and its expense to taxpayers, they called for less government regulation and interference. This sentiment resulted in the federal Indian policy of *termination*, which aimed ostensibly at "emancipating" American Indians by terminating federal Indian trust responsibilities.[1] Most American Indians certainly were eager to diminish the influence of the BIA in their political and social lives, but not at the cost of the federal government's legal obligation to protect their tribal governments and sovereignty, the nontaxable status of reservation lands, their treaty rights, and their access to federally supplied services. Galvanized by their involvement in World War II, American Indians pledged to fight termination, and in the process mobilized for their drive toward self-determination.[2] In their struggle for sovereignty, Native people employed pacifist and militant tactics modeled by leaders of the African American civil rights and Black Power movements. As historian Sharon O'Brien explains, "Proud of their heritage and determined to protect their political, cultural, and land rights, Indian people across the nation organized, demonstrated, and protested."[3] Primarily college-educated Indian youths made "Red Power" the rallying cry for the movement they led. Many of their families had moved off their reservations, either during the war to work in wartime industries or later as part of a BIA relocation project.[4] Returning to their reservations in the 1960s, the activists brought with them political and cultural agendas that stressed Indian culture, tribal sovereignty, and self-determination.

In this context, the all-Indian rodeo circuit emerged in the mid-1950s and 1960s to accommodate the changing dynamics between Indians and Anglo Americans, as well as within and between Indian communities. Although political differences and reports of racial prejudice continued to strain Indian-white relationships, many non-Indians had gained a newfound respect for American Indians and their cultures as a consequence of the distinguished service of twenty-five thousand American Indian servicemen in World War II. Consequently, many whites, particularly from the East, became more eager to support burgeoning tribal tourist enterprises during their jaunts to the American West. The American Legion also grew more interested in American Indians as potential members and opened additional branches on reservations, some of which sponsored reservation rodeos.

Relationships and perspectives within and between northern Plains Indian communities were also changing in a way that fostered an all-Indian rodeo circuit. Many tribes sought to reverse the effects of the BIA's program of relocating American Indians from rural enclaves to urban cities by revitalizing their local reservations.[5] As one way to improve their tribal economies, tribal councils on the Northern Cheyenne, Crow, Rosebud, and Pine Ridge reservations initiated tribal tourist enterprises. They used their existing tribal fairs and rodeos as tourist attractions to capture the attention of non-Indian visitors and to encourage them to visit the reservations. Many of these tribes opened the postwar decade by staging fairs and rodeos to appeal to a non-Indian tourist audience. The Crows did this by playing up the Indian character of the event, calling Crow Fair the "Teepee Capital of the World." The Rosebud Sioux went the opposite direction by scheduling carnivals, stock car races, and bowery dances alongside their Indian dances, parades, and rodeo. Both tribes continued to feature rodeo, knowing it was a favorite among non-Indians and Indians alike.

On each of these reservations—Crow, Northern Cheyenne, and Lakota—women and men continued to participate in rodeos. As they did, rodeo families, families whose members by blood or marriage consistently participated in rodeo, began to emerge. Many of the members of these rodeo family were women, who assumed a more visible role competing in rodeos and presiding over them as rodeo queens. Since 1929, when bronc-rider Bonnie McCarroll was killed competing in the Pendelton Round-Up, rodeo promoters had severely limited the place of women.[6] According to Mary Lou LeCompte, when the Rodeo Association of America was formed that same year, its system included no events for women. By 1948, a group of cowgirls changed this by forming the Girls Rodeo Association, later known as the Women's Professional Rodeo Association (WPRA). The WPRA was successful at working with local rodeo producers as well as the PRCA. They were able to make cowgirls' barrel racing a standard rodeo contest at a majority of PRCA-sponsored rodeos.[7] As reservation rodeos followed this trend, cowgirls' barrel racing became a more prominent event.

At a time when intratribal divisions were causing dissension on the reservation, Plains Indians continued to find common ground at these reservations rodeos. It was also a time when pan-Indian solidarity was reaching its zenith with the proliferation of intertribal political activist groups and with the popularity of cultural activities like powwows and the Native American Church, so it was inevitable that rodeo would follow the trend. Crows, Northern Cheyennes, and Lakotas continued to allow and even to encourage non-Indians to compete in their rodeos. Eventually, many of these tribes would take a chance on their audiences and institute all-Indian rodeos.

By the mid-1960s, Native cowboys had established organizations like the All-Indian Rodeo Cowboy Association (AIRCA) and the All American Indian Activities Association (AAIAA) to promote all-Indian competitions, particularly rodeos, in the Southwest and northern Great Plains, respectively. In 1958 Navajo cowboys created the first regional all-Indian rodeo association, the All-Indian Rodeo Cowboys Association, as a "non-profit organization, committed to developing and promoting organized Indian rodeos on the Navajo Nation."[8] Pius Real Bird, the arena manager of Crow Fair's rodeo, brought the trend to the Northern Great Plains in 1962 by declaring Crow Fair's rodeo to be an all-Indian rodeo where the winner would earn the title of "champion Indian rodeo performer of North America."[9] Subsequently, an Absalooka cowboy, Delmar Eastman, helped launch the All American Indian Activities Association (AAIAA) in the mid-1960s. He and others intended the AAIAA to sanction a variety of tribally sponsored events in the northern Great Plains, but their focus remained on the sponsorship of Native rodeos. The AAIAA began to promote and sanction intertribal rodeos at Crow Agency and Wolf

Point in Montana; at Pine Ridge, Rosebud, and Lower Brule in South Dakota; and at Fort Totten, New Town, and Fort Yates in North Dakota. Competing in sanctioned rodeos meant that contestants could expect more equitable prizes, standardized rules, and standardized events.[10] Local efforts in these reservation communities determined the number of AAIAA-sanctioned rodeos.[11] On reservations like Crow Agency, Pine Ridge, and Rosebud where the local enthusiasm was considerable, tribal fair and Fourth of July rodeos were consistently sanctioned by the AAIAA. Native cowboys including Pete Fredericks, Joe Chase, and Jay Harwood gained approval for Indian rodeo contestants to compete in both Professional Rodeo Cowboys Association (PRCA) rodeos and AAIAA-sanctioned rodeos and to allow their scores to count toward their PRCA standings.[12] The level of competition at these reservation rodeos was heightening. From 1958 to 1976, a time when Indians were rallying for self-determination, many Plains Indians determined themselves to be Indian-rodeo cowboys, who preferred to perform in an all-Indian rodeo circuit.

## THE POSTWAR PERIOD AND TERMINATION

Following World War II, American Indians took up the fight for tribal sovereignty, which began with their battle against the federal policy of termination. After John Collier retired as commissioner of Indian affairs in 1945, Indian-policy reformers once again began to champion the goal of complete assimilation of American Indians into mainstream American society. The reformers' rhetoric and reasoning were eerily similar to that of their late-nineteenth-century counterparts who had been eager to initiate the process of assimilating Indians and immigrants arriving from southern and eastern Europe, thereby incorporating their bodies, souls, services, and lands into America's fabric.[13] Reminiscent of the logic that led to the General Allotment Act of 1887, postwar reformers attempted to dissolve communal reservations. They were convinced that reservations were "antiquated relics of a bygone age," and "if reservations could be eliminated, their acreage fully divided into property, and individual Indians freed from the restraint of federal bureaucracy . . . Indians would be better able to reach their full potential."[14]

In the postwar years, the fervor of Indian-policy reformers was intensified by a pervasive American commitment to a democratic ideology that vilified Communism as well as by a renewed conviction that Indians deserved to be integrated into American society, whether they wanted to be or not. The vigorous participation of Native Americans in World War II provided the rationale for both conservative and liberal government officials to abandon John Collier's multicultural Indian New Deal policies. While conservative Republicans favored turning Indian affairs over to the states, liberal Democrats in the Truman administration also called for the "liberation" of the Indians from the fetters of federal paternalism.[15] These early proponents of termination used liberal rhetoric, attacking the poverty and what they misunderstood to be the segregation of Native Americans residing on reservations. In reality, the off-reservation experiences of many American Indians who had served in World War II or who worked in wartime industries reaffirmed their Native self-image and inspired them to advocate for increased tribal sovereignty. For them, reservation lands, whether they lived there or not, had become an enduring symbol of their Indian identity. Failing to realize this, policy makers assumed that the large numbers of American Indian soldiers who fought in World War II did so as "an unquestionable act of loyalty to the United States, . . . an American Indian effort to prove themselves worthy of 'mainstream society.'" Indian-policy reformer O. K. Armstrong claimed that Indians "who return from service [will] seek a greater share in American freedom" and not be satisfied "to live in a shack and loaf around in a blanket."[16] In his 1945 article for *Reader's Digest* entitled "Set the Indians Free!", Armstrong urged Congress to "emancipate" American Indians by removing the roadblocks imposed by federal trusteeship. He suggested that only then would Native American communities be liberated to soar to new heights.[17] The call for the "emancipation" of Native Americans from a restrictive Bureau of Indian Affairs eventually took the form of the federal Indian policy known as *termination*.[18]

Termination, which was advocated from the late 1940s to 1970, attempted to assimilate Native Americans by extinguishing the federal government's trust responsibilities toward Indians. Ever since the postcolonial United States government began making treaties with American Indians, it had acted as the guardian to "domestic dependent" Indian nations. As such, the federal government was bound to protect American Indian tribal governments and sovereignty, the nontaxable status of reservation lands, treaty rights, and access to federally supplied services. Motivated by the mood of the postwar period, Congress passed House Concurrent Resolution 108 in 1953, which provided the power to terminate federal relations with individual tribes.[19] This drive to terminate federal trust responsibility harbored potential disaster for Indian America.[20]

Throughout the 1940s and 1950s, American Indians, politicized by their off-reservation exposure, organized to protest this policy as well as the injustices they had confronted off their reservations. During World War II, a number of Indian servicemen and workers in wartime industries had gotten a glimpse of the world outside the reservation. The Bureau of Indian Affairs Relocation Program of the 1950s coaxed many more off their reservations and into cities. In American cities, American Indians saw firsthand the overwhelming disparity between Indian and non-Indian economies, education, health care, and general quality of life.[21] They also confronted racial discrimination, which they resolved to protest in each instance. A reporter for the Pine Ridge reservation's newspaper, the *American Indian: Shannon County News*, urged a boycott in response to one such incident that occurred in Chadron, a reservation border town, during the Chadron Rodeo in 1947:

> A deplorable incident occurred in Chadron last week when a restaurant keeper, in a fit of anger, deliberately picked up a piece of pie and slapped it in the face of the respectable reservation woman and it is further alleged he pushed her head back until he caused her injury to her neck. This ungentlemanly act it is said was perpetrated when the lady questioned the value of a piece of pie he had placed before her. Indians are denied some privileges throughout every town surrounding the Pine Ridge reservation and there is very little we can do about it. The only policy we can follow is to patronize those business people who are friends of Indian people. Stay out of the places where Indian trade is not wanted and we believe an Indian boycott will bring some Indian haters to their senses.[22]

In their quest for equal treatment off the reservation and for equal standards of living on it, American Indians mobilized to demand the right of self-determination owed to them as semi-sovereign nations. To Indians, self-determination meant that they would have a primary role in implementing programs affecting their reservations' economies, education, health, law enforcement, and housing. Led by the National Congress of American Indians, tribes mounted an effective opposition to termination that eventually resulted in the restoration of affected tribal groups. Formed as a direct response to termination and relocation and led mostly by Native college students, the Red Power movement of the 1960s borrowed its name and tactics from the African American civil rights movement and stressed Indian culture, tribal sovereignty, and self-determination. Through fish-ins, blockades, and occupations of Alcatraz Island, in 1964 and 1969, groups such as the National

Indian Youth Council and Indians of All Tribes and the American Indian Movement emerged to defend Indian rights.

In this politically charged atmosphere of the 1960s, many American Indian youths returned to their reservations from universities, colleges, and cities and brought with them their radical political and cultural agendas. They were products of the Red Power movement and had participated in Native American studies classes and in Indian pride and Indian rights activities. In *Shared Symbols, Contested Meanings: Gros Ventre Culture and History, 1778–1984*, Loretta Fowler explains the growing cultural awareness of Indian youth, saying that "youths became motivated and encouraged to be Indian, or were channeled into an interest in and commitment to being Indian in new ways."[23] Popular supratribal activities like powwows and Native American Churches were all expressions of this. Historians such as Steven Cornell, James H. Stewart, Robert K. Thomas, Omer C. Stewart, Morris W. Foster, Ben Black Bear, and William K. Powers have documented this pan-Indian cultural phenomenon.[24]

Indian rodeos were a part of this trend toward pan-Indian activities. During and following the war, members of reservation communities had scattered. Many people left their reservations as part of the Bureau of Indian Affairs Relocation Program as well as for combat and war industries jobs. A number of Indians were more prosperous as a result of their war-related job opportunities and could afford cars for the first time. With easier access to transportation and better roads built during the New Deal, Native Americans could travel farther from their reservations to intertribal events. Like the burgeoning powwow circuit, reservation rodeos provided an opportunity for Crows, Northern Cheyennes, and Lakotas to gather as tribal and pan-Indian groups. Throughout the 1960s, rodeos frequently accompanied powwows.[25] Just as the political and social pan-Indian movement facilitated the development of the all-Indian rodeo circuit, so too did the economic trend of northern Plains Indians sponsoring tribal tourist enterprises designed to attract non-Indian visitors and their dollars to existing reservations.

## TRIBAL RANCHING AND TOURIST ENTERPRISES

Northern Plains Indians communities responded to federal attempts to break up their reservations by shoring up their tribal resources and expanding their tribal economic enterprises. During the termination era, northern Plains Indian tribal cattle enterprises—often begun with New Deal funding and composed of cattle herds that were raised, marketed, and sold by and for the benefit of tribal members—were buffeted by attempts by the Bureau of Indian Affairs to undermine tribal land bases and economies. With its emphasis on dissolving supposedly antiquated reservations, federal Indian policy diminished many northern Plains Indian cattle enterprises that Indian ranchers had successfully revived during the Indian New Deal. For example, in an attempt to purchase at auction tribal land that the bureau had authorized to be sold, the Northern Cheyenne tribe liquidated their tribal steer enterprise in 1955. The former BIA director of education during the Collier years, Willard W. Beatty, assessed the BIA's role in the reduction of the Northern Cheyennes' steer enterprise and land in 1959.

> The Bureau deliberately defeated the attempt of the Northern Cheyenne ... to buy the key tracts of individual land which the Bureau authorized sold. The tribe had money in the U.S. Treasury. Some technicality was advanced by the Bureau for a refusal to release the money to bid on these land parcels. The tribe sold much of its livestock to raise the money, and again the Bureau refused to make available the money. . . . Thus the land went to non-Indians.[26]

By the 1960s, tribal leaders like John Wooden Legs on the Northern Cheyenne reservation had responded to these attempts to liquidate reservations with a tenacious determination to make their reservations' economies self-sufficient. Except during the Indian New Deal years, the Bureau of Indian Affairs had worked resolutely to persuade Indians to be self-supporting and to view themselves as individuals rather than as members of a tribe, yet many Plains Indians had proved to be equally committed to the right of their tribes, as semi-sovereign nations, to function as tribes.[27] Once Indians had effectively challenged the termination policy, Bureau of Indian Affairs officials eventually woke up to this reality and began to support tribal enterprises aimed at bringing prosperity to the tribe as a whole and to individual tribal members. With John Wooden Legs presiding as president of the Northern Cheyenne Tribal Council, the Northern Cheyennes fought for and received a BIA land loan of $550,000 in 1962 after "three years of effort to get it." Wooden Legs explained, "This means whatever can be developed on this land will belong to us." After Wooden Legs' augmentation of tribal lands, the restoration of the Northern Cheyenne Steer Enterprise followed in the same year, along with improved reservation employment statistics. He was pleased to report these achievements, saying, "Now for the first time in many years, all our land is being used by the enrolled members and by our Tribal herd. The Steer Enterprise is up to almost 5,000 head. So far it is holding its own. It has helped a few people by providing some employment."[28]

Recognizing the widespread appeal of tribal fairs and rodeos in the previous decade, the mounting interest of Americans in the West, and the recently acquired notoriety of Indian servicemen, many northern Plains Indian communities also viewed cultural tourism as a potentially profitable tribal enterprise. With a booming postwar economy, Americans had more disposable income with which to purchase automobiles and to see America. They traveled more often, especially to the American West, as westerns became the most popular film and television genre in the 1950s. In an age of intense nationalism, it was not unusual for Americans to look west to celebrate their sense of exceptionalism, as Frederick Jackson Turner had done in 1893. Although historic antagonisms, which began over disputes involving reservation resources or discrimination, continued to exist between Indians living on reservations and whites living in border towns, many non-Indians living there and elsewhere became more respectful of Indian people. Many had served alongside American Indian servicemen or were aware of their distinguished service in the Second World War. Heralded individuals like Pima Indian Ira Hayes, who had been immortalized as one of the marines photographed raising the American flag on Iwo Jima, and groups such as the Navajo Codetalkers, who had used their language to form an unbreakable code during the campaign in the Pacific, exemplified American Indian valor.[29] Through tourist enterprises, American Indians began to replenish their tribal coffers by capitalizing on mainstream America's positive recognition of their service in World War II. This trend met with varied reactions on the Northern Cheyenne, Crow, and Lakota reservations.

In an attempt to preserve the Northern Cheyenne reservation, John Wooden Legs supervised the creation of a tourist center enterprise. Wooden Legs collaborated with the Bureau of Indian Affairs to launch the project. Peter Iverson describes his dogged efforts to counter the assimilationist goals of termination with tourism:

> Wooden Legs saw his people as back on war ponies, for he knew they had to fight to save the land and thus salvage the future. He rejected the forced integration of the Cheyennes into the mainstream of American life; he rejected forcing his people 'into the slums of the city.' This did not mean 'trying to keep the Cheyennes in a blanket.' It did mean making the reservation attractive to people."[30]

The tribe's first step was the implementation of part one of their Community Development Program, which attempted to secure the land base of the reservation in order to "keep and utilize their own lands and resources, now and in the future." To devise an auxiliary plan that would suggest appropriate uses of their lands and resources, Wooden Legs and the Northern Cheyenne Tribe hosted an Economic Development Conference in December 1960. The conference bore fruit as its participants conceived and launched the Northern Cheyenne Tribal Tourist Enterprise as part two of their Community Development Program. The stated purpose of the Tourist Center Enterprise was to "develop tourist and recreational facilities on the reservation" by creating "a retail outlet on the reservation for authentic crafts of the Northern Cheyennes, and to provide a seasonal job for the manager of the Center." The plan of operations for this enterprise included a five-person board of directors composed of three tribal members and two non-tribal members appointed by the council.[31] The Northern Cheyenne Tribal Council had been established under the Indian Reorganization Act and was composed of an elected tribal chairperson and members from designated electoral districts on the reservation. Some American Indians, like the Crows who had rejected the IRA, ridiculed the tribal governments organized under the act, claiming that they were "puppets of the BIA." Yet tribal councils, formed with or without the BIA's direction, undeniably "made possible the perpetuation of the concept of tribal sovereignty that . . . would play a dominant role in relations between the Indians and white society."[32] By initiating and administering their tourist enterprise, Northern Cheyennes were demonstrating what self-determination meant to them.

With support from Indian and non-Indian sources, Northern Cheyenne artists and craftspeople made the Northern Cheyenne Tribal Tourist Enterprise a success. The 1962 General Report of the Northern Cheyenne Tourist Center Enterprise concluded in recognition of the joint efforts of Indian and non-Indian supporters of the project. It stated that "only because certain individuals, both Indian and non-Indian, were determined to see this project launched did it finally come to pass. Without the increasing cooperation and effort of the Indian people themselves to make the project succeed, it surely would have failed."[33] The Association on American Indian Affairs, a national citizens' organization composed primarily of non-Indians, was among the groups mentioned that had assisted the Northern Cheyenne tribe in implementing their tourist enterprise. As he campaigned for reelection as tribal chairperson in 1964, John Wooden Legs proudly described the success of the Northern Cheyenne Arts and Crafts Association that "has been operating three years now. It has paid over $16,000 worth of crafts. Because this group has done so well, the Tribal Council and the Bureau applied for and got a training program for beadworkers."[34] Women played a large role as crafts-people in these burgeoning tourist markets, principally as beadworkers.

Lakota tribal leaders also cooperated with the Bureau of Indian Affairs to promote tourism on the Rosebud, Pine Ridge, Crow Creek, Cheyenne River, Sisseton, and Standing Rock reservations, where rodeos were among the main attractions. In 1965, the Rosebud Sioux Herald: Eyapaha published an article on the "newly emerging recreation and vacation industry operated by Indian tribes in South Dakota." On many Lakota reservations, rodeo was mentioned among the various tourist attractions. On the Rosebud reservation, "people put on pageants, native dances, [arranged] trail rides, pow-wows and rodeo events." The Crow Creek and Cheyenne River reservations offered summer activities that included "rodeos at Ft. Thompson and Eagle Butte, Indian fairs, handicraft displays and pow-wows." The Sisseton and Standing Rock reservations also "put on horse shows, fairs, and rodeos." The article concluded that "on the Fourth of July, nearly every reservation will have some special celebration, and these affairs are always colorful and exciting."[35]

As part of the effort to promote their reservation and its culture to outsiders and to expose Lakotas to the attributes of urban life, the Rosebud Sioux and their Indian agent proposed a student exchange program. Harold Schunk, the part-Lakota superintendent of the Rosebud reservation from 1959 to 1968, was a controversial figure on the reservation for his commitment to the advancement of Indians through acculturation, which he believed was a necessary part of the process. In 1964, he and Chicagoan David Gray initiated a unique experiment of a grassroots cultural exchange similar to a foreign student exchange program. The exchange provided that for one year, Indian families would host Chicago students during school vacations, and the following year, the young Indian students would live with their former guests' families in the city. In the first year, Chicago youth came to live on the reservation, and in the second year, a dozen Indian youths from Rosebud went to live with families in Chicago. According to Schunk, "Howard Bad Hand, the first Indian to go the city, took to city life like a native and is clamoring to return. Meanwhile, Charles Annen of Arlington Heights, Illinois, took up rodeoing during his summer on the reservation and became very good at it."[36] The young man from a Chicago suburb, who came to the Rosebud reservation in South Dakota to learn about modern Lakota culture, had discovered that rodeo was an integral part of it. The exchange proved to be a success as both the Indian and non-Indian student participants gained a greater appreciation for the other's culture.

In 1968 the Bureau of Indian Affairs sponsored a tourism campaign that they billed as "see America first with the first Americans." It was intended to "encourage more summer vacationists to visit Indian reservations, become better acquainted with Indian life and history, enjoy the hunting and fishing, and buy Indian arts and handicrafts." Two television personalities—Dan Blocker and Forrest Tucker—made radio and TV spot announcements. Thus, Hoss Cartwright of *Bonanza* and Sergeant O'Rourke of *F Troop* were "in there pitching for the American Indians." The Bureau urged tribal councils to determine how they could make best use of the anticipated increase in tourist dollars—they were "expected to improve existing tourist facilities, build new ones, and in some cases, employ guides to show tourists highlights of reservation life."[37]

Not everyone agreed with the emphasis on tourism. Former Crow superintendent and tribal chairperson Robert Yellowtail was not in favor of relying on tourist dollars as a principal source of tribal revenue. During his tenure as Crow superintendent, he was an advocate of Crow political, cultural, and economic independence. Although he utilized the Crow Fair and Rodeo effectively to promote the tribe's culture and political agenda to Indian and non-Indian visitors, he did not want the Crows to rely on tourism to sustain their individual incomes. In 1965 he expressed his conviction that tourism could not bring about economic rehabilitation. In a letter to K. W. Bergan, coordinator of Indian affairs, who had proposed a Manpower Training Project for Crows in beadwork and leatherwork, Yellowtail responded negatively: "I am not too hot on this matter. The salvation of the Indian people is economic rehabilitation. . . . Tourism is alright in so far as it brings in cash to tribes who happen to have attractive spots but again it cannot substitute for the basic individual economic rehabilitation, nor will it bring in enough dough to supply the cash needs of the individuals of any tribe."[38]

As a result of the rising American economy and a greater interest in the American West, tourism had been on the rise on the Crow reservation and throughout Montana since the end of World War II. In 1947 the *Hardin Tribune-Herald* reported that "for the first time in the history of Glacier National Park, travel has passed the quarter-million mark. New arrivals on August 18 brought the season total up to 252,483. A sharp increase in travelers from the Southern and Eastern states has been recorded."[39] In 1950 an increase was noted in tourist entries at the Crow reservation where "7,126 visitor cars were greeted at Crow Agency," marking "an increase from 5,718 to 7,126 vehicles."[40] Bureau of Indian Affairs officials encouraged tourism on the Crow reservation, as elsewhere. After visiting the Crow Fair in 1962, Assistant Commissioner of Indian Affairs E. Reeseman Fryer commented on the tourist potential of Crow Fair and Rodeo, as well as the reservation's natural resources that would allow "boating, fishing and vacationing on the banks of the Yellowstone reservoir." After attending the rodeo and celebration, Fryer predicted, "With community cooperation between the Crows and non-Indians the annual celebration could be a drawing card that would attract people from everywhere."[41] Yellowtail had, of course, recognized this almost three decades earlier. He had in effect unleashed Pandora's box by promoting Crow Fair and Rodeo so zealously from 1934 to 1945. In the decades following World War II, the Crows took up where Yellowtail had left off and made Crow Fair and Rodeo a drawing card for both Indian and non-Indian visitors from all over the globe.

## "THE TEEPEE CAPITAL OF THE WORLD" AND THE EMERGENCE OF CROW RODEO FAMILIES

The Crows desired to promote both pan-Indian solidarity and non-Indian tourism at Crow Fair and Rodeo. The fair and rodeo was never a big money-maker itself, but tribal leaders hoped it would prompt visitors to consider the reservation for other recreational and investment opportunities. By showcasing highly visible aspects of their culture such as the tepee encampments and daily parades, the Crows lured Native Americans and the growing tourist market to their reservation.

Beginning in the 1950s, Crow Fair was often advertised as the "Teepee Capital of the World" to attract both Indian and non-Indian guests. While the encampment was designed to promote tourism, it also served to solidify the Crows' tribal and intertribal relationships. A perceptive journalist in 1955 recognized that Crow Fair and Rodeo's significance surpassed that of other "tourist attractions." He astutely described the fair's cultural significance for the Crows: "It is not a tourist attraction. It is for the Crow people—with a parade in the morning, a rodeo each afternoon, and feasting and dancing each evening. It's a deep-rooted institution where each year the Crow people come together to enjoy the simplicity and hospitality that is distinctly theirs." He further conveyed the nature of the tepee encampment reunion: "Hidden along the banks of the Little Big Horn this weekend is perhaps the biggest teepee encampment to be found at any celebration in Montana, but . . . it is not a commercial affair in any sense. . . . The word 'fair' is an anachronism now, but the institution itself bids to last another century. It has found a place in the hearts of the Crow people."[42] In recognition of the fiftieth anniversary of the Crow Fair, an article entitled "Crow Indians Celebrating 50th Annual Fair" was published in the *Great Falls Tribune* in 1955. The article's appearance in a western Montana newspaper underlined the state and nationwide attention given to the Crows' annual event in the 1950s. The article described the evolution of Crow Fair and Rodeo from an industrial fair to a community cultural celebration and rodeo. The article recalled the second Crow industrial fair in 1905, for which Superintendent Reynolds had blanketed the reservation with posters. The posters revealed the agricultural emphasis of the early fairs: "Crows Wake Up: Your big fair will take place early in October. Plant a Good Garden. Put in Wheat and Oats. Get your Horses, Cattle, Pigs, and Chickens in Shape to Bring to the Fair. Cash Prizes and Badges Will Be Awarded to Indians Making Best Exhibits."[43] The newspaper feature went on to explain the increasingly intertribal nature of the fair: "As the years went by, the emphasis began to change. The Crows, always hospitable and friendly, entertained more and more Indians. . . . The Indian was once more doing things his way. . . . By 1912 the exhibits began to diminish, and by the early 1920s, they had disappeared, yet the annual gathering continued." The journalist recalled that Superintendent Robert Yellowtail had "reactivated the industrial side of the fair" during his tenure in office from 1935 to 1945, but "Yellowtail's retirement and the dislocation caused by the war ended the competitive and exhibitive side of the fair." According to this contemporary observer of the 1955 Crow Fair, it was the "social aspect" that remained and drew Crows from every district of their reservation, as well as Indians from other reservations, yearly to the Crow Fair and rodeo:

> During the half century of its existence, the fair has fulfilled a need for the Crow people. Their reservation is large—the largest in Montana—and distances are great. At least one hundred miles separate the colony at Pryor from those living at Wyola, and not often during the year do these people have the opportunity of visiting each other. . . . Each family pitches its camp in the same

location. Visitors from other reservations still attend and each year a number of non-Indian friends are invited.[44]

As the Crows gained complete autonomy over the direction of Crow Fair and Rodeo in the postwar years, it became an increasingly intratribal and intertribal event, culminating in the creation of an all-Indian rodeo in 1962. Phillip Bull Mountain, secretary of the 1953 Crow Indian Fair and Rodeo, boasted to Eugene Fisher, president of the Northern Cheyenne Tribe in 1953, that Crow Fair was an "all Crow Indian sponsored event."[45] The fair and rodeo was no longer under the supervision of the Bureau of Indian Affairs superintendent as it had been before World War I and again during the Yellowtail administration. Thus, the "all Crow" board of directors accentuated Indian parades, dances, and rodeo, and largely ignored the agricultural exhibits that were prevalent before 1920 and from 1934 to 1945.

Donald Deernose, chairperson of the Crow Fair committee in 1948, emphasized the intertribal character of Crow Fair and Rodeo. He proclaimed that "the biggest teepee encampment in the nation would be at Crow Agency" and promised that "tribes from all over" would make up the "largest Indian parade in the nation, with all the participants clad in their full tribal regalia." He pointed out that it would be "a good opportunity for visitors to observe the differences in costumes among the various tribes."[46] A year later, the Crows invited the public to attend another impressive intertribal tepee encampment:

> Fifteen buffalo from the Crow tribal herd will be killed . . . for the entire Indian camp composed of all prairie Indian tribes from Canada to Oklahoma, the Dakotas, Oregon and Washington. The Crows will be host to every plains Indian tribe. . . . The largest encampment of Indians ever gathered will be housed Crow style in the tepee, home of the plains Indians. The tepees will be pitched in a semicircle one-half mile in diameter located at the fairgrounds one mile from Custer battlefield. . . . The Crow tribe has extended a cordial invitation to the public to celebrate the annual occasion with the Indians.[47]

A daily Indian parade was usually scheduled "with various tribes in full regalia taking part."[48] In 1956 a "record crowd, with representatives of Indian tribes throughout the entire nation" attended the fair and rodeo.[49] In 1957 Crow Fair was again billed as "one of the few places in the country where the colorful Indian encampment may be observed."[50] The Crows held intertribal events because they recognized their commonality with other Northern Plains Indian communities, as each attempted within and across tribal boundaries to claim the right to determine the character of their economic, cultural, and political lives.

As part of their resolve to govern their own tribal affairs, Crows endeavored to select appropriate leaders who would represent their interests on the tribal, state, and national levels. On the national level, Robert Yellowtail spoke before a Senate Committee on Interior and Insular Affairs in 1952, entreating them to "allow the Indians a voice in the selection of the Commissioner of Indian Affairs." Yellowtail believed that political patronage played a large part in the selection and appointment of Indian commissioners. He concluded, "The 450,000 Indians of the continental United States and Alaska are a part and parcel of the body politic of our country" that merits a voice in choosing who will head the Bureau of Indian Affairs and represent their interests.[51]

The Crows looked among themselves to discover appropriate representation on the tribal level. Crow political and economic leaders often sought roles at the Crow Fair and Rodeo. Many Crow men and women involved on Crow Fair and Rodeo boards of directors, on rodeo committees, and as rodeo princesses and queens were also influential in tribal politics and cattle ranching. As people engaged in Crow community affairs, they recognized the status that many Crows had affixed to the fair and rodeo and its leaders. Many of these Crow representatives were members of families who had been active in Crow Fair since its inception in 1904. This fact was not lost on one journalist who underscored the fact that the Crow Fair and Rodeo had become a breeding ground for tribal leaders. He observed that the "names of persons prominent on the reservation today—Yellowtail, Deernose, Crooked Arm— were included among the winners that first year."[52] Yellowtail, Deernose, Whiteman, and Cummins were among those family names that consistently appeared on Crow Fair committees throughout the 1950s and 1960s.[53] Like Robert Yellowtail and Donald Deernose, Edward P. Whiteman served both in tribal politics, as chairperson of the Crow Tribal Council, and on the Crow Fair board of directors, as its chairperson in 1957.[54] Others followed suit, including Clarence (Toots) Stewart, who was the vice secretary of the Tribal Council as well as Crow Fair secretary.[55] Similarly, members of prominent cattle ranching and rodeo families—such as the Bird-in-Ground, Small, Not Afraid, and Real Bird families—emerged to direct Crow Fair's rodeo events. For instance, Ivan Small was elected manager of the rodeo portion of the fair for the 1957 event.[56] In 1959 Gilbert Bird-in-Ground was the rodeo arena director.[57] Women such as Crow Fair and Rodeo Secretary Velma Holds were also elected as board members.[58]

Bureau of Indian Affairs officials also recognized the stature and responsibility that Crow Fair and Rodeo leaders held. BIA official K. W. Bergan affirmed this in a letter to Daniel LaForge, who had recently been elected as chairperson of the Crow Fair and Rodeo board in 1962. Bergan extended his congratulations to LaForge, assuring him that "we were very pleased to read the newspaper item appointing you chairperson of the Crow Indian Fair and Rodeo. It is a great honor as well as a great responsibility that has been placed on your shoulders. We wish you success in this venture."[59] LaForge's response to Bergan's letter exuded his confidence in the abilities of the members of the executive board of the fair and rodeo, which had been meeting monthly in hopes of staging "one of the biggest and best fairs since its inauguration."[60]

Women played an increasingly prominent role as Crow Fair and Rodeo officers, royalty, and rodeo contestants in the 1950s. As pan-Indian events became more common, so too did the titles of rodeo princess and queen. In the 1930s and 1940s, western Native communities like the Crows had begun to select or elect princesses to represent their tribes in ceremonies. In the 1950s, the Crows began to select a princess from each district on the reservation and one queen who represented their entire tribe at tribal and intertribal events, including rodeo. Morgan Baillargeon describes the late-twentieth-century procedure for selecting rodeo queens: "Rodeo queens are usually drawn from competitors in the women's events. A contestant is rated on her knowledge and ability to handle horses. Judges interview each contestant, who answers general questions about horses and then guides a horse that she has never ridden through a series of commands. The contestant is also judged on her appearance, poise, and knowledge of her Native heritage."[61] In 1952 the Crow board added the title of Crow Indian Fair and Rodeo queen. Along with the new title came an expanded role as representative of the tribe and its traditions. Seventeen-year-old Dora Old Elk won the title in a competition against three other young Crow women.[62] Crow women skilled in rodeo were also chosen to represent non-Indian communities such as Hardin, Montana, where Crows had excelled in the annual Big Horn County Rodeo for decades. Clarice Hawks of the St. Xavier district of the Crow reservation was chosen rodeo queen at Hardin's first postwar rodeo in 1946.[63] In 1950 Crow cowgirl Sharon Old Elk was selected to represent Hardin in the rodeo arena as their representative in ladies' barrel racing at the Regional High School Rodeo.[64]

Throughout the 1950s, Crow cowgirls and cowboys continued to collect prize money and gain recognition in reservation and local rodeos. In these postwar decades, members of several Crow families emerged as consistent rodeo contestants and victors. As rodeos continued to appear frequently on and around the Crow reservation, so did the names of individuals from the Not Afraid, Bird-in-Ground, Real Bird, Fitzler, Small, and Pickett families in the winners' lists. Members of some families such as the Bird-in-Grounds and Not Afraids had been successful in rodeo throughout the twentieth century. Other active rodeo families emerged in the postwar years, including the Real Birds, Fitzlers, Smalls, and Picketts. These families did not have to look far to find rodeos in which to compete. Organizers and audiences welcomed and followed them to various rodeo grounds.

On the Crow reservation, Fourth of July reservation rodeos, especially the St. Xavier and Lodge Grass Rodeos, provided increasingly professional arenas.[65] The National Rodeo Cowboys Association approved the Lodge Grass Rodeo in 1955. This added prestige to the event and attracted more competitive riders because the performances of cowboys who belonged to the National Rodeo Cowboys Association could contribute to their professional rodeo ranking. Even as the competition became more intense, the rodeos remained community events for Crows, who came for the dancing and feasting as well as for the rodeo events. The 1959 Lodge Grass Rodeo was typical in its scheduling. The rodeo events occurred at 1:30 each afternoon and included roping, team tying, saddle bronc riding, bareback bronc riding, bulldogging, girls' barrel racing, jackpot cow-riding, and a special cow-cutting (herding) contest. The final day was designated an "All-Indian Day" with "dancing through the camp, a feast, and a buffalo barbecue."[66] These Fourth of July rodeos welcomed young and old rodeo contestants. A number of Crow youth became interested in rodeo through their involvement in 4-H clubs, which were often government-sponsored. In conjunction with the 1959 Lodge Grass Rodeo, the 4-H club sponsored a youth fair. A number of younger Crows participated in its rodeo, which concluded with the scramble in a cloud of dust. The rodeo's finale was a scramble calf roping rodeo where "seventeen 4-H club members struggled through dust, their competitors and flying feet to capture 17 calves in the 'calf scramble.'"[67]

Off the reservation, Crows competed more regularly in the Hardin Rodeo than in any other non-Indian rodeo, a record that testified to their positive experiences there. Although Robert Yellowtail had once scolded the people of

Hardin, Billings, and Sheridan for being unsupportive of the Crow Fair and Rodeo, the organizers of the Hardin Rodeo had always courted the Crows' participation in their annual rodeo, and their performances had consistently won the praise of local reporters. The Crows had competed in what had been called the Big Horn County Fair annually throughout the century, but the event and its rodeo were suspended during World War II. When the Hardin Rodeo resumed in 1946, Crow cowboys and cowgirls were there to compete. Promoters promised that "all the chills, thrills and spills that spectators witnessed at the Hardin rodeos held here each year before the war will be repeated for reminiscent audiences. . . . The Hardin rodeo was known as one of the best in the West before it was discontinued five years ago due to the war. Many of the same performers will return again to make the show as exciting as ever."[68] As promised, many of these performers returned and many were from Crow rodeo families.

The Not Afraids and Bird-in-Grounds were two such identifiable families whose relatives had gained attention in rodeos throughout the twentieth century.[69] During the 1950s Cedric, Ed, and Gary Not Afraid carried on the tradition begun by their predecessors' notable 1920s appearances at the Lodge Grass and Hardin Rodeos.[70] Employing their considerable talents, they won many regional and local titles. The Northwest Cowboy Association recognized several Crow rodeo cowboys, including Cedric Not Afraid, among the top point winners for the 1952 season.[71] In 1957, Gary Not Afraid took home the All-Round Cowboy Award at the invitational rodeo held at Lodge Grass after winning first in calf roping and third in bareback and saddle bronc riding.[72] The Bird-in-Ground family name had been linked to rodeo since Sampson Bird-in-Ground became the first Indian to ride a buffalo at the 1915 Miles City Roundup.[73] More than four decades later in 1958, Sam Bird-in-Ground earned $63.75 for calf roping at the Hardin Rodeo and was again a top prizewinner in 1959.[74]

Members of the Real Bird, Fitzler, Small, and Pickett families also emerged as rodeo luminaries. As cattle ranchers on the prime ranching land of Medicine Tail Coulee, near where the Battle of the Little Bighorn took place, the Real Birds were born in the saddle and grew up riding, roping, and steer wrestling. It is no wonder then that a journalist reporting on the 1948 Hardin Rodeo referred to one of the Real Birds as "Scrap Iron" Real Bird for his tenacious bronc riding performance in winning a prize of $35.62. At the 1957 invitational rodeo held at Lodge Grass, Richard Real Bird was recognized for calf roping. Other families like the Fitzlers made notable rodeo appearances throughout the decade in more unusual ways. In 1951, Crow Indian Glen Fitzler of Pryor, Montana, performed at the Hardin Rodeo and was billed as one of the "best known rodeo clowns in the business." Like all skilled rodeo clowns, he was prepared to provide both "amusing antics" and the "more serious business of 'bull fighting' during the Brahma bull riding event." At least one of his children would follow his lead and later become a rodeo clown.[75]

The Small family, which had members on the Crow and Northern Cheyenne reservations, produced a number of outstanding rodeo cowboys and cowgirls. Between 1946 and 1960, members of the Small family ranked at or near the top time after time at the Hardin Rodeo. Among the members of the Small family that excelled during those years were Victor, John, Ralph, Clinton, Mark, Junior, Corline, Ed, Dale, Melvin, and Caroline.[76] In the first postwar Hardin rodeo, Ed Small placed in calf roping, as did Victor Small in team tying. In 1958, Dale Small earned $146.40 for bulldogging (steer wrestling). A year later, Clinton, Dale, Vic, and Melvin Small were again successful at the Hardin Rodeo. The women and men of the Small family also competed successfully in reservation rodeos. Caroline Small made a showing in the barrel race at the 1957 invitational rodeo held at Lodge Grass, and Vic and Clinton Small won the jackpot roping there two years later.[77]

A number of young Crows also gained national rodeo recognition as high school cowboys and cowgirls in the 1950s and 1960s, demonstrating their competitiveness with white cowboys. Lloyd Pickett, whose son would later become involved in rodeo, was among them. At the first annual Montana Championship High School Rodeo, Hardin offered seven entries. Three of them, including Pickett, were from the Crow and Northern Cheyenne reservations. A year later, three Crow Big Horn County high school students placed in the annual state championship high school rodeo. Lloyd Pickett ranked in the breakaway roping contest and became eligible to compete in the national high school rodeo. The success of Pickett and members of other Crow families such as the Not Afraids, Bird-in-Grounds, Real Birds, and Smalls had contributed to their families' legacy of rodeo. By the mid-twentieth century, rodeo had become a crucial tradition for many Crow and Plains Indian families and tribes.[78]

# THE INAUGURATION OF AN ALL-INDIAN RODEO
# AT CROW FAIR

At Crow Fair's rodeo, American Indian contestants and stock had always been featured, but non-Indian cowboys, rodeo stock, and judges continued to participate until 1962. As the Crows began to focus on tourist enterprises, they promoted Crow Fair and its rodeo to tourists as one of the reservation's greatest cultural events. For many years, they also believed that they needed to include non-Indians not only as spectators but also as contestants to sustain their rodeo. In 1948 the *Hardin Tribune-Herald* reported that "a rodeo will be a feature of the program every day of the fair. Both white and Indian contestants may enter, and all the usual rodeo events will be included." As it would for the Lodge Grass rodeo, the National Rodeo Cowboys Association sanctioned Crow Fair's rodeo in 1953. The Crows counted on sanctioning to draw larger numbers and more competitive contestants, many of them non-Indians, to the rodeo. Crow Fair rodeo officials boasted that the rodeo would be an NRCA-approved show and that the winning rodeo contestants would split a handsome $700 purse. The Crows also placed advertisements in the *Hardin Tribune-Herald* that underscored the use of both non-Indian and Indian-owned stock in the race meets and rodeo at Crow Fair. One such advertisement read: "Crow Fair and Rodeo: 5 Races Each Day Plus 5 Rodeo Events, Feature Race Saturday Afternoon for Big Horn County Owned Horses Only, Feature Race Sunday Afternoon for Crow Indian Owned Horses Only." Through printed advertising and word of mouth, the rodeo at Crow Fair grew in size and popularity. In 1956, the rodeo that was held the first three days of Crow Fair was said to be one of the most successful in the history of the event. The advertisement in the *Hardin Tribune-Herald* for Crow Fair and Rodeo reflected that "Crow Nation Will Stage Annual Rodeo and Celebration August 21, 22, 23." The rodeo that year included both amateur and professional NRCA-sanctioned events.[79]

Crow women also became more involved as contestants in Crow Fair's expanding rodeo. In 1956, Crow Fair's rodeo included a "cowgirls barrel race each day" in addition to the standard events of "calf roping, team tying, bareback bronc riding, wild cow milking, saddle bronc riding and steer riding." Ladies' barrel racing was again one of six featured events in the daily rodeo held each afternoon during the fair and rodeo in 1959.[80]

As the numbers of Indian contestants rose, the Crows began to see that it would be possible to stage their rodeo without non-Indian contestants, judges, and stock. In doing so, they accelerated the trend toward establishing all-Indian rodeos on a statewide level.

It was only appropriate that the Crows' "Teepee Capital of the World" should exemplify one of the first established all-Indian rodeos. By 1962, the Crow Fair and Rodeo board of directors declared their rodeo to be an exclusively Indian event. They did this in large part to accommodate the ever-increasing number of Indian rodeo cowboys and cowgirls on the Crow reservation and throughout the northern Great Plains. As an all-Indian event, Crow Fair and Rodeo enhanced both pan-Indian and Crow solidarity. According to Pius Real Bird, Crow Fair rodeo's manager in 1962, the all-Indian rodeo at Crow Fair was designed to name the "champion Indian rodeo performer of North America." In a 1962 interview with the *Hardin Herald-Tribune*, Real Bird assured local non-Indian cowboys that the rodeo was just responding to the increasing numbers of Native rodeo cowboys and cowgirls. He also professed to be simply following the trend toward all-Indian events. He explained that "the change had been made because the Crows feel there is a real need for a final championship competition among top Indian rodeo performers. . . . There are many national Indian competition events such as dance championships, all-Indian basketball tournaments, and the Miss Indian America pageant but none in the field of rodeo."[81]

Although some Plains Indian rodeo contestants insisted on an all-Indian rodeo because of their desire to create an Indian championship, others had expressed concerns regarding the degree of fairness with which they had been judged by non-Indians. In an interview given in 1995, Pius Real Bird acknowledged that the committee's decision was also a reaction to the racial prejudice Indian cowboys had experienced from non-Indian judges. Rodeo contestants, especially in timed events, are particularly vulnerable to the decisions of judges. Real Bird explained, "We had a lot of good cowboys, especially bronc riders, and we got tired of them [non-Indians] judging our rodeo."[82] Hal Borland's When the Legends Die, published in 1963, depicts the frustration many Indian rodeo cowboys felt with the biased treatment they had received in the National Rodeo Cowboys Association.[83] Thus, the combined desire of the Crows to compete with and among other Indians and to be judged impartially by Indian judges motivated them to take the chance on initiating an all-Indian rodeo.

As an all-Indian rodeo, Crow Fair and Rodeo attracted Indian cowboys and spectators from all over the West for intertribal camaraderie and rivalry. Initially, there was some reluctance among those board members who feared that there would not be enough Indian contestants to equip an all-Indian Crow Fair rodeo. Real Bird, however, predicted that an all-Indian rodeo would be a success based on the prolific history of northern Plains Indians in rodeo.

> Indian horsemanship reached its peak here in the Northwest, where horse and rider were especially trained for the buffalo chase and horseback battle. Descendants of these hard-riding nomads of the northwest plains have done well in the field of rodeo competition throughout the years. Some years ago, top Indian bucking riders like Ben Youngbird of the North Dakota Gros Ventre Tribe, Perry Eastman of the Northern Cheyenne, Jim Carpenter and Jim Cooper of the Crow Reservation and other Indian top hands all challenged one another in real old fashioned bronc riding, right here in Montana."[84]

Real Bird went on to mention some of the top Indian bronc riders who would compete at Crow Fair rodeo; they included Pete Fredericks, Joe Chase, Clinton Small, and Bud Fitzler. He added that he had also heard of some top team ropers among the San Carlos Apaches. He summarized his endorsement by declaring that "the ability is there, traditional intertribal rivalry is still strong, and this is rodeo country!" At Crow Fair's first all-Indian rodeo, Real Bird's expectations were met. Western Indians, including "Crees and Bloods from Canada, Arapahoes and Shoshones from Wyoming, Blackfeet, Assiniboines, Gros Ventre, Northern Cheyennes and others from Montana, and Southern Cheyennes from Oklahoma and even a few Navajos" traveled to Crow Agency for the event. In 1964, "the best Indian riders and ropers in the country" were once again crowned at what the Crow rodeo producers claimed to be "the only all-Indian championship rodeo in the United States."[85]

With the inception of the all-Indian rodeo, Crow unity was enhanced as they came together en masse to defeat the other tribes and secure the championship. In the previous two years, "there were two celebrations, sponsored by different factions. . . . But this year, all of the 4,500 Crows have gotten together for their big show and party." The Crow rodeo arena directors intensified the spirit of intertribal rivalry by presenting a traveling trophy to the tribe that amassed the most points; it took three consecutive wins to make the trophy a permanent possession of a tribe. In 1962, the Crows were pleased to have kept the "tribal championship on their home reservation" as "they compiled more

points in all events than any other tribal group." In addition, "three individual championships also stayed at home." Members of two of the Crows' leading rodeo families, the Not Afraids and the Real Birds, won them. The local
newspaper listed the Crows' victories: "They were the calf roping crown, won
by Gary Not Afraid of Lodge Grass, the top spot in team tying, earned by Dee
and Wayne Not Afraid of Lodge Grass, and the saddle bronc championship,
which went to Richard Real Bird of Crow Agency." The Crows' neighbors and
longtime Crow Fair and Rodeo participants, the Northern Cheyennes, were
the runners-up, followed by the ranking of "Blackfeet, Gros Ventre, Fort Peck,
Assiniboine Sioux, Blood Indians of Canada and Rosebud Sioux." In the second year of the all-Indian competition, arena directors Gerard and George
Bull Tail offered purses of $150 for each event except saddle bronc riding, for
which $200 was offered, and the "girls' barrel race," which paid only $50 plus
entry fees. That year the Northern Cheyennes seized the title from the Crows,
but the Crows were pleased with gate receipts that indicated record attendance. Despite initial apprehensions, the all-Indian rodeo had proved itself to
be exceedingly popular among Indian and non-Indian visitors alike.[86]

Crow Fair and Rodeo continued to bolster intratribal and intertribal affiliations and competition. In 1964, just as in the previous years, "the Crows and
their visitors from many tribes [camped] at the tribal ground, near the arena."
During their stay, they participated in and watched the rodeo and horse races
in the afternoon and the dancing at night. Representatives from Crow rodeo
families often seized the spotlight at the rodeo. In 1964, Crow cowboy Wayne
Not Afraid won best all-around cowboy title. The following year, the Crows
displayed the trophy saddle presented to the best all-around cowboy in the
Crow Tribal building. The Indian cowboys were vying for that individual title
as well as for purses of $250 for most events. Clinton Small of the Northern
Cheyenne reservation was the all-around champion, taking first in saddle
bronc riding and in team roping with his brother Junior Small. Other Crow
Indian titleholders included Wayne Not Afraid for calf roping and Jennifer
Bird-in-Ground for barrel racing. A year earlier, Jennifer Bird-in-Ground had
been elected rodeo queen. As a winning rodeo contestant and Crow Fair
Rodeo Queen, Bird-in-Ground was another representative of her family's rich
rodeo tradition. Winners also included other notable Plains Indian rodeo
cowboys such as Lakota Charlie Colombe of Mission, South Dakota, for saddle bronc riding; Blood Indian Pete Bruised Head from Carston, Alberta, for
bareback bronc riding; and Gros Ventre Janice Cauliflower of Hays, Montana,

for barrel racing. The participants also included children such as Clyde Little Light of Crow Agency, who competed and won in kids' cow riding.[87]

Members of the prominent rodeo families the Smalls and the Real Birds again played important roles at Crow Fair's rodeos in 1967 and 1968. The accent was on youth at the 1967 Crow Celebration and All-Indian Rodeo. Ivan Small, seventeen and college bound, served as president, while Mary Beth LaForge, eighteen, served as treasurer—the first female to be an officer other than secretary of the celebration. That year the top performers in each rodeo event received silver trophy spurs, which were touted as an innovation in rodeo awards in Montana.[88] In 1968 tribal chairperson Edison Real Bird, who had himself competed in bareback and bronc riding events in the 1950s, announced the rodeo events. Real Bird had "in later years . . . traded in his spurs for a microphone" at both all-Indian and non-Indian rodeos throughout the American West.[89] *Hardin Tribune-Herald* photographer Richard Bowler captured Cory Real Bird's impressive bronc ride in 1967. The caption read, "Airborne bucking bronc 'Cream Puff' was determined to unseat Cory Real Bird. . . . But try as he did, the mare just couldn't rid herself of Cory."[90] He was one of many Crows to receive silver spurs for his efforts at the all-Indian rodeo.[91] The decade closed with Indian rodeo contestants traveling from Montana, North and South Dakota, Wyoming, and Canada in the northern Great Plains; Oklahoma in the Southern Great Plains; and Arizona in the Southwest to attend the Crows' all-Indian rodeo.[92] This scene belied the original conception of Superintendent S. G. Reynolds and other Indian officials of Indian industrial fairs as events that would serve to detribalize and assimilate American Indians while keeping them closer to home.

## RODEO FAMILIES AND ALL-INDIAN RODEOS ON THE NORTHERN CHEYENNE, ROSEBUD, AND PINE RIDGE RESERVATIONS

The success of the all-Indian rodeo at Crow Fair would inspire the creation of all-Indian rodeos on other northern Plains Indian reservations. In the meantime, Northern Cheyennes and Lakotas on the Rosebud and Pine Ridge reservations met and competed at various reservation fairs and rodeos.

In 1958 the Northern Cheyennes staged their own fair at Lame Deer, but unlike Crow Fair, it was limited to members of the Northern Cheyenne Indian tribe or Indians living on the Northern Cheyenne reservation. Its content also remained closer to its original incarnation as an industrial fair in that it retained its agricultural contests and lacked a rodeo. As tribal council president, John Wooden Legs remained intent on bolstering the economic status of his tribe. Consequently, he collaborated with Bureau of Indian Affairs officials in staging a truly agricultural fair. In an effort to make the fair more appealing to the Northern Cheyenne community, Wooden Legs also offered barbecue and tribal dancing.[93]

While their own tribal fair lacked a rodeo, Northern Cheyennes took advantage of other opportunities to meet with and compete in rodeos against other Indians. In 1959 Northern Cheyenne stock contractors and cowboys participated in the pan-Indian St. Labre Diamond Jubilee. The religious at the St. Labre Mission sponsored the event in the Northern Cheyenne reservation town of Ashland, Montana. The Roman Catholic missionaries, realizing the mounting enthusiasm among American Indians for rodeo and their expectation that it be a part of their cultural celebrations, staged a pan-Indian event attended by Arapahos, Crows, Gros Ventres, and Lakotas. For three days, rodeos and Indian dances took place at the celebration. It was a rodeo in which professional Indian rodeo cowboys like the Smalls competed against amateurs.[94] Northern Cheyenne cowboys like Austin Two Moons, who had competed in rodeos in Sheridan, Crow Agency, and Hardin, were able to rodeo against other Indian cowboys on their home reservation. One Northern Cheyenne rodeo family emerged when John Fisher of the reservation town of Birney provided the broncos for the rodeo and his relative Al Fisher competed in the steer riding events. Indian cowgirls like Clair Courtney, a Lakota from Pine Ridge, South Dakota, took advantage of the rare opportunity to participate in saddle bronc riding, an event that was reserved for men in professional rodeos.[95] Subsequently, a number of Northern Cheyenne horsemen and -women also participated in the Red Lodge Rodeo in Red Lodge, Montana, in 1960.[96]

In the summer of 1964, the Northern Cheyennes staged a celebration and rodeo of their own in the reservation town of Lame Deer, Montana. Along with their annual Indian parade and Memorial Day ceremonial, the Lame Deer Saddle Club hosted a rodeo in the afternoon and Indian dancing at night.[97] In 1965, the Northern Cheyennes inaugurated their annual Fourth of July intertribal powwow, another type of pan-Indian celebration that was becoming increasingly popular in the 1960s. Powwows varied from one region to another and evolved over time by incorporating new dance categories and elements. At powwows, like tribal fairs, American Indians competed and paid homage to past and present through particular dances, honoring songs, the giving of gifts, and the selection of head singers, dancers, and other ceremonial leaders.[98] Their 1968 powwow was dedicated to the Indian soldiers in Vietnam. Memorial dances were held "for each of the Northern Cheyenne boys who lost their life in Vietnam," and others were held in honor of the Indian boys then fighting in Vietnam. The powwow was widely attended, with five hundred Indian families from a "dozen different Indian tribes of the Northwest . . . present. Each family pitched a tent in brotherhood with the other tribes for the colorful event."[99] Eventually, rodeos would accompany many such intertribal powwows.

Held prior to the founding of their own all-Indian rodeo, Rosebud Sioux communities frequently hosted open rodeos within their reservation. Although they remained open to all, Lakotas provided much of the equestrian talent and the stock. Many of these gatherings included a blend of adopted activities like baseball and barn dances as well as adapted Indian activities like rodeo and Indian dances. Independence Day provided one such occasion for the reservation communities of St. Francis, Spring Creek, Parmelee, and Okreek to come together and enjoy a picnic of buffalo barbecue and "a big rodeo, fast ball games, dances and other entertainment." In the evenings, Lakotas and their non-Indian guests also attended Indian dances as well as barn dances or country-and-western dances.[100] The 1950 annual Indian Celebration and Rodeo hosted by the Rosebud Sioux of Parmelee offered prizes totaling $800 to its rodeo champions. One reporter gushed that "in addition to the usual good rodeo for which Parmelee is noted," there was "a big Indian celebration and Indian dancing dressed in full regalia."[101] In another event, the members of the Rosebud Roping Club sponsored a Fourth of July rodeo at the Rosebud Fairgrounds. The program included an "All Jackpot Events program of calf roping, bulldogging and horse racing" and Indian dances each afternoon and evening.[102]

As rodeos continued to spring up on the Rosebud reservation, Rosebud Sioux rodeo families like the Walns, the Whipples, and the Colombes came to the fore, contributing to the sport as stock contractors, contestants, and judges. The stock contracting company Waln, Whipple and Bradford often furnished the livestock for reservation and local rodeos, and family members like Sonny Waln and Stanley Whipple competed and won trophy buckles.[103] In 1965 Joe Waln was one of the judges for the rodeo events at the Rosebud Sioux Fair and Rodeo.[104]

Many of these rodeos occurred in Mission, South Dakota, in the heart of the Rosebud reservation. When American Legion Mission Post 287 sponsored the Mission Rodeo in 1957, the group promoted it with posters covering the reservation, announcing, "Rodeo! Mission, South Dakota S.D.A.R.A. approved . . . $75.00 purse all events." Although many of the Indian and non-Indian contestants were amateurs, those who were professionals could use their scores toward their National Rodeo Cowboys Association rankings.[105] Twelve miles west of Mission, the Rosebud Sioux members of the Parmelee 4-H Club introduced the annual Soldier Creek Rodeo in 1960.[106] It remained a popular reservation rodeo in 1965.[107]

The Rosebud Sioux sporadically hosted a rodeo, which became an all-Indian rodeo in 1967, at their reservation-wide fair. Following World War II, the reservation's American Legion post and its Lakota membership organized the Rosebud Fair and Rodeo. Like the Crows, the Lakotas initially staged the fair and rodeo to appeal to a non-Indian tourist audience but gradually shifted the focus to their Indian guests. To generate enthusiasm among local non-Indians and to maintain Indian support, they included many of what had become standard Indian fair activities such as a big rodeo each day, Indian dances, Sioux Indian arts and crafts, Indian parades, and the obligatory agricultural exhibits, which included "fine specimens of needlework." From 1948 to 1953, the roster of events varied widely, but rodeo was a mainstay. The competition and prize money continued to draw contestants and crowds. Reportedly, the "rodeo staged each day pleased the crowds with some good riding and roping" as Indian and non-Indian cowboys again competed for awards totaling $816 and the title of "best all-around cowboy."[108]

Along with the rodeo, the Rosebud Sioux scheduled various events at their tribal fair that were designed to attract non-Indians, especially non-Indian residents from the local area. The schedule varied from year to year but might include evening bowery dances, baseball games, bike races, footraces, and the occasional carnival or stock car race.[109] There were years between 1953 and 1960 when the Lakotas changed their strategy for attracting tourists and shifted their emphasis toward events perceived by non-Indians as typically Indian. In 1956, for example, the Rosebud Sioux Tribal Council worked with the BIA's County Extension Service to sponsor an "Indian Celebration" at Rosebud that featured garden exhibits, canned goods exhibits, and arts and crafts exhibits. Visitors saw Indian dances and regalia and feasted on barbecued buffalo, served each day. In 1959 the agricultural and arts and crafts aspects of the fair had become important enough that when a fire destroyed the exhibit building at Rosebud Fairgrounds, Lakota contestants moved their exhibits to a new venue in Rosebud.[110]

During his tenure as Rosebud Superintendent from 1959 to 1968, Harold Schunk hoped to use the fair, as Yellowtail had done during the Indian New Deal, as a forum for Indians to showcase their modern culture and to discuss their political concerns. As a proponent of Indian cattle ranching on the Rosebud reservation, Schunk encouraged the return of rodeo to the Rosebud Sioux Tribal Fair while continuing to endorse the display of agricultural exhibits and "historical dances in their beautiful ceremonial costumes." The Rosebud Sioux Tribal Council supported Schunk's vision. Tribal councilmen doubled as members of the fair committee at the 1963 Rosebud fair. Tribal council officer Charles Kills in War oversaw the exhibits in the agricultural and arts and crafts divisions, while Superintendent Schunk himself presented trophies for the rodeo and agricultural events. The response of non-Indian and Indian guests alike was overwhelmingly positive. In 1960 the Rosebud Sioux once again featured rodeo at their tribal fair, which "attracted a record breaking crowd of local and tourist people . . . over three thousand." Photographers captured some scenes from the Rosebud Fair and Rodeo in 1965 and 1966, including one from 1966 in which a caption described the skillful cow-tying demonstrated there: "A local roper finds the mark in the calf-roping section of the rodeo—which found local cowboys testing their eye and know-how."[111]

In the 1960s, the Rosebud Fair and Rodeo provided a public forum for Lakotas to discuss pressing political issues, particularly those surrounding termination and non-Indian land leases. The main speaker at the 1962 tribal fair and rodeo was the assistant commissioner of Indian affairs for legislation. He was scheduled to speak on congressional bills affecting the Lakotas, especially the federal policy of termination and its implications. His speech centered around an amendment to Public Law 280, the law that was the centerpiece of termination legislation and that gave certain states criminal and civil jurisdiction on reservation lands.[112] The proposed amendment would prove crucial to the fight against termination because it "would require the consent of the tribes before any state takes jurisdiction over law and order on Indian reservations."[113] Many Lakotas who did not want federal trust responsibilities to be handed over to state governments were glad to hear that their dissenting voice would be heard. They suspected that state politicians would be likely to favor non-Indians, particularly regarding Indian land holdings. Lakotas on the Rosebud Sioux reservation had recently clashed with local ranchers over tribal jurisdiction to collect taxes from non-Indians leasing Indian lands.

> Several local white ranchers have refused to pay tribal taxes and at least one was expected to tangle with the Rosebud Sioux Tribe in the next few days. . . . The ranchers, who lease Indian land, have clashed with Tribal jurisdiction, which gives the Tribe the right to cancel leases if tribal assessments are not paid. The same reports said the rancher would come armed with this lawyer for a legal "shoot-out" with the Tribe (which is bringing in its own attorney for the event.)[114]

Antagonisms also festered among different factions of Lakotas on the Rosebud and Pine Ridge reservations. In "Spontaneous Combustion: Prelude to Wounded Knee 1973," Akim D. Reinhardt describes the divisions that were developing on the Pine Ridge reservation in the 1960s; similar divisions were also present on the Rosebud reservation. Broadly, one group comprised those who lived in rural reservation areas, remained fluent in the Lakota language, adhered to the Lakota religion, and showed concern for treaty rights; the other group comprised those who "tended to live in reservation towns, [and] were more apt to be Christian-English speakers who adhered to middle-class American values."[115] As Reinhardt suggests, these factions became evident in the locations and types of residences that individual Lakotas chose as the federal government began to build federal cluster housing on the Pine Ridge reservation in 1962 as part of its renewed effort to assimilate Indians. The latter group embraced these "contemporary, urban-style dwellings as symbols of progress, while proponents of traditional Lakota values often stayed in isolated homes that . . . were situated on family allotments."[116] Despite these distinct intratribal differences, a cross-section of Lakotas from both factions continued to congregate at their reservation fairs and rodeos.

By August 1967, the Rosebud Sioux had transformed their fair and rodeo into an all-Indian rodeo where Lakotas could put aside their disputes and find common ground. That year they announced their own All American Indian Championship Rodeo and Pow-Wow. The rodeo took place on the Rosebud Fairgrounds, and the events included saddle bronc riding, bareback bronc riding, calf roping, bulldogging, bull riding, team tying, and barrel racing. There was a $15 entry fee and a $150 purse for each event with the exception of barrel racing, which awarded $75. "Sterling silver-gold plated" trophy buckles were also awarded for each event. While non-Indians could not act as

competitors, the Lakotas encouraged them to attend as spectators. Admission
was $1.50 for adults and $.75 for children ten and above.[117]

The Lakota Sioux community found some degree of solidarity at the 1968
tribal rodeo. At the Rosebud Fairgrounds, they honored the Lakota soldiers
serving in Vietnam. They and their guests "prayed for peace in Vietnam, for
the Sioux fighting there as well as others." They also prayed for the goals of
both progressive and traditional Lakotas, asking, "for health and prosperity
for the Sioux people, and for education of the Indian youngsters. . . . Help all
Indian people, whether mixed or full blooded, to enter together in the pipe
society and take part in prayer and the ritual using a peace pipe."[118] A 1969 letter to the editor of the *Rosebud Sioux Herald: Eyapaha* praising the Lakotas'
display of cohesiveness at the Rosebud Sioux Fair and Rodeo recognized the
social function that the event served in the Rosebud community:

> Dear Editor:
> I would like to congratulate the people of the Rosebud reservation for pre-
> senting such a fine pow-wow, fair and rodeo at Rosebud. What makes me so
> happy is that this event was organized, planned, and operated with 100 percent
> Indian skill and talent. It shows and proves that Indians can do things for
> themselves without having some white man tell them how to do it. I am proud
> of the fact the people worked together for a common goal—a good Rosebud
> Fair, and they did not involve personalities, politics and grudges. A special
> thanks should go to John Waln who so freely devotes his time, talent and ener-
> gies to making the rodeo a success. For the past two years he has supervised
> one of the finest rodeos in South Dakota. I hope that we learned something
> from this—the Rosebud people can solve a lot of problems when they are will-
> ing to put the personal things aside, and all work together for a common goal
> and the good of all the people. —Name Withheld, Rosebud.[119]

Throughout the 1960s, Jake Herman, an Oglala Lakota rodeo cowboy and
clown, provided a running commentary on Pine Ridge Sioux rodeo and politics. In his editorial column, "WA-HO-SI," in the *Shannon County News*, the
Pine Ridge newspaper, Herman bore witness to the enduring affection many
Oglala Lakotas continued to share for rodeo. Herman pointed out that a
number of Lakota cowboys from the Pine Ridge reservation were charter
members of the Tri-State Old Time Cowboys Association, formed in 1963.
The members, who had "cowboyed 30 or 35 years," comprised a "permanent
association of saddle-hardened residents of Nebraska, Wyoming and South
Dakota." In 1964 Herman attended and promoted, as he had before, "the old
ex-rodeo cowboys' reunion at Mission and at White River."[120] In 1966 the

old-time cowboys again met for a breakfast. Herman wistfully recounted the morning's events, which he attended with fellow Lakota cowboy Emil Red Fish. After they had heard speeches and posed for group photos, Herman mused, "These old time cowboys meetings are beautiful and sad as many are now at the end of the old cowboy memory trail—days that were, days that will never return. Old time cowboys who have reached the end of the trail, leave only their memories and experiences of the colorful past.[121] Jake Herman shared some Indian rodeo cowboy yarns in his newspaper column in 1963. Revealing the way that rodeos fostered Lakota camaraderie, one anecdote recounts the time that Lakota rodeo cowboy Charles Yellow Boy saved Herman's life at a rodeo.

> This happened at a rodeo some years back: A fierce range bull was put in a chute. A steer rider mounted this bull. The bull unseated his rider then he charged a cowboy standing near by. This bull hooked the cowboy and threw him way up in the air. Then the bull spotted me. I was in the arena in front of the chutes. This bull charged at me before I had time to set myself to try to side step the charging bull. Suddenly, appeared Charles Yellow boy. He dashed out on horseback. Charles had a saddle rope about 45 ft. long. He threw that loop and caught the bull by the hind leg. Then he set his cow horse. Charles stopped the bull cold in his tracks. This gave me a chance to run like a scared Jack rabbit which I did and I dove over the fence. This was one of the most welcome timely beautiful rope catchers I had ever seen. Charles Yellow Boy was a real top cowboy. Charles is no longer here on mother earth. He died a few years back. I'll always remember Charles Yellow Boy. My Kola who saved me.[122]

Herman was confident that future generations of Oglala Lakotas from Pine Ridge would continue the Lakotas' impressive record of rodeo. He profiled several of the rising Indian rodeo cowboys in 1965. Among them was Ed Two Bulls Jr., aged 26, of the Red Shirt Table district of the Pine Ridge reservation, who had been "playing rodeos for the last three years." Herman also mentioned Tuffy Sierra, who had been riding bulls and riding bareback at many rodeos since the early 1960s. According to Herman, Sierra had "the know how and the makings of a future top rodeo rider. He has won and placed in Brahma Bull riding and bareback riding." As Herman predicted, the Sierra family would continue to produce rodeo champions. Dugan LaBeau, a nineteen-year-old bareback and bull rider, was also on Herman's list. Herman predicted in 1965 that LaBeau and Sierra were "going places in the rodeo world. Next year these two top rodeo riders will make the big time. They are

*Jake Herman, rodeo clown, and his mule, Cheyenne River Annual Rodeo, 1926.*
State Historical Society of North Dakota (Fiske 4250).

both young and love to ride and my guess is that they will make it pretty rugged for any riders who compete with them. Good luck, boys."[123]

Throughout the 1960s, Oglala Lakotas compiled a record of success at professional open rodeos that anticipated the creation of their all-Indian professional circuit. In 1966, Jake Herman praised the successes of Pine Ridge cowboys in the SRCA (the Sioux Rodeo Cowboys Association), an informal precursor to the Great Plains Rodeo Association that was formed in 1976 along with the INFR.

> The S.R.C.A. rodeo association takes in five states—South Dakota, Montana, North Dakota, Nebraska, and Wyoming. . . . What most people don't realize is that five of the top performers on the S.R.C.A. and one in the N.R.C.A. who have a high rating are all from the Pine Ridge reservation. Dugan LaBeau of Pine Ridge village stands first in the bull riding. Louis Twiss of Cuny Table stands second. . . . Curtis Coomes of Manderson stands 3rd in bronc riding. Tuffy Sierra of Pine Ridge village stands third in the N.R.C.A. riding. Keith Lockhart of Porcupine stands first in calf roping. . . . If these top rodeo riders and ropers win at the last four shows they will bring honors to South Dakota and the Pine Ridge reservation.[124]

By 1962, the Oglala Sioux Fair and Jack Pot Rodeo was an all-Indian rodeo. It featured a rodeo along with Indian dances and agricultural exhibits.[125] At the rodeo, representatives of notable rodeo families from the Crow, Northern Cheyenne, Rosebud, and Pine Ridge reservations took home prize money. The "Colombes, Walns and Whipples, Sullys, and Parkers kept the Rosebud reservation in the prize money offered at the tribal rodeo," while Crow cowboys Gary Not Afraid, Junior Small, and Clinton Small placed in bulldogging and calf roping.[126] The Oglala Sioux Fair and Rodeo had become a pan-Indian event, as had the Crow Fair and Rodeo and the Rosebud Sioux Tribal Fair and Rodeo.

As part of their drive for self-determination, American Indian leaders instituted Native rodeos and organizations in the 1950s and onward. The burgeoning all-Indian rodeo infrastructure simply made official what had long been a reality: rodeo was a pan-Indian event. The increased participation of Indian men and women, the latter of whom competed as barrel racers and rodeo queens, made possible the formation of an all-Indian rodeo circuit. The emergence of rodeo families like the Not Afraids and the Real Birds on the Crow reservation; the Smalls and the Fishers on the Northern Cheyenne reservation; the Walns, Whipples, and Colombes on the Rosebud reservation;

and the Sierras and Twisses on the Pine Ridge reservation ensured its future. Even as they excluded non-Indian contestants from their rodeo arenas, Crows and Lakotas encouraged their attendance. In a renewed effort to revitalize their reservations and to improve their economies, they continued to promote non-Indian tourism at their tribal fairs and rodeos like the Crows' "Teepee Capital of the World." By naming it thus, the Crows completed the transformation of their Indian fair, which Superintendent Reynolds had introduced ironically to assimilate them, into a veritable all-Indian celebration.

CHAPTER FIVE

# "Talking Broncs"

## TRADITIONS OF INDIAN RODEO CHAMPIONS AND COMMUNITIES

### 1970 to the Present

AFTER THIRTY-FOUR-YEAR-OLD BULL RIDER DALE David "Tazz" Big Plume of the Tsuu T'ina Nation in Alberta, Canada, died on February 10, 1994, his family placed a remembrance in the *Calgary Herald* with a list of the many relatives who survived him as well as those who had passed before him. The family went on to express their love for Tazz and to wish him well as he went to meet his deceased rodeo partner Bob Noel "at the Creator's Rodeo Office [where] together they will continue on their trail of peace in that circuit, with their fees paid in full."[1] Tazz Big Plume, an American Indian rodeo cowboy, is representative of an American Indian horse-and-cattle culture adopted by Southwestern, Great Plains, and Canadian Indians in varying degrees between the late sixteenth and twentieth centuries and adapted by each subsequent generation of American Indian horsemen and cowboys. It was appropriate that Tazz Big Plume's family should end his memorial where most rodeos begin—with the recitation of "A Cowboy's Prayer." By doing so, they recognized that although he was "taking that last inevitable ride to the Country up there," his legacy as a skilled horseman and American Indian cowboy would continue through the many men, women, and children competing in the "arena of life" known as the Indian rodeo.[2]

From 1970 on, Indian rodeo devotees like Tazz Big Plume and his family have increased in numbers and have helped the all-Indian rodeo circuit to grow. With a new federal Indian policy of self-determination in effect, Native Americans were free to institute all-Indian rodeo as a pan-Indian activity. In his July 8, 1970, "Message to Congress on Indian Affairs," President Richard Nixon called for a new federal Indian policy that would abandon the goals of assimilation and grant American Indian tribes the power of self-determination. Nixon explained that under such a policy tribal governments would be able to function in a more autonomous manner befitting their semi-sovereign status, without excess interference from the BIA. In *The American Indian's Fight for Freedom: Red Power*, Alvin M. Josephy underlines the significance of the tone and intent of Nixon's message. It signaled a

> firm rebuttal by a chief executive of the nation of the white man's conviction—countenanced officially for many generations—that American Indians were incompetent to control their own affairs. . . . It showed that a national administration had at last listened to and accepted their [the American Indians'] ideas of what they needed and wanted. It would no longer be "either-or" for Indians (either a white man or an Indian). Forced assimilation into the mainstream, the most benign aim of federal policy since colonial days, would be abandoned by Richard Nixon.[3]

Although change would be gradual, self-determination fundamentally redirected federal policy. The capstone legislation of this policy was the Indian Self Determination and Educational Assistance Act, which passed in Congress in 1975. It instructed the secretaries of departments like the Department of Health, Education, and Welfare to make contracts directly with individual Indian tribes. In response, northern Plains Indian communities took the initiative to revitalize their reservation economies, education systems, and cultures.

The most radical of the newly formed Native American activist groups was the American Indian Movement, or AIM, formed on the model of the Black Panther Party in 1968. In 1972 AIM orchestrated a march on Washington, D.C., known as the Trail of Broken Treaties, that numbered some two thousand people from more than one hundred reservations. When government officials reneged on their previous agreements, some four hundred AIM members seized the Bureau of Indian Affairs headquarters and held it for six days. The climax of AIM's protests took place in Wounded Knee, South Dakota, on the Pine Ridge reservation, where at least three hundred Lakotas had been massacred in 1890. In 1973, the hamlet of Wounded Knee became the site of a standoff, brought on by mounting antagonisms within the reservation, in which AIM and "various arms of the federal government" became involved.[4] The ensuing seventy-one day armed conflict became the focal point of AIM's campaign to reassert Native sovereignty as they and their Oglala Lakota comrades declared the enclave the Independent Oglala Nation. Following the events at Wounded Knee, radicalism waned as President Richard Nixon began to comply with Native American demands. He rejected termination in 1970 and signed the Indian Self-Determination and Educational Assistance Act in 1973.

In this setting, northern Plains Indians have maintained and promoted rodeos as a favored form of intratribal and intertribal gathering and competition on their home reservations and beyond. They have done so by creating organizations to commemorate Indian rodeo notables and by fostering the sport of rodeo within their families and communities. As pan-Indian events, all-Indian rodeos were taking place on a regional and national level as professional all-Indian rodeo associations developed and sanctioned numerous events. From its inception in 1976, the Indian National Finals Rodeo has remained the culmination of the all-Indian rodeo circuit and the Native solidarity the circuit has nurtured. The success of the growing all-Indian rodeo circuit has been buoyed by the dedication of many Lakota, Northern Cheyenne, and Crow cowboys and cowgirls who have continued to participate in rodeos in a variety of contexts. Through generational training, competition, hard work, and camaraderie, these Indians have fostered family, tribal, and intertribal ties. Within reservation communities, all-Indian rodeos have often been held as memorial and charity competitions and in conjunction with tribal fairs and community celebrations. Thus, the enduring presence of and tribal participation in reservation rodeos like the Crow Fair rodeo and the Rosebud Sioux Tribe rodeo have strengthened tribal affiliations and have made all-Indian rodeo a part of the shared experience of many northern Plains Indian communities. By the first decade of the twenty-first century, rodeo has become part of the identity of many Lakota, Crow, Northern Cheyenne, and Canadian Indian horsemen and -women, residing in their collective memories and folklore.

## HONORING CHAMPIONS:
## THE INDIAN NATIONAL FINALS RODEO

By the mid-1970s, Native Americans were seeking new ways of recognizing past and present Indian cowboys of rodeo fame. When the American Indian

Hall of Fame (AIHF) was formed, its organizers considered Indian rodeo cowboys to be among Native America's finest athletes. In 1972, three BIA institutions, including Haskell Indian Junior College, joined a number of newly minted tribal colleges, including Oglala Lakota College on the Pine Ridge reservation and Sinte Gleska College on the Rosebud reservation, to form the American Indian Higher Education Consortium. A year later, Haskell Indian Junior College (later to become Haskell Indian Nations University) established the American Indian Hall of Fame in Lawrence, Kansas, as one place where American Indian athletes, rodeo cowboys among them, would be honored. The Hall of Fame was designed to venerate outstanding Native athletes in hopes of inspiring young people with the accomplishments of their forebears. Accordingly, the preamble of the American Indian Hall of Fame declared:

> In the belief that the athletic achievements and sportsmanship of many American Indians stand as a tribute to the will and abilities of the athletes involved and in the belief that these achievements stand also as inspiration for young Indians seeking to develop rewarding and productive lives, this organization is founded to provide suitable recognition to these athletes and their achievements and to preserve records of their attainments and memorabilia incident thereto for the Nation and prosperity.[5]

Given their long-standing record of success dating back to George Defender, it is not surprising that a number of Lakota rodeo cowboys were suggested as potential American Indian Hall of Fame members. Father Paul Quinn, a Catholic priest and observer of the Rosebud reservation, recommended a number of Lakota rodeo cowboys as candidates. In his letter, Quinn wrote, "I don't suppose cowboys are considered athletes in the sense that they consider—there has been an Indian or several who did well. Maybe some still are doing well." With his letter, he enclosed a list of Lakota cowboys. Among those mentioned on Quinn's extensive list of "S.D. [South Dakota] great rodeo men in the early days" were members of the Rosebud rodeo families— the Walns, Whipples, and Colombes (including Dave Colombe Sr., Chris Colombe, Charles Whipple, and Joe Waln). He also mentioned other Lakota rodeo notables like Mary Strike ("great lady rider"), Jake Herman ("great cowboy and clown"), Steve Janice, Billy Pourier, and Pete Fredericks.[6] "Jake Herman Sioux Cowboy" appeared on at least one official list of outstanding American Indian athletes as a result of Father Quinn's suggestion.[7]

Part of the American Indian Hall of Fame's professed mission was also to foster a deeper respect for American Indians among non-Indians. To this end, the preamble to their preliminary report on the hall of fame stated, "The American Indian Hall of Fame . . . will attempt to develop an active dialogue and feelings of mutual respect among all Americans. It will . . . build a complex depicting the life of the Indian and amplifying present possibilities for growth by linking the past with the present to build a better future for all Americans."[8] Since 1890, many northern Plains horsemen and -women had been linking their "past with the present" and seeking to improve the futures of their progeny by incorporating cattle ranching and rodeo into their reservation lives. By 1972, as the American Indian Hall of Fame developed, it was clear to reservation observers like Father Quinn that Native cowboys had been successful in their attempts to cultivate rodeo within their families and communities. Ultimately, only Jackson Sundown was inducted into Haskell's Hall of Fame, but the serious consideration given to Native athletes demonstrated their renown.

The idea for another hall of fame, the Sioux Nation Cowboy Hall of Fame, was conceived in March 1981 to "promote and ensure the continuity of the sport of rodeo in reservation settings."[9] In a 1980 issue of the Sioux Nation Cowboy News (a monthly periodical published in Kyle, South Dakota, on the Pine Ridge reservation), its Lakota writers proclaimed, "We hope this paper will initiate a future Sioux Indian Cowboy Hall of Fame." They promoted the idea by including stories and photographs of successful Lakota cowboys such as Jumbo Montileaux, Pete Longbrake, Charlie Colombe, and Roger Lawrence. Jumbo Montileaux was a Pine Ridge Sioux bronc rider from Kyle, South Dakota. A photograph with the story was captioned "Jumbo riding to a win at Wall, South Dakota in 1947." Pete Longbrake was recognized as "many times past Saddle Bronc Champion of the SDRA [South Dakota Rodeo Association] and NRCA [National Rodeo Cowboys Association]." Charlie Colombe was from a family that was omnipresent in rodeo. He was said to have been "one of the top Indian professional bronc riders of the 60s and 70s." The caption under his photograph read "Pictured is Charlie winning at . . . Deadwood, South Dakota in 1966. Charlie is always willing to help our young Indian cowboys coming up."[10] A photograph of Roger Lawrence was also included, with a caption that read "Roger as the Champion Saddle Bronc Rider at the SDRA in 1970, and runner-up of the title from 1963 to 1973. Aren't you young saddle bronc riders glad that Roger gained a 'little weight' and retired from the rough stock?"[11] Although the Sioux Nation Cowboy Hall of Fame remained a dormant idea, in 1996 the Oglala Nation Rodeo committee once again decided to build an Indian Rodeo Hall of Fame. Committee member Gerald Big Crow argued, "From the 1930s to the present there have been numerous tribal members with great rodeo accomplishments." He and others sought to establish a Rodeo Hall of Fame in 1996 to ensure that Indian rodeo luminaries were not forgotten and that others would follow their lead.[12] Several years later, the construction of the Indian Rodeo Hall of Fame in Fort Pierre, South Dakota, remained on hold.

Many of these rodeo notables and their families had made their claim to fame in the burgeoning all-Indian rodeo circuit. Throughout the 1970s, numerous all-Indian regional Indian rodeo associations were appearing.[13] These associations were modeled after the first formal Indian rodeo association, the All Indian Rodeo Cowboys Association (AIRCA, later the All Indian Professional Rodeo Cowboys Association), which Dean Jackson, Jack Jackson, and Roy Spencer had founded in the Southwest in 1957. Soon other Native managers followed their lead and established Indian rodeo associations in their regions as local rodeo activity was mounting. In a number of ways, these associations brought standardization and increased professionalism to Native rodeos. They helped to hone the skills of both judges and rodeo competitors by sponsoring judging and rodeo schools. They also worked with stock contractors to improve the quality of the broncs and bulls used in their rodeos. Moreover, to coordinate a more predictable schedule of rodeos, which would reduce scheduling conflicts, Indian rodeo associations collaborated more closely with rodeo sponsors.[14] While the all-Indian rodeo circuit was improving the caliber of Native rodeos, it was also improving the quality of the experience for those who competed in it. Native contestants did not have to travel as far or pay entry fees as steep as did participants in the professional rodeo circuit. Most importantly, all-Indian rodeos, often held in conjunction with powwows, fostered a spirit of camaraderie among Native people who participated in these rodeos as organizers, competitors, and spectators.

Prior to opening day of any Indian rodeo, a number of women would have committed themselves and a great deal of their time as rodeo secretaries and secretary-treasurers. As presidents and vice presidents of all-Indian rodeo associations, men would have helped plan and advertise the overall event. Nevertheless, women, many of whom had competed as barrel racers and whose ranching and rodeo families often included husbands and children involved in rodeos, played vital organizational roles. As secretaries and secretary-treasurers, they "kept books, accepted entry fees, and responded to a steady stream of telephone calls concerning upcoming rodeos."[15] Joe Waln, a Rosebud Sioux rodeo producer, praised the rodeo secretary's time-consuming responsibility as a principal rodeo coordinator: "Prior to a rodeo the secretary has the responsibility of staying glued to the phone at least 24 to 36 hours prior to the rodeo. In addition she must schedule the contestants into the program. Not an easy task when many cowboys ride in more than one rodeo miles apart in a single weekend."[16] On the role of women in all-Indian rodeo organizations, Peter Iverson muses, "One is reminded of a phrase uttered by an Indian woman—that 'men are the jawbones of our communities but women are the backbones.'"[17]

By the mid-1990s, the all-Indian rodeo circuit had evolved to include fourteen regional rodeo associations, five of them in Canada and nine in the United States: the Indian Rodeo Cowboys Association (southern Alberta), the Indian Professional Rodeo Association (Alberta), the Western Indian Rodeo and Exhibition Association (British Columbia), the Northern Alberta Native Cowboys Association, the Western States Indian Rodeo Association (Washington and Oregon), the Prairie Indian Rodeo Association (Saskatchewan), the United Indian Rodeo Association (Montana), the Rocky Mountain Indian Rodeo Association (Wyoming and Idaho), the Great Plains Indian Rodeo Association (North and South Dakota), the All-Indian Rodeo Association of Oklahoma (also including Kansas and Texas), the All-Indian Rodeo Cowboys Association (Arizona), the Southwest Indian Rodeo Association, the Navajo Nation Rodeo Cowboys Association, and the Eastern Indian Rodeo Association (Florida).[18]

As the all-Indian rodeo circuit grew, competitors, organizers, and audiences became eager to establish an event that would determine its champions. In anticipation of a national finals rodeo, regional Indian rodeo associations began to institute events that would crown regional champions. In 1971 the All American Indian Activities Association (renamed the Great Plains Indian Rodeo Association in 1974 as it shifted its focus exclusively toward Native rodeo) held such an event in Malta, Montana.[19] Eight Rosebud Sioux were among those who took part in the regional rodeo finals. The winners included cowboys from Rosebud rodeo families like the Walns, the Whipples, and the Colombes, who placed in calf roping, team roping, steer wrestling, bull riding, and saddle bronc riding. Cowgirl barrel racer Vi Colombe also won.[20]

In 1976 a group of Native leaders launched the Indian National Finals Rodeo to honor the "world champions" of the expanding all-Indian rodeo circuit. The event was similar to the National Finals Rodeo that the Professional Rodeo Cowboys Association (PRCA) had initiated in 1955. Clem McSpadden, general manager and cofounder of the Indian National Finals Rodeo, recalled the early days of the INFR. From the event's beginning, McSpadden—grand-nephew of Will Rogers, operator of the Bushyhead Ranch in Chelsea, Oklahoma, a former state senator and congressman, and a PRCA Hall of Fame member and rodeo announcer of the year—used his penchant for showmanship to make the INFR a momentous event.[21] In a 1996 interview that took place at the INFR in Saskatoon, Saskatchewan, the part-Cherokee INFR general manager remembered many of the talented Native ranchers and rodeo devotees who were responsible for the inception of the all-Indian rodeo national finals:

> In 1976, in our bicentennial year, a group of Indian rodeo enthusiasts got together and said let's have an Indian National Finals, and three of those men are still on our commission: Mel Sampson, who is a former chief, except the Yakama tribe calls him manager; Fred Gladstone, a very fine gentleman from the Blood Reserve, Standoff, Alberta; and Pete Fredericks, who is a rancher from Holiday, North Dakota, and a former professional PRCA bareback rider, and the idea was born.[22]

Other committed people from the northern Great Plains as well as from the Northwest and Southwest provided essential leadership in the INFR's first decade. For the first seven years, Jay Harwood, a Blackfeet health care executive originally from Montana, served as president; he was then general manager for three years. Melvin Sampson from Wapato, Washington, one of those whom McSpadden mentioned, succeeded Harwood as INFR president, while also serving as president of the Western States Indian Rodeo Association. In addition, Dean C. Jackson from the Navajo Nation (who founded the American Indian Rodeo Cowboys Association in 1958) and Bob Arrington of Sapulpa, Oklahoma (who joined the INFR board in 1977 and later became its vice president) helped to commence a successful national all-Indian rodeo championship.[23]

At once the annual Indian National Finals Rodeo became a source of pan-Indian, family, and community pride. One of the reporters for the *Sioux Nation Cowboy News* conveyed this sentiment in his description of the opening ceremonies at the 1979 INFR, which began, "'We the Indians of North America,' . . . as Jay Harwood introduced the presidents of eight All Indian Rodeo Associations of the U.S. and Canada . . . " The reporter concluded with

Harwood's declaration that "this is our finest hour." One reservation community that had reason to feel proud of their record at the INFR was Pine Ridge reservation, thanks in part to the performances of the Jacobs brothers. Jim Jacobs, an Oglala Lakota cowboy from Porcupine, South Dakota, "brought home the World buckle" in bareback riding in 1979, just as his brother Chuck Jacobs had done a year earlier as the 1978 World Champion Indian Bareback Rider. The *Sioux Nation Cowboy News* praised the ability of the Jacobses to develop and maintain a rodeo tradition within their family: "Our congratulations go out to the Jacobs brothers, for they've kept the title within their family."[24] For many on the Pine Ridge reservation, rodeo had become part of their bloodline, as it had elsewhere in Indian country.

Over the years, contestants and spectators traveled to destinations throughout the West to partake in Indian rodeo's culminating event. In its first years, the INFR was held in the Salt Palace in Salt Lake City. In 1981 the board of commissioners relocated the INFR to the Tingley Coliseum at the state fairgrounds in Albuquerque, New Mexico, where it remained for thirteen years. Eventually, Native participants hailing from the north raised objections to the expense of the long trip because it cost them in terms of the wear and tear it inflicted on their horses, which affected their performances in steer wrestling, calf and team roping, and barrel racing.[25] In response to these complaints, as well as to other difficulties involved with booking the event at Tingley, the board chose to move the finals to the Rushmore Plaza Civic Center in Rapid City, South Dakota, in 1994.[26]

Even as the INFR became a more commercial and professional enterprise like the PRCA's National Finals Rodeo, it remained essentially an event by and for Indians. As the event's size and popularity grew throughout the 1980s and 1990s, corporate sponsors became more eager to invest in it. By 1981, the number of all-Indian rodeos, the number of contestants involved in them, and the amount of prize money they and the INFR could offer were swelling. The *Lakota Times* reported with pride the expansion of the all-Indian rodeo circuit: "In 1981 all-Indian rodeos were held in practically every state west of the Mississippi, and pay off amounted to nearly one and a half million dollars. Indian rodeo boasts a total membership of 3,000 contestants in the eight regional rodeo associations that compete at the INFR." At the Seventh Annual Coors Indian National Finals Rodeo, which took place at the Tingley Coliseum, 160 contestants competed for copious prize winnings. Of the rising stakes at the 1982 world championships, the *Lakota Times* reported, "The total payoff will amount to approximately $61,500 plus special awards in all events, for a total of well over $75,000 at stake." The Adolph Coors Brewing Company provided "a major portion of the prize money." In conjunction with the rodeo, a powwow offering $7,000 in prize money for winners of the various dance competitions was held at the Horse Arena.[27] A year later, the total prize money payoff at the INFR amounted to "approximately $66,000 plus special awards in all events, for a total of well over $80,000 at stake."[28] In 1994 prize money of approximately $150,000 and special awards such as saddles, buckles, and championship rings were added incentives for those in the Southwest and elsewhere to travel to Rapid City, South Dakota.[29] Two years later, changes in management, scheduling conflicts, and an attractive offer from the Federation of Saskatchewan Indian Nations motivated the INFR board to stage the 1996 Indian National Finals in Saskatoon, Saskatchewan. Additional corporate sponsors—including Labatt's, Pepsi, Nelson Homes, Saskatchewan Indian Gaming Authority, SaskTel, and Confederation Bingo—contributed to the "largest payoff in the history of Indian rodeo," amounting to $200,000 in cash and prizes.[30] Of the generous prizes, McSpadden boasted, "There are but a handful of PRCA rodeos that offer this much prize money," and he predicted that the Indian National Finals Rodeo would only "get bigger because there are so many casinos on reservations now that can afford to sponsor something, and this is good public relations."[31]

As the competition grew more spirited, Indian cowboys and cowgirls began to request that non-Indian as well as Indian judges, staff, and stock contribute their expertise. In 1996, McSpadden calculated that of the 200 finalists competing at the INFR, 125 to 130 of them also competed in the PRCA. Thus, Indian national finalists were coming to demand equal standards of quality in the INFR, and because it attracted better corporate support, it could afford them. As Indian cowboys and cowgirls requested the best judging staff and livestock, this often meant including non-Indians and their stock. INFR General Manager McSpadden recollected in 1996, "Our contestants came to us a few years ago and said, for our judges could you get Wrangler judges? Wrangler sponsors all the judges at the professional level PRCA. . . . There are several that are Native Americans, but it is who is available on this week's date, so we have three judges: one is a Native American, two are not."[32] Times had changed since the all-Indian rodeo circuit's inception, when there was an expressed concern about discrimination by non-Indian judges. McSpadden recognized that some PRCA judges in previous decades might have let their racial biases alter their judgments, yet he maintained that the situation was vastly different by the 1990s and felt confident that "judging today is about as near color-blind a set of judges as I've ever seen."[33]

The 1996 Indian National Finals included both Indian and non-Indian owned stock as well as professional rodeo announcers and clowns. Of the rodeo announcers, Dr. Randy Taylor and Joe Braniff, both were Indians, while one rodeo clown was Indian and the other was not. Each rodeo clown was chosen foremost for his bullfighting ability to protect the contestants, but a sense of humor was also essential. The broncs and bulls were also divided between those provided by Indian and non-Indian stock raisers. On a regional level, according to McSpadden, all-Indian rodeos more often relied on "native stocks or what we call amateur stock; they couldn't afford to hire professional stock. So they would use local stock. That is not to say a few head of those were not good enough to go into anyone's professional string."[34]

Still, the INFR has always remained essentially different from its PRCA counterpart. The most obvious distinction is that American Indians have continued to make up all of its contestants, all of its executive committee, and a vast majority of the spectators. In 1993 about 85 percent of the 27,895 spectators at the INFR were Indians.[35] In the PRCA rodeos, Indian cowboys and cowgirls could often be distinguished from their non-Indian counterparts in the arena. While Native American and non-Native cowboys require identical equipment, clothing has frequently been distinctive, as many have chosen to don traditional ribbon shirts.[36]

American Indian women have also found a larger role as contestants in the all-Indian rodeo circuit and in its national finals than in the PRCA rodeos. Since 1992, women have had a more active role in the all-Indian Rodeo circuit than in the Professional Rodeo Circuit, as cowgirls' breakaway roping was added as a trial event at the Indian National Finals Rodeo. The INFR board did so in an effort to increase women's participation. They knew that a growing number of cowgirls had been competing in breakaway roping contests in high school, college, and reservation rodeos. Since that time, Indian cowgirls of all ages have been successful in barrel racing and breakaway events at the INFR. The Best All-Around Cowgirl title was added in 1993 to recognize the top female competitor in both events. Young Native cowgirls now had an additional incentive to become stronger competitors who would be capable of competing on a national level. A number of these girls and women made it to the 1996 Indian National Finals, where a nine-year-old girl, an eleven-year-old girl, and a thirteen-year-old girl qualified to compete against adult women.[37]

Two decades after its inauguration, the Indian National Finals Rodeo was continuing to generate pan-Indian tribal solidarity. When the Federation of Saskatchewan Indian Nations hosted the 1996 INFR to commemorate the fiftieth anniversary of the Union of Saskatchewan Indians (later the Federation of Saskatchewan Indian Nations), they were building on the tradition of northern Plains Indian communities that rodeoed to celebrate historic tribal and intertribal occasions.[38] The Indian National Finals Rodeo, Incorporated, which coordinates the annual championship rodeo, has maintained its non-profit status as an organization whose aim is to honor the talents and cultures of Indian cowboys and cowgirls. As such, its dual purpose is to determine the world champions of the Indian rodeo circuit and to "bring people of all cultures together to share our rich Indian history and culture." The 1996 INFR accomplished its purpose through its rodeo, which was accompanied by a powwow and American Indian trade fair. The result was an event "considered by many Indian people throughout North America as something not to be missed."[39] The Native people who made up more than 75 percent of the audience, having traveled from all over the United States to the remote Canadian town of Saskatoon, agreed. Of those who won the coveted title of World Champion, the program proclaimed: "Only a few will win the championship, and for those that do, with that title comes the responsibility of representing Indian people, as well as the sport of rodeo to the North American public."

Tribal groups have seized the opportunity to display their nation's best Indian rodeo talent. In 1996 for the first time, the Eastern Indian Rodeo Association brought a group of enthusiastic contestants and fans all the way from Florida to the event in Canada. They were pleased to see Perrie Brett Whidden of the Brighton Seminole Tribe of Florida win the title of Miss Indian Rodeo America. As McSpadden put it, "They have one-hundred people up there. They are like the pom-pom girls at a Dallas football game." As is often the case at all-Indian rodeos, the success of a member of one's tribe or region brought honor to other tribal members.[40]

## LAKOTA RODEO COWBOYS AND COWGIRLS
## FOSTER FAMILY AND TRIBAL TRADITIONS

One of the abiding obligations of those singled out as Indian rodeo champions has been to perpetuate the sport of rodeo within their families and their communities. This has often involved the training of the younger generation. Representatives from Crow, Northern Cheyenne, and Lakota rodeo families who were finalists at the 1996 Indian National Finals Rodeo testified to the endurance of Indian rodeo as a family tradition. Among them were Crow steer wrestler Mike Not Afraid, Northern Cheyenne barrel racer Sharon Small, Pine Ridge Lakota bull rider Smiley Sierra, and Rosebud Lakota bareback rider Guy Colombe.[41]

Indian rodeos have provided a place where families can support one another's endeavors in a variety of arenas. One Miss Indian Rodeo America contestant elaborated on the extent of her family's involvement, explaining that her mother braids her hair, her father pays the bills, and her brother gets the horse ready. Based on his decades of experience, McSpadden concluded about Indian rodeo, "So you can see, it's a family affair."[42] Customarily, Native family and community members have also acted as the first teachers of rodeo to Indian youth. Although many women and girls have continued to compete, it is usually older male relatives such as grandfathers, fathers, uncles, and brothers who provide most of the rodeo training, which often takes place on their family's ranch. To supplement this training within families, many champion riders have hosted rodeo schools for their reservation communities, and many Indian cowboys and cowgirls have continued training as members of high school and college rodeo teams. Indian rodeo has remained a sport taught by one generation to another within family and community groups. It is no wonder then that many Indian rodeo cowboys interviewed in recent years preferred the all-Indian rodeo circuit to the professional rodeo circuit. Many of the men, women, and children who have been competing in Indian rodeos throughout the northern Great Plains and Canada have described rodeos as tribal and family traditions—times of competition, hard work, and fellowship.

The Pine Ridge and Rosebud Lakota reservations have continued to produce renowned rodeo cowboys as well as much of the prime bucking stock used in all-Indian rodeos. In the 1970s, Oglala Lakota Howard Hunter became one of South Dakota's top cowboys among both Indian and non-Indian competitors. In many ways, Hunter was typical of outstanding northern Plains Indian rodeo cowboys and cowgirls. His experiences—in the role of his family and tribe in advancing his rodeo career, in his travel schedule, in his work experience in raising horses and ranching, in his elevated status within the Lakota community, and in his effort to pass on the skills of rodeo to Lakota youth—were all representative of what others have gone through. Hunter's lineage seemed to predetermine his legendary status on the Pine Ridge reservation. His birth and initial introduction to rodeo were described in an article entitled "Howard Hunter, the Cowboy from Wounded Knee." In it, the author proudly bound Hunter's heritage inextricably to that of the Oglala Lakotas.

> It was the last bloody fight of the Indian Wars, and they called it the Battle of Wounded Knee. . . . That night a blizzard covered the area, and the following morning Indian searchers under guard found an infant, not yet dead, wrapped in a blanket and buried in snow. The baby survived and grew up to have children and grandchildren, among them a sinewy youth named Howard Willard Hunter, who was born Feb. 4, 1951, at Pine Ridge, S. Dak., just outside the Pine Ridge Indian Reservation. . . . He learned to ride horses, doctor calves, shoot coyotes and hunt deer. But what captured his interest above all was rodeo.[43]

Hunter's family and Oglala Lakota community nurtured his talent as a rodeo cowboy from his earliest years. The diminutive Indian cowboy, who has been described as standing "5-foot-5, [weighing] 130 pounds with boots and spurs and [wearing] scraggly chin-whiskers" and a "bashful smile," was raised on the Pine Ridge reservation in South Dakota, one of eight children.[44] His parents, both Oglala Sioux, had a ranch on the Pine Ridge reservation. Hunter's mother, Ethelyn Hunter, also excelled in rodeo.[45] In a 1980 article for the Rapid City Journal, Hunter described his childhood training as a cowboy: "Dad had a ranch when we were kids and tried to break horses. I started bareback when I was ten years old and rode five broncs the year I became thirteen."[47] Like most rodeo cowboys and cowgirls, Hunter grew up practicing his rodeo skills by riding calves and colts. He entered his first Little Britches rodeo at the age of ten where he won third place in the bareback bronc riding.[47] By 1969, Hunter was considered a "one-man rodeo team" at Oglala Community High.[48] Single-handedly, he won the team traveling trophy for Oglala Community High School.[49] Many in the Oglala Lakota community were thrilled with his success and how well he represented them. When Hunter won bareback and bull riding in the regional high school finals and was unable to afford the costs of travel to the national finals, "the tribe scratched up $240 to send him to the national high school finals but the cosmopolitan splendors of San Antonio, Texas, were too much for him. He fell off everything except one bareback."[50] Undaunted by his disappointing performance, Hunter dusted himself off and persevered. In 1970 he decided to try his luck as a professional rodeo cowboy.[51] A year later in Rapid City, South Dakota, his talent was reaffirmed when he won a saddle as the South Dakota Rodeo Association's top saddle bronc rider.[52]

Like other members of his tribe who have firmly believed in the benefits of rodeo for Indian youth, Lakota cowboy Charlie Colombe generously aided Hunter's efforts to advance his rodeo career. Through his repeated victories, Hunter caught the eye of Colombe, a successful Lakota bronc rider from a long-standing rodeo family. Colombe, who was also a member of the Rosebud Sioux Tribal Council, had been deeply concerned about the problems of youth in "the fresh air ghettos." Like those who formed the American Indian Hall of Fame, Colombe believed "it would be good for the young to have their own sports heroes." That conviction motivated Colombe to promote Howard Hunter and to organize an Indian Athletic Recognition Day in 1972.[53] In his effort to help Hunter, Colombe asked Shawn Davis, a non-Indian three-time world champion saddle bronc rider from Montana, if he would watch Howard ride. Davis had been an advocate of Indian rodeo since 1970, when he went to South Dakota to recruit Indian cowboys for the Rodeo Far West outfit's European tour. In 1971 the Blackfoot Indian tribe adopted Davis as an honorary member. In appreciation of the honor, Davis resolved "to do something for the Indians and the thing he knew best was bronc riding." In May 1972, he scheduled an Indian riding school in Blunt, South Dakota, that coincided with Colombe's Indian Athletic Recognition Day. Hunter attended the school, and Davis was duly impressed by his performance.[54] As a result, Davis decided to "haul Hunter for the rest of 1972—that is, pay his travel expenses and put up his entry fees in exchange for a share of his winnings."[55]

Hunter went on to compete in both the Professional Rodeo Cowboys Association's "big building rodeos" and in the developing all-Indian rodeo circuit. In 1973 he won about $6,000 in prize money in PRCA rodeos.[56] Lakota commentators predicted that he would be rated "Rookie of the year in the Professional Rodeo Cowboys Association," but he was not.[57] The following year, Hunter's abiding commitment to his family prevented him from the extensive travel necessary to win enough money to qualify for the 1974

National Finals Rodeo (NFR). His mentor, Davis, confirmed this, saying, "The only reason he hasn't been to the Finals is because he won't go hard enough on the road. . . . He's got a family and is the type of guy who puts their concerns and needs first in his life."[58] Hunter was also successful in the all-Indian rodeo circuit, in which he placed first in the saddle bronc at the 1973 All-Indian Rodeo held in the Cow Palace in San Francisco. At its annual meeting and awards banquet, the Great Plains Indian Rodeo Association (GPIRA) honored Hunter as their 1974 all-around cowboy. (The GPIRA also presented awards to other cowboys from the Rosebud, Pine Ridge, and Crow reservations with familiar rodeo family names. Among them were Smokey Whipple, Rosebud; Louis Twiss, Pine Ridge; and Gary Not Afraid and Ivan Small, Lodge Grass.)[59]

By 1975, Hunter was on his own and was focusing on qualifying for the 1976 National Finals Rodeo and Indian National Finals Rodeo. Hunter told one reporter, "I want to make the Finals . . . and what I really want to do is win a championship. . . . That's my ultimate goal." Through a series of flawless performances, Hunter realized his goal in 1976. Over the course of the year, he placed at sixteen rodeos altogether, confining his competition to saddle bronc riding. At Cheyenne Frontier Days, Hunter won better than $8,300, including $2,700 for first in saddle bronc riding.[60] "San Antonio rodeo—Hunter Rides On!" read a 1976 headline proclaiming Hunter's first place win in saddle bronc riding at the Livestock Exposition Rodeo in San Antonio, Texas. The article declared Hunter to be on a hot streak: "The 25-year-old cowboy . . . has been hot this season at the winter rodeos. . . . His total earnings climbed to $5,380."[61] He finished the 1976 season with $14,714 in earnings. Hunter had qualified to compete in the Indian National Finals rodeo in Salt Lake City, but he tore some muscles and had to return home to recuperate for his very first NFR.[62] With $24,500 in earnings, he qualified for the NFR again in 1979 and placed second.[63] By 1980, Hunter had "twice qualified and turned in good performances at the Professional Rodeo Cowboys Association National Rodeo Finals."[64]

As a professional rodeo cowboy, Hunter struggled to balance his time between traveling on the rodeo circuit, raising a family, and making a living raising horses and ranching on the reservation. Like many northern Plains Indian rodeo cowboys, his reservation profession meant working horses. He spent some years rodeoing part-time, working on Charlie Colombe's ranch and rodeoing on weekends.[65] In a 1977 feature article in *Hoof and Horn* on

Howard Hunter, Bob Childress provided a glimpse into Hunter's family and ranch life on the Pine Ridge reservation: "Home is where his wife, Betty Anne, daughter Stacy, who is six, and four-year-old Howard, Jr. wait for dad to show up between rodeos. Home is also a business place, as Howard manages to find time to buy, sell and trade fifty or so horses a year." Hunter aspired to accumulate enough equity through rodeo to become a cattle rancher like his father. Hunter told Childress, "I'm gonna start gathering up cattle . . . and I'm definitely going to ranch. I'll rodeo long enough to get the money to buy cattle . . . but I don't like to travel." To qualify for the NFR in 1976, Hunter had traveled to seventy-six rodeos. His frequent travels ultimately contributed to his future ranch as he added more than $2,000 to his "cattle-buying fund" at the NFR.[66] In 1979 Hunter estimated that he had competed in between seventy-five and eighty PRCA rodeos. In a 1980 interview for the *Rapid City Journal*, Hunter discussed the rigors and expense of travel. His strategy had always been to aim "mostly for those that pay at least $500 or more in an event, and are close to home. It's hardly worth the effort if the payoff is just $100 as you may spend $1,000 to get there." Hunter also confided that he "used to get quite lonesome" while traveling the circuit and "still do if I'm away from home long enough."[67]

As an acclaimed Lakota bronc rider, Hunter had become a hero to many Indians who esteemed his equestrian talents. In a 1971 article on Howard Hunter entitled "One of State's Top Cowboys," Dawn Little Sky from the Standing Rock Reservation in South Dakota offered several explanations for the elevated status of bronc riders within Native communities: "A bronc rider, a good one, is our idea of the greatest athlete. Horses have always been important to us. They were a form of wealth. And Indians respect bravery."[68] Hunter had proved his skill and courage by riding some first-rate rodeo stock. When asked about great bucking horses, Howard quickly replied, "'Descent'" but allowed that "the best one still in action is 'Frontier Airlines.'"[69] His handling of these strong horses elicited praise from Lakotas as well as from Indians of all tribal backgrounds who were involved in Indian rodeo. According to one observer in 1977, Howard Hunter had become "the pride and joy of Indian rodeo. They just refer to him as 'Howard' and you're supposed to know who they're talking about."[70]

Lakotas from Pine Ridge were especially proud of Howard Hunter and often tapped him as a representative of their tribe because of their shared values of horses, family, and community. Hunter was also among the first people honored when the Oglala Nation Rodeo committee established an Indian Rodeo Hall of Fame in 1996. By that time, he had acquired four Indian National Finals Rodeo saddle bronc championships in addition to his two victories at the NFR. During the Oglala Sioux Tribal Fair and Rodeo, Howard Hunter and his mother, the late Ethelyn Hunter, were among the four individuals honored by the Indian Rodeo Hall of Fame for their contributions to the sport of rodeo. Even past his prime he continued to compete into the 1990s, and although he had been seriously injured while competing at the Crow fair rodeo in 1995, Hunter made a special appearance at the Oglala Sioux Tribal Rodeo to receive his community's honor, which was accompanied by star quilts and plaques. Committee member Gerald Big Crow related his goals for the future of the Indian Rodeo Hall of Fame, saying, "I hope the younger generation will continue honoring rodeo champions in the future."[71] Big Crow, like many Oglala Lakotas, was committed to maintaining the tribe's rodeo tradition.

Hunter sought to repay the support his fellow Lakotas had given him by dedicating himself to the perpetuation of the sport of rodeo among young Lakotas. Like many Indian rodeo cowboys, Howard Hunter endeavored to teach rodeo skills to the next generation of Indian cowboys. The advice Hunter has given to aspiring young bronc riders is to start as he did with National High School Rodeo. He warned, "A young fella shouldn't ride 'over his head' or without any instruction." But as a writer for *Hoof and Horn* observed, "That advice comes from a guy that climbed on his first bareback horse at the age of ten. He waited until he had a little age on him to ride saddle broncs. He was twelve."[72] In an effort to properly train younger Lakotas, Hunter teamed up with Pine Ridge rodeo notables Jim Meeks and Tuffy Sierra to offer the Broken Arrow Rodeo School in May 1982. The advertisements encouraged youngsters to "Learn from Pros!" Afterward, students could test their new skills at the jackpot rodeo that followed the school.[73]

Throughout the 1970s, 1980s, and 1990s, Lakota cowboys on the Rosebud and Pine Ridge reservations continued their efforts to train reservation youths in the sport of rodeo. They often organized rodeo schools and Little Britches rodeos. In 1970 the Rosebud Sioux Tribal Rodeo Association provided the stock for the Second Annual Rosebud Little Britches Rodeo.[74] In 1971 Rosebud's tribal rodeo association also planned to inaugurate an annual reservation rodeo school "to train Indians in the art of bareback-riding, saddle bronc and bull riding."[75] On the Pine Ridge reservation, riders like Howard Hunter and the Twiss brothers were training young rodeo cowboys and cowgirls. In 1982 the Oglala Lakota brothers Maurice, Louis, and Lloyd Twiss hosted the fourth annual Lakota Rodeo School. Maurice Twiss, a state rodeo champion himself, explained that he started the school in 1979 to "teach safety rules to boys and girls on the reservation who want to learn rodeo. . . . Without the school, boys will just go ahead and enter a rodeo with no instruction—and therefore with far more chance of getting hurt." In the Twisses' three-day rodeo school, almost two hundred Lakota youngsters practiced bull riding, bronc riding, calf roping, barrel racing, goat tying, and pole bending. Actual competition followed the school on Saturday. Boys and girls as young as eight years old had eagerly arrived for training—even in riding the bulls. Louis Twiss attempted to prepare the novices for the bulls they would ride that day. He warned: "The ones that buck high and kick their legs high are tough to ride. And the ones that spin around and kick are the toughest." An observer described one novice, Tony Cofford, in his first ride, in the school's Junior Bull Riding Contest:

> Tony Cofford, from Red Cloud, rode one of them: A coal-black bull that kicked and spun around as hard as it could to get him off. But the bull lost. Tony hung on to beat the buzzer, as the bull doubled up and bucked all the way over to the other side of the arena. Tony, decked out in purple chaps and a pink shirt, became first place winner in the Junior Bull Riding Contest.[76]

The Twiss brothers had taught proper rodeo skills and instilled in their students an enthusiasm for rodeo. The reactions among the winners reflected their success, as when ten year-old Darrell Hunter looked down proudly at his silver buckle, engraved "1982 Lakota Rodeo School Champion." He had won first place in novice bull riding that morning. According to one bystander, when asked how he felt, Hunter looked at the bright buckle and shyly said, "Wonderful." Hunter further proved he had the constitution of a bull rider when he was asked "Was he nervous before he got on the bull?" and "Did it hurt when he fell off?" To the questions, he responded, "No" and "Nope."[77]

The Pine Ridge community also showed their support and enthusiasm for the Lakota Rodeo School: "Cars from across the reservation pulled up and parked all around the ring to watch, honking their horns loudly as a young rider rode home to victory, or a girl whipped around the posts at top speed. It lasted until twilight, when the final awards were given out." Most mothers heartily endorsed these schools for the character they believed that rodeo could build in their children, but a few remained apprehensive about its potential dangers. Hard knocks were good if they weren't too hard.

> One young mother said she thought rodeo-riding was a good idea. "I think it builds character," she said. "My son said he'd do it—and so now he has to go through with it." She said she also thought getting used to some knocks and bruises, and learning to be able to take pain, was good for the kids. And they also learn they can't win every time, she added. But another Pine Ridge mother disagreed. "I'm going to teach my son to play the piano," she said, "he's gonna stay off those damn cows!"[78]

Young adults have furthered their training and experience in high school rodeos and a growing college rodeo circuit. On the development of high school rodeos, INFR General Manager McSpadden explained, "Since World War II, a high school rodeo competition started and thirty some states now have State High School Rodeo Finals . . . so you'll find a lot of Native American kids from New Mexico, Nevada, Oklahoma, the Dakota country, Montana . . . that are learning at the high school level."[79] Lakota cowgirls as well as cowboys were following in the hoofprints of Howard Hunter, who first tasted championship victory in regional and national high school rodeo competitions.[80]

Following high school, a number of Lakotas have developed their talents in the growing college rodeo circuit. From the mid-1960s through the 1970s, Congress passed extensive legislation relating to Indian education. The result was that Indian communities, beginning with the Navajos and followed immediately by the Lakotas and other Indian nations, founded tribal colleges such as the Navajo Community College (later Diné College), Oglala Lakota Community College, and Sinte Gleska College (later University) on the Pine Ridge and Rosebud reservations.[81] Along with other institutions of higher education, these tribal colleges became a part of the college rodeo circuit. By the mid-1980s, the circuit encompassed twelve regions around the country with the Great Plains region being the largest. At that time, twenty-one-year-old Alan Goode was the most prominent member of Oglala Lakota College's rodeo team. Like many Indian rodeo cowboys, Goode helped run a cow and calf operation with his father near Eagle Nest Butte on the Pine Ridge reservation. He predicted, "I'll probably end up in accounting and business to help out with the ranch." At Oglala Lakota College, he was preparing for that career in the cattle business while experiencing the intense competition and travel involved in rodeo. Of sixteen teams that competed in the Great Plains Region,

Goode helped put Oglala Lakota College's rodeo team in sixth place after the fall series of rodeos. To accomplish this, Goode competed in rodeos stretching from South Dakota in the west to Michigan in the east. His tribal college paid most of his gas expenses; otherwise, Goode said, "I just wouldn't be able to make it." To qualify, the individuals and teams were required to place first or second in their region. In 1984 Goode's competitive zeal helped him qualify to compete in the national college rodeo championships held each year in June in Bozeman, Montana. When asked why he participated in rodeo, Goode answered, "I like the competition, it's me against everyone else."[82]

## NORTHERN CHEYENNE AND CROW COWBOYS CONTINUE A RODEO TRADITION

Northern Cheyenne rodeo aficionados like Phillip Whiteman Jr. have helped to ensure the continuance of Indian rodeo in their families and communities. According to Whiteman, "Riding is a tradition in my family." In addition to the five bronc-riding schools he attended in Montana, he also "learned to rodeo in the usual way, at home and from his elders. His grandfather, Frank Whiteman Sr., who owned horses, and his father, Phillip Whiteman Sr., were his first teachers."[83] Two notable northern Plains Indian saddle bronc champions, Crow Indian Mel Williamson and Blackfeet Indian Chuck Lewis, also helped hone Whiteman's skills. Once he had achieved his own success, Phillip Whiteman Jr. began, in 1990, to return these gifts by conducting a bronc riding school for three days every summer, thus helping the next generation of Northern Cheyenne rodeo cowboys to succeed in life and in the rodeo arena. On his home reservation, he has also taught bilingual education in schools like the Busby School of the Northern Cheyenne Tribe, and he helps younger rodeo competitors, just as his elders had lent him a hand.[84]

In 1994 Whiteman was first in the standings for the Rocky Mountain Indian Rodeo Association. He thereby earned a spot in the Indian National Finals Rodeo for his ninth trip to the apex of the all-Indian rodeo. Whiteman had competed vigorously in both the Indian and non-Indian rodeo circuits. A member of the Rocky Mountain Rodeo Association, the Northern Rodeo Association, and the Professional Rodeo Cowboys Association, he has excelled in all three groups as one of the top riders in saddle bronc riding and team roping, often attending three or more rodeos in a weekend. While he has been successful in both circuits, he relishes all-Indian rodeos, where he has often

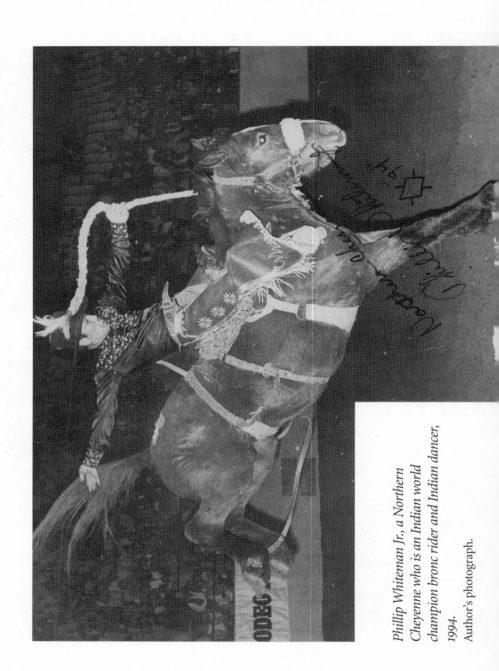

*Phillip Whiteman Jr., a Northern Cheyenne who is an Indian world champion bronc rider and Indian dancer, 1994.*

Author's photograph.

*Traditional Crow dancers performing during night dances, Crow Fair, 1971.*
Left to right: *Eugene Old Elk and David Jefferson.*
Photo by Dennis L. Sanders. Hardin Photo Service, Hardin, Montana (Photo #255).

been able to shine, both on the back of a bronco and as a champion grass
dancer in the concurrent powwow events. Although Phillip Whiteman Jr.'s
favorite rodeo remains the Navajo Nation Fair and Rodeo, the second largest
all-Indian rodeo is held adjacent to his home in southeastern Montana—the
Crow Fair and Rodeo.

At the Crow Fair and Rodeo, the Crows have continued their long-standing rodeo tradition, which reaffirms the value they place on family and community ties. Crow Fair rodeo has bred a number of rodeo families on the
Crow reservation who earned their first spurs there. Members of the Bird-in-
Ground, Not Afraid, Passes, Small, and Real Bird families have often been
listed in Crow Fair and Rodeo programs from the early 1900s on. After 1930,
each of those families has been consistently represented.[85] Since the New Deal

years, events such as rodeos, powwow contests, and tribal parades have become mainstays.[86] Many have considered the rodeo to be the main event, however. A special feature of the August 1994 Crow Fair rodeo was a three-horse relay race in which Crow equestrians rode bareback and moved from mount to mount. These breathtaking feats were interrupted for twenty to thirty minutes at a time for the Crows to practice the giveaway, another tradition long associated with their community gatherings. Through an announcer, Crows accomplished in academics, athletics, the military, or other activities gave away presents such as Pendleton blankets to their clan uncles, aunts, and family members who had contributed to their success. The giveaway predated Crow reservation life as a means of "honoring and repaying" clan members.[87] The Crows had adapted the giveaway and allowed it to persist as a cultural expression that served a function similar to the rodeo that it accompanied. According to Frederick Hoxie, that function was to "cement family and clan ties, focus the activities of reservation districts and protect their followers from outsiders."[88]

In 1994 the principal giveaway occurred on the last day of Crow Fair and Rodeo, when members of the Crow Fair board, Crow Fair rodeo officers, district princesses, Miss Crow Nation, and the Crow Fair rodeo queen, gave away. Eighteen-year-old Della Big Hair, 1995 Miss Crow Nation, explained the ritual, which signifies the Crows' enduring belief in demonstrating one's gratitude and respect for another generation through gift giving:

> They [my family] have to dance this Crow Fair because I'm giving away. Each princess gives away to their clan aunts and uncles and friends first. I'll give-away, and then I'll dance and my friends and family have to dance. . . . They'll say my name and my Indian name and my accomplishments, and then I'll dance around and my family follows along. There's a long line of people dancing with me. Then . . . I'll take all my blankets and everything I want to give away. Then I'll tell each person to come up because I want to give them something and they give me a wish. . . . You have to do that on your own and it costs lot. But you do that because you're thankful. . . . One generation takes care of another.[89]

Similarly, a skilled rodeo cowboy or cowgirl, taught by family and tribal members, is obligated to share his or her talents with the next generation.

Like their Lakota counterparts, a number of Crow cowboys and cowgirls acknowledged that family and tribal members had trained them. In 1994 seven Crow rodeo cowboys responded to a questionnaire that inquired about

*Billy Three Irons, Crow Indian, 1984.*
Photo by Dennis L. Sanders. Hardin Photo Service, Hardin, Montana (Photo #726).

their experiences in rodeo, including the source of their training. All had received their training on their home reservations, while three had also attended rodeo schools. Randy Falls Down got his training "out in the hills."[90] Likewise, Crow bull rider Willis Tsosia, member of the All-Indian Rodeo Cowboys Association, the Rocky Mountain Indian Rodeo Cowboys Association, and the Great Plains Indian Rodeo Association, seized all chances to practice his skills: " If you had the opportunity to get on a bull competing or not, you'd go for it."[91] Albert "Apple" Caphill Jr., who was trained by "riding horses at home, also broke horses to gentle horses. And later on [he got more training at] a rodeo school in Miles City, Montana."[92]

Like so many Indian rodeo cowboys, these Crow cowboys have been raised in families that have been involved with horses, cattle, and rodeo for generations. Marlon B. Passes, a member of the Great Plains Indian Rodeo Association, stated his familial rodeo record very clearly: "I was raised around horses and cattle at the place along the Banks of the Little Big Horn River. I guess we are all horsemen, fathers, cousins, brothers, nephews, uncles, based on a family tradition."[93] In fact, Passes' father, Lloyd Pickett, went to the Indian National Finals Rodeo three times and at the age of sixty-one "won a trophy saddle in team roping at Torrington, Wyoming, September, 1994."[94] Lloyd Pickett's grandson and Marlon Passes' nephew, Kelly D. Passes, related that he was "a second generation saddle bronc rider. My father, Don Passes, was an Indian and a Pro Rodeo Champion." Following his father's lead, Kelly was a contestant in the Indian National Finals Rodeo in 1994. Kelly's brother Victor also competed in saddle bronc riding.[95] Marlon Passes has reason to trust that rodeo will continue to be a way of life for his family because his daughter was also taking part in barrel racing and his sons were competing in team roping and steer riding.[96]

Other Crow cowboys like Lonn Fitzler and Albert Caphill Jr. have fathers, brothers, or both who competed in the rodeo circuit and got them interested in the sport. Rodeo could be part of one's family in a variety of ways. As bull-dogging and team roping competitor Lonn Fitzler explained, "My Dad rode bulls and [was a] rodeo clown for over twenty years for the R.C.A. [now the Professional Rodeo Cowboys Association]."[97] Like his father, Albert Caphill Jr. has entered bareback riding events but has also been a full-time rodeo announcer. As of 1994, Caphill continued to enjoy announcing because it allowed him to extol an important part of his family's and many American Indians' history by "giving the background of the American Indian cowboy."[98]

## INTERTRIBAL COMPETITION, HARD KNOCKS, AND CAMARADERIE

In addition to fostering family and tribal ties through generational training, all-Indian rodeos have afforded opportunities for intratribal and intertribal competition, hard work, and camaraderie. Many Plains Indians, whose social gatherings have long involved competition and wagering on horse races, have relished the competitive feature of all-Indian rodeos. At all-Indian rodeos, spectators and contestants have joined in the excitement of intertribal competition as they have rallied behind members of their own tribes. American Indian fans of the all-Indian rodeo circuit have attended rodeos "to hear the name of someone they know or the name of someone they didn't know and to hear that that contestant was from their town or their tribe."[99] Regional Indian rodeo association alliances have often determined the nature of competition between tribes. An observer of Indian rodeos since the 1950s affirmed this, saying, "Oh yeah, a Navajo will try to beat an Apache, or a Cherokee will try to beat a Creek, but when they come from one region they are all pulling for each other, you know. You'll have an Apache hazing a steer for a Navajo if they are from the same region."[100]

Oral history also suggests that different regions have excelled in different events. Terry Gray, a Rosebud Sioux rodeo cowboy and archivist of Sinte Gleska University, made this observation in 1996. INFR General Manager McSpadden speculated that cowboys from the Southwest often have been "better timed-event people, and your better bronc riders usually come from the Northern tier states and Canada." The large numbers of horses found on many northern Plains reservations partially explained this trend. He spoke from experience as a horseman and rancher when he explained this rationale.

> I can remember the old timers telling me that in the twenties, when professional producers would get so many bucking horses from reservations because Indian people always wanted to own large numbers of horses. When you own large numbers of horses you also, by the temperament of the devils, you are going to have a large percentage of bucking horses, and if you own them and try to ride them as a young man you are going to learn to ride bucking horses better than someone who doesn't own horses.

McSpadden also warned against generalizations, recognizing that kids want to do what's popular. "If a kid wants to start today in being a rodeo performer in Canada, he wants to ride bucking horses. Of course in the last two to three years, bull riding has gotten big with the bull riding tour so you'll see good bull riders anywhere."[101]

The Rosebud Sioux have often hosted intertribal rodeos that have challenged in competition other northern Plains Indian tribes, including Lakotas from other agencies. Male and female representatives of prominent Crow, Northern Cheyenne, and Lakota rodeo families, including the Not Afraids, the Bird-in-Grounds, the Smalls, and the Twisses were among the winners at the 1977 Rosebud Sioux Fair and Rodeo.

Cowboys from four states took the top rodeo honors at the Rosebud Sioux Tribal Fair Saturday and Sunday at Rosebud. Over 325 cowboys from 11 states and one Canadian province competed in the two-day event. . . . In calf roping the winners were Wayne Not Afraid, Lodgegrass, MT, first . . . Wilfred Bird In Ground, Garryowen, MT, fourth; Clinton Small, Ashland, MT, fifth . . . Team Roping winners . . . Darrell Twiss, Pine Ridge . . . John Small and Arnie Bends, Busby, MT . . . Barrel racing . . . Candy Not Afraid, Lodgegrass, MT . . . A Lodgegrass, MT, man, Henry Small, took first in the steer wrestling.[102]

In 1978 the Antelope community of the Rosebud reservation sponsored a rodeo that pitted teams composed of members from the Pine Ridge, Cheyenne River, and Rosebud reservations against one another. The Rosebud Sioux team captured first place, while the Cheyenne River Sioux team came in second, and the Oglala Sioux team came in third.[103]

Crow Fair's all-Indian rodeo has also continued to provide a proving ground for cowboys and cowgirls from different tribes. In 1982 Crow Fair's program predicted, "Approximately one thousand Indian cowboys and cowgirls, representing the tribes from throughout the U.S. and Canada, will compete for an estimated $85,000 in prize money."[104] Most cowboys relished rodeo action as a time for competing and for "the natural high of the ride itself."[105] While rodeo contestants vied against one another for standings in each event, the stock they encountered in the arena often determined their performance. In that sense, the luck of the draw partially determined the excitement of one's ride. Crow Indian Willis Tsosia said he entered Indian rodeos "to see if I get to ride a bull that's been to the Indian National Finals. This depends on the drawing of the bull's number to your name."[106] Beyond the competition that takes place in the arena, Indian rodeo managers competed over the relative quality of their rodeos. Marlon Passes, Crow Fair rodeo manager in 1993, explained this particular kind of rivalry: "You want to prove to other tribes that you've got a good rodeo. . . . As far as putting the show together . . . it's sort of a major competition among tribes."[107]

In addition to the challenges of competition found at all-Indian rodeos, there have been hardships.[108] Rodeo cowboys and cowgirls have constantly exposed themselves to danger in the arena, and their travel schedules have been rigorous. Both Indian and non-Indian cowboys have endured the inevitable hard knocks encountered in the rodeo arena. As Crow cowboy Albert Caphill Jr. phrased it, "They both wear boots, wear hats, and both get bucked off."[109] Joe Waln, an Oglala Lakota rodeo producer since 1951, observed in a 1977 newspaper interview that with "rodeo comes a curious mixture of fun and brushes with tragedy." He continued about the latter: "Accidents bother me more now than they used to." In his years with rodeo Waln described seeing riders injured, maimed, and killed. "There's always a second there where everybody just stares in shock before they can do anything but after awhile you learn what to do fast to help that cowboy. . . . But for every somber moment in a rodeo there is also something humorous, something that lifts spirits."[110] Every Indian rodeo cowboy and cowgirl has also dealt with the issues of travel and expense when following the all-Indian rodeo circuit. When asked how Indian cowboys have managed the expenses incurred on the rodeo circuit, Clem McSpadden replied, "Same as any other person, you pay your fees and if you win, you win money, and if you don't you go home, work, and practice till you think you are ready to come to another one." He also estimated that only the top 25 percent of those who have competed in the all-Indian rodeo circuit have actually made money.[111] The traveling involved in following the circuit poses one of the hardships of rodeo. Kelly D. Passes wrote in 1994 that he tried to hit "three to five rodeos in a week. . . . I have been to fifty rodeos since Memorial Day weekend [about four and a half months]. Traveling gets a little hectic at times, since I'm a single parent of two children, a boy and a girl."[112] Crow rodeo cowboys explained that they usually attend one to four rodeos a weekend. All of the traveling proved to be too burdensome for Lonn Fitzler who admitted that he "cannot rodeo anymore because of work."[113] By 1994 he restricted himself to local team roping competitions.

As a result of their common experiences, those who have traveled the all-Indian rodeo circuit have often developed relationships with men and women from other tribal affiliations. One Indian cowboy expressed a commonly held view when he wrote, "long time ago we were traditional enemies, but today the Crow-Sioux-Cheyenne-Blackfeet-Bloods-Cree-Gros Ventre-Assinaboine-Navajo-Southern Tribes—we all laugh together. Even travel together. Borrow from each other—horses-money-equipment."[114]

## COMMUNITY EVENTS: MEMORIAL, CHARITY, AND TRIBAL FAIR RODEOS

Although the all-Indian rodeo circuit has fostered competition and camaraderie between tribal groups, memorial and charity reservation rodeos have

reaffirmed relationships within them. Such community rodeos became com-
monplace on northern Plains reservations from 1976 on. These rodeos have
reinforced community cohesiveness, allowing tribal members to honor their
dead, especially deceased rodeo cowboys, as well as to offer emotional and
financial support to those in distress. Often, to help defray the hospital or
funeral costs of someone who has been injured or recently lost, family members, other relatives, or community members will host a benefit rodeo, or a
bull riding or team roping contest, as cattle are less expensive than other
rodeo stock.[115]

Despite the turmoil surrounding Wounded Knee on the Pine Ridge reservation in the early 1970s, Lakotas have frequently staged memorial rodeos
there and on the Rosebud reservation. On the Rosebud reservation in 1974,
the *Mellette County News* reported, "A crowd gathered at Parmelee over the
weekend to observe and compete in the Memorial Rodeo and Pow-wow."[116]
In honor of their own renowned Rosebud Sioux rodeo cowboy John Waln, a
group of Lakotas organized a memorial rodeo in conjunction with the Rosebud Sioux Tribe Fourth of July celebration in 1978. They helped to keep
Waln's legacy alive by offering the John Waln Memorial Trophy. The rodeo
was an Oglala Sioux Indian Rodeo Association-approved rodeo, which meant
that scores affected the regional rankings of cowboys competing in the all-
Indian rodeo circuit.[117] Also on the Rosebud reservation, the Soldier Creek
community sponsored a two-day memorial rodeo over the Fourth of July
weekend in 1980. The same year as the Soldier Creek memorial rodeo events,
the Rosebud Sioux Tribe hosted an all-Indian rodeo at the Rosebud Fairgrounds.[118] In 1977 Oglala Lakotas on the Pine Ridge reservation began host-
ing the annual Roger Mills Memorial Roping contest in memory of another
respected Lakota. It remained a community event in 1981, as participants
came together at St. Ann's Cemetery to memorialize Mills prior to the rodeo.
At the rodeo, those who won team roping events received trophy buckles.
Afterward, everyone shared a "free noon meal."[119] In honor of Bill Horn
Cloud, the Horn Cloud Family sponsored the Third Annual Bill Horn Cloud
Memorial Rodeo in 1996.[120] Memorial and charity rodeos have continued to be
a place where Lakotas could show their respect and support for one another.

Tribal fair rodeos have also become a part of the community fabric shared
by many Lakotas and Crows. From the late nineteenth century to the 1970s
and 1980s, Rosebud reservation residents had taken part in the Rosebud Sioux
Fair and Rodeo as contestants, spectators, donors, rodeo staff, and stock con-

*Edison Real Bird Memorial Rodeo, 1981.*
Photo by Dennis L. Sanders. Hardin Photo Service, Hardin, Montana (Photo #507).

tractors. Once it had been sanctioned by various all-Indian rodeo associations, the Rosebud fair's rodeo was able to offer larger purses and more intense competition. By 1970, the Rosebud Sioux Tribe Pow-Wow and Rodeo had become an all-Indian rodeo approved by the All American Indian Activities Association.[121] *Eyapaha*, the Lakota news section of the *Todd County Tribune*, anticipated that "thousands of people from all over the nation will gather on the Rosebud for the annual All-Indian Rodeo Fair and Pow-Wow. . . . The IAA-sanctioned [Indian Activities Association-sanctioned] rodeo boasts a $2000 purse plus entry fees. Total pow-wow purse is $1720."[122] Enthusiastic Indian audiences and competitors attended to be entertained by one another and by the rodeo action. The newly formed Great Plains Indian Rodeo Association sanctioned the Rosebud Fair and Rodeo in 1974 and again offered a total purse of $2,000 plus entry fees. To cover general expenses, the Rosebud Fair and Rodeo committee charged rodeo admission fees of $2.50 for adults and $1.00 for children above the age of ten.[123] Within two years, the GPIRA-approved Rosebud Sioux Fair rodeo was offering a startling $8,000 in prize money for the rodeo and $7,355 for the powwow.[124] By 1977, the Rosebud

Sioux Fair rodeo had become "the largest amateur show in South Dakota and with a purse of $500 per event." With such generous purses, it offered "more than most RCA [Rodeo Cowboys Association, later the Professional Rodeo Cowboys Association] shows in the area." The result was that Indian competitors came "from as far away as New Mexico and Canada with the bulk coming from Nebraska, Wyoming and North Dakota." While most cowboys and fans enjoyed the intensified competition, some criticized the emphasis on prize winnings. According to Joe Waln in 1977, rodeo had changed over the years and "rodeo activity at Rosebud has not been an exception. The rodeo which now offers attractive purse money to top cowboys nationally for long years was an event for local cowboys and offered jackpot prizes."[125]

Concerned that the rodeo was becoming commercialized, a group of traditionalist Lakotas reduced the prize winnings in order to reemphasize Lakota "brotherhood." In 1979 the Oglala Sioux Indian Rodeo Association staged the 102nd Rosebud Sioux Fair, Powwow, and Rodeo and offered a $3,500 purse.[126] Purses were again a source of some debate at the 1981 annual Rosebud Fair and Rodeo. The purse for the all-Indian rodeo, originally advertised as $2,550, was subsequently reduced to $2,250. Tribal public relations officer Frank Dillon Jr. explained their efforts to reject European American values that emphasized individual self-interest, stating, "If money is to be our main reason to attend the Fair, then we have truly become 'wasicu' [his spelling of a Lakota word for white man]. This year's event is billed as 'Returning to Tradition.'" Even amidst controversy, the rodeo was the highlight of the fair. One reporter praised it: "Probably the most colorful of the events held over the weekend— attracting an estimated 3,000 on Sunday alone—was this year's All-Indian Rodeo, which kicked off each day with a grand entry into the John Waln Memorial Arena. The grand entry featured clown and bullfighting acts to the delight of spectators. Observers say the rodeo was one of the best professionally-run rodeos featured in recent years."[127] The final assessment of one observer was that "traditionalists . . . brought together a sense of brotherhood to many who attended."[128] In time, the Rosebud Sioux Fair and Rodeo once again became a lucrative event for winning rodeo cowboys. In 1983 the South Dakota Rodeo Association, the Oglala Sioux Rodeo Association, and the National Rodeo Cowboys Association approved of the Rosebud Fair rodeo, which offered a purse of $5,000.[129]

The controversy over the large purses did not detract from the intratribal camaraderie that the fair and rodeo fostered. Many Lakotas attended the

Rosebud Sioux Fair and Rodeo to come together with other tribal members. A 1975 newspaper account of the fair and rodeo described the event as a reunion, noting, "Many out-of-town relatives and friends of Rosebud Reservation residents can be seen throughout the Todd-Mellette counties area this week as people gather and prepare for the big annual Rosebud Sioux Tribe Fair and Rodeo."[130] Similarly in 1978, Retired Master Sergeant Moses Broken Leg, "a man who was born on the Rosebud Sioux reservation and fought World War II and the Korean Conflict with war hero Audie Murphy returned, as he does every year, to enjoy the Rosebud Sioux Fair. . . . [He] returns to Rosebud for the peace pipe ritual, in which he reaffirms his pure Indian heritage."[131] In 1979 the tribe offered a "free meal daily" as a gesture of hospitality at the 103rd Annual Rosebud Sioux Fair.[132]

As the Rosebud Sioux Fair and Rodeo became the centerpiece of Rosebud community life, the tribe and its backers put their money into improving the fairgrounds. In preparation for the 1976 Centennial Rosebud Sioux Fair and Rodeo, a new rodeo arena and grandstand, seating approximately two thousand people, was built north of Rosebud to provide additional seating. The *Mellette County News* described the remodeling as well as the scale and character of the rodeo, which was meant to entertain Lakotas and their Indian and non-Indian visitors:

> The new grandstand seating approximately 2,000 began to take shape this week. This will provide seating in addition to the older grandstand, which was moved across the rodeo arena to accommodate the construction of the new grandstand. The area beneath the crow's nest in the rodeo arena is now filled with new bright green metal stock chutes, part of the all-steel rodeo facilities, which are being installed. The new arena and grandstand will also be used to present performances of country-western singers Wanda Jackson and Johnny Rodriguez.[133]

Other improvements included "modern restrooms, improved roads with curb and gutter, improved fire protection, camping facilities, and security fencing."[134] According to Joe Waln, as of 1977 the rodeo arena had become "one of the best in the nation. . . . The only thing we're lacking is barns and they aren't really necessary."[135]

Joe Waln was one of many Lakotas who remained involved in the management of Rosebud Sioux Fair's rodeo. Over the years, Waln contributed as both a rodeo producer and stock contractor. His B & W Rodeo Company supplied rodeo stock in 1978.[136] In 1977 Rosebud's local newspaper, the

*Mellette County News*, featured Waln, whom they recognized as "another long-time associate of the fair and in particular its rodeo. . . . For the past 15 years, Waln has been involved in making the rodeo at Rosebud Fair a success." Like many Indian rodeo cowboys, he learned to ranch, rodeo, and raise horses from his father. He recounted his rodeo roots, explaining that he "began riding saddle broncs at the age of 15 and learned the basics of handling a rodeo string from his father, Bob Waln." Along with his wife, Grace, he traveled the rodeo circuit for two or three years. Waln's saddle bronc days came to an end in the 1950s as a result of an injury he sustained at his ranch. The injury, he recalled, "was the event that turned his attention to producing rodeo instead of participating in it."[137]

Waln's career as a rodeo producer was similar to that of a rodeo cowboy in terms of family, horses, and travel. In 1977 Bud Whipple, also from an esteemed Rosebud Sioux ranching and rodeo family, replaced his father, Bob Whipple, as Waln's partner.[138] The quality of their horses was evident in that they sold their first two strings to RCA (Rodeo Cowboys Association) producers. Waln noticed that horses had become less abundant on reservations, stating that "years ago it was easier to get stock, good stock, with the abundance of horses in the country then. Things have changed, however, and the search for good stock is more difficult now." On the nature of rodeo stock, Waln explained that appearances can be deceiving: the broncos and bulls that seem so ferocious in the arena are actually quite mild. He said of the saddle broncs, "They're like men after the rodeo and start lining up to be loaded know'n' they're go'n' home." Waln's travel schedule, like that of most Indian rodeo cowboys, was rigorous. He described his company's routine during the spring and summer rodeo season.

> At Parmelee the rodeo season starts a little earlier than most places around here due to an indoor arena. The season starts in April with Little Britches. The season continues through Labor Day with the rodeo company producing a rodeo every weekend through the height of the summer. . . . When B & W Rodeo Company hits the road it takes three semi-trailer trucks, two 20-foot horse trailers, two pick up men, a group of four girls to flank the horses and unsaddle the broncs, usually an announcer and of course Whipple and Waln.[139]

A number of Rosebud community members, including many from the Waln and Whipple families, contributed their efforts to the Rosebud rodeo as contestants, staff, and rodeo queens. In 1974 Joe Waln served as arena director and Gary Whipple served as announcer. Waln believed "the announcer can make or break the show with his style of announcing."[140] In addition, Booger Waln acted as "Arena Flag Judge," Calvin and Roger Waln were "Pick Up Men," and Carol Waln was a "Time Keeper."[141] In 1976 young women also competed for the role of Miss Rosebud Rodeo Queen '76 at the Rosebud Centennial Fair and Rodeo. According to coordinator Ann Wilson, selection was based on equestrian and public relations abilities, including "horsemanship, personality, and appearance." Contestants were also required to "live on the Rosebud Reservation and be at least ¼ Indian." The young woman who was selected as Miss Rosebud Rodeo Queen was then eligible for the Great Plains Indian Rodeo Association regional contest where she would represent her tribe and its equestrian heritage.[142] The annual Rosebud Sioux Fair and Rodeo continued to engage tribal members, who claimed it had been a reservation gathering since 1877.[143] With more than a century of participation in the Rosebud Sioux Tribal Fair and Rodeo, many Lakotas considered it to be a part of their common culture.

By the 1990s, Crow Fair and Rodeo had also become a part of the community identity of many Crows—both men and women—who held it in their collective memory and folklore. Like the Rosebud Fair and Rodeo, Crow Fair and Rodeo largely appealed to Crows as a reservation reunion where Crows from all districts could meet. District princesses had joined board members in representing these districts in the 1930s. By the 1990s, Miss Crow Nation and the Crow Fair rodeo queen were also representing both their districts and their tribe at their fair, particularly in the parades that began each day, in the Parade Dance that took place on the final day of Crow Fair, and at pan-Indian rodeos and powwows. Unlike a district princess, who was selected by her own district, Miss Crow Nation was chosen at the Miss Crow Nation Pageant held in Lodge Grass in December. The Crow Fair board sponsored the competition, and the judging was "based on speech, dance, costume and knowledge of the Crow language and clan system."[144] Della Big Hair was Miss Crow Nation for 1995, and she explained her responsibilities as a tribal representative: "I have to represent them in each town I go to, telling people to come to the powwow, kind of like advertising for the Crow Fair."[145] Della is an accomplished fancy-shawl and grass dancer, and in years past, she has represented her district as a princess.

The young women chosen as district princesses and Crow Fair rodeo queens have often possessed both impressive lineage and talents. Patricia Real

Bird was a Crow Fair princess representing her district of Wyola in 1992. The daughter of Gordon and Bernadine Real Bird and the granddaughter of Pius and Cordelia Real Bird and Gloria and Bernard Cummins, she was an honor roll student and was given the award for Best Female Athlete of the Year. Similarly, Melissa Shane, the Reno District princess in 1992, was a sixth-generation descendant of the renowned Crow chief Pretty Eagle.[146] She also excelled in powwows and pageants. She had been selected as Miss Plains Indian 1989, Special Guest at the Nineteenth Annual Stanford University Powwows in 1990, and Women's Jingle Dress Dancer in the 1990 Indian National Finals Pow Wow and Rodeo in Albuquerque, New Mexico. Crow Fair rodeo queens were also selected yearly. They were often from long-standing Crow rodeo families such as the Not Afraids and the Bird-in-Grounds and often competed in barrel or breakaway rodeo events. In 1975 Danielle Not Afraid was senior rodeo queen and Agnes Bird-in-Ground was junior rodeo queen.[147]

The Calcutta auction is another featured event at the Crow Fair rodeo that has involved the entire community. In 1995 Pius Real Bird explained that the Calcutta began when he and his committee established Crow Fair's rodeo as an all-Indian event in 1963. He maintained that it has continued to be one of the most popular events. As part of the unique event, the top ten Crow bronc riders were selected and auctioned off to individuals or groups of bidders. The top rider would usually go for $500, while the lesser riders would go for around $150. After the rodeo, the Crows who "bought" them would garner the riders' winnings or suffer their losses.[148] Curtis Real Bird explained the pressure put on the cowboy by certain Crows' monetary and emotional investment in the Calcutta. He explained, "You still have to impress the judges, you still have to put up a good ride, and that ain't half the pressure they put on you because these guys are going to buy you in Calcutta and they're going to come over and say, hey, you better ride boy."[149] Charles Real Bird remembered a time at Crow Fair rodeo when his sons Tim and Shawn were being auctioned off in the Calcutta. Although Shawn went for almost $500, his younger, skinnier son went unsold until Charles bought him for about $25. The surprise was that Tim won the day and his father collected all the winnings for having had faith in his son.[150] The Calcutta auction is one way that Crow Fair's rodeo has continued to bind Crows and their families together. Over time, the rodeo at Crow Fair cultivated mutual respect for one another. Just as it has among the Lakotas, riding broncs, which demonstrates facility with horses, affects one's status in the Crow community. Crow Indian cowboy Shawn Real Bird explained that people might say, "He's a good bronc rider. Or they might say he's starting bronc riding. But that's the way you carry your stripes in society."[151]

As most Crows grew up competing in and watching the rodeo at Crow Fair, it has become integral to their community's identity and evident in its folklore. Many Crow Indian rodeo cowboys have a cache of stories to tell about Crow Fair's rodeo. Among them is usually one about their first ride at the fair as well as one about the Calcutta auctioning of the top ten bronc riders. The Real Bird family, whose ranch land stretches out along the banks of the Bighorn River, is no exception. According to bronc rider Curtis Real Bird, Crow Fair's rodeo was a place to see and be seen. It was "probably the greatest rodeo in the world. . . . Heck, I used to tell girls, you know, one of these days you're going to pay to watch me perform and by God, when I got to the Crow Fair, they did. They paid for their seats and they watched me ride a bronc."[152] Even though Curtis "bought some real estate" the day of his first bronc ride at Crow fair, it was a sterling memory because "these kids you grew up with, they're standing there watching. You're the big cowboy, getting all the attention."[153] Seven-year-old Cotton Real Bird was already riding sheep in preparation for his first bronc ride at Crow Fair's rodeo. Shawn Real Bird was fifteen when he first rode in kids' bareback riding and placed second. He remembered how his initial defeat inspired him for a subsequent victory. "Boy, I was mad. I could have won that buckle. That summer I just thought about it and thought about it. I even knew the rodeo manager then. I asked him what size the rodeo buckle was. . . . It was something like $3^1/2$ by 3, so I got a piece of paper and made a buckle and said, I think the buckle is going to be about this size." The following year he won that buckle.[154] A younger cousin, Paul Hill, was still in high school and was just beginning bronc riding when he first competed at Crow Fair and Rodeo. His cousin Curtis good-humoredly recalled that Paul "got dumped on his head. The horse jumped out of there and piled over him. We had to go find a backhoe to dig him out!"[155] Despite his less-than-glorious first performance in the rodeo, Hill enthusiastically declared of the rodeo, "Yes. I love it."[156]

Rodeo has become such an integral part of the Crow community that it has found its way into the tribe's humor in the 1990s. In *From the Heart of Crow Country: The Crow Indians' Own Stories*, Crow tribal historian Joseph Medicine Crow related one such story. The anecdote told of an Indian bareback rider by the name of Joe Stinks. His friends, who were also Indian cowboys, encouraged him to change his name for his upcoming rodeo performance, saying, "As it is, the whites like to make fun of our names and look down on us." They gave him twenty-five dollars to get "a good white man's name, like Jones, Smith or Johnson." When Joe emerged from the chute the next day, the announcer cleared his throat and boomed over the public address system, "Ladies and gentlemen, we have a real treat for you! The bucking horse of the year, W. O. Gray, is now in chute number six and the cowboy on him will be Joe Stinks No More!"[160] Although the rodeo cowboy was willing to amusingly modify his name to suit his situation, he was clearly unwilling to deny his birthright, his Indian identity, which by the 1990s included being a Native rodeo cowboy.

Given unprecedented autonomy by the federal policy of Indian self-determination, Plains Indians determined that rodeos, particularly all-Indian rodeos, would remain a part of their individual and collective identities. Just as rodeos have fostered family ties by making rodeo training part of one's Indian inheritance, they have accentuated intertribal and tribal affiliations. As pan-Indian events, all-Indian rodeos have distinguished and honored Indian rodeo champions. These role models have encouraged others to partake in the camaraderie and competition offered by the all-Indian rodeo circuit on a regional and national level. Within reservation communities, rodeos have remained expressions of a community's pride, generosity, and solidarity. Tribal members have staged rodeos as memorials to honor the departed, as benefits to ease the financial burdens of the injured, and as reservation reunions or tribal fairs to celebrate their tribe and its culture. Rodeos like Crow Fair's rodeo and the Rosebud Sioux Tribal Fair's rodeo, which have existed for nearly a century, have brought communities together and have created a collective memory. But it has been the consistent participation and openhandedness of Indian men and women, often from rodeo families like the Hunters, the Walns, and the Whipples among the Lakotas; the Cratons among the Blood Indians; the Smalls among the Northern Cheyennes; the Not Afraids, the Bird-in-Grounds, and the Real Birds among the Crows, to name a few, that have perpetuated the sport of Indian rodeo at its grassroots. By continuing to share their training, experiences, and folklore with the next generation of Indian rodeo cowboys and cowgirls, they have ensured that rodeo, and particularly all-Indian rodeo, will endure as a northern Plains Indian family and tribal tradition.

# Celebrating Native Solidarity

S CENES FROM THE 1996 INDIAN NATIONAL FINALS RODEO
in Saskatoon, Saskatchewan, attested to the endurance of Native
solidarity, nurtured over a century at the rodeo. After his remark-
able eight-second ride, an elated Indian world champion bull rider
from Pine Ridge, South Dakota, threw his cowboy hat in the air.
Everyone in the overwhelmingly Indian audience erupted in applause, charged
with his adrenaline. Another such moment occurred as a young cowgirl and
accomplished barrel racer from the Brighton Seminole tribe won the title of
INFR Rodeo Queen. All in attendance cheered, but none so wildly as her
Seminole family, fans, and fellow cowboys and cowgirls who had traveled all
the way from Florida to the remote Canadian city to wave posters and support
their tribal members. Despite late-nineteenth-century assurances of imminent
Indian doom—and aggressive attempts by the Bureau of Indian Affairs,
missionaries, and Indian reformers to detribalize and assimilate them—
American Indians remained a people who prized their tribal and eventually
intertribal connections. Remarkably, northern Plains horsemen and audiences had used government-sanctioned arenas to foil the BIA's plans to assimilate them. Through rodeo, an activity with Hispanic, Native, and Anglo
American roots, northern Plains Indians had reinforced their commitment
to long-standing values that cherished horses, family, community, generosity,
and competition.

The great irony of the federal government's aggressive assimilation campaign is that Indians managed to respond to its initiatives in way that strengthened their identity. As they made the transition to reservation life between 1880
and 1920, northern Plains Indians refused to surrender their distinct identity,

yet they remained willing to reconstruct it. In its most intense period of adherence to assimilation, the federal government insisted that Indians become ranchers or preferably farmers on individual plots of land, give up their traditional religions, and send their children to off-reservation Indian industrial boarding schools. With the buffalo gone, Sun Dances outlawed, and their children deported for most of the year, northern Plains Indians found new ways to remain essentially Indian. Overwhelmingly, they chose cattle ranching and rodeo. Both activities resonated with their existing cultural priorities. Until land allotment and leasing fragmented their reservation lands, many enthusiastically took up cattle ranching, which allowed them to work with horses, together, and out of doors.

They also flocked to rodeos that offered a chance for reunion, celebration, and competition as their pre-reservation summer rendezvous and Sun Dances had once done. Throughout the summer months, northern Plains Indians performed in rodeos at Wild West shows, professional rodeos, Fourth of July celebrations, and county and state fairs. American national holidays like Independence Day provided ideal opportunities for Indians to stage government-approved community celebrations and rodeos. While the Indian Office tolerated these activities, they remained particularly concerned about the "show Indians'" image and their extended absences from their crops. To keep their Indian charges closer to home and to excite them with an interest in agriculture, Indian agents introduced Indian industrial fairs in 1904. By inaugurating Indian industrial fairs, Indian agents quite unintentionally provided one of the greatest forums for Indian cohesiveness. Enthusiastically, Crows on their reservation and Lakotas at Pine Ridge and Rosebud seized the opportunity to gather at these Indian industrial fairs where Indian organizers, overseen by their Indian agents, immediately incorporated rodeo alongside the requisite agricultural contests. As northern Plains Indians tightened tribal ties at reservation rodeos, children at government-run Indian boarding schools began to foster a sense of pan-Indian unity by forming new relationships with students from other tribal groups.

While missionaries and Indian agents continued their efforts to "uplift" Indians throughout the 1920s, they slightly relaxed their assimilationist efforts. Northern Plains Indians experienced greater freedom of cultural expression as a result of these subtle changes and because of the steady flow of leasing dollars into their reservations.[1] In response, Indian cowboys and community members, many of whom were raised on reservations, asserted their preference for rodeo as their reservation's primary social activity. Crows and Lakotas replaced their government-sponsored agricultural fairs with Indian-organized rodeos such as the Crows' Indian rodeo and the Lakotas' annual Pine Ridge rodeo. Fourth of July rodeos also emerged as reservation-wide events in Lodge Grass, Wyola, and St. Xavier on the Crow reservation and on the nearby Northern Cheyenne reservation. As rodeo grew more popular for Indians and non-Indians following World War I, northern Plains Indians also competed in local rodeos and summer fairs, and in more distant professional rodeos.

During the Indian New Deal from 1933 to 1945, Commissioner of Indians Affairs John Collier attempted to dismantle the policies of his predecessors. As he encouraged cultural and economic revival, Collier encouraged his Indian agents to resuscitate dormant Indian fairs. As a result, government-sponsored tribal fairs replaced the Indian-organized reservation rodeos of the 1920s as the reservations' primary gatherings. Among the Lakotas, Indian agents who were relatively culturally sympathetic allowed Lakotas a voice in determining the content of their tribal fairs. At the Oglala Sioux Fair and the Rosebud Sioux Fair, Lakotas did not abandon the rodeo as a favored form of community celebration. Rather, they included rodeo events alongside their adapted Indian dances and ceremonials. It was under Crow Indian Superintendent Robert Yellowtail's leadership on the Crow reservation that Indians demonstrated most dramatically what they could accomplish when they possessed complete cultural autonomy. The cultural content of the fair and rodeo was not designed as their white Indian Agent perceived it but as the Indians saw it. The Crows featured rodeo in their cultural display by staging a rodeo on at least three of the fair's five days. By featuring Indian buffalo riding throughout this period, the rodeo further exemplified the Crows' successful integration of their past and present realities as well as their desire to attract tourists. As the Crow Fair and Rodeo became a Plains Indian event from 1934 to 1945, the enduring presence of rodeo there predicted its own future as a pan-Indian event.

Galvanized by their involvement in World War II and their fight against the policy of termination, Native Americans began their drive toward self-determination. From 1945 to 1970, many determined themselves to be Indian rodeo cowboys, who preferred to perform in an all-Indian rodeo circuit. As the numbers of Indian rodeo competitors grew and their pan-Indian sensibilities intensified, American Indians forged the all-Indian rodeo circuit. In

1958 Navajo cowboys created the first regional all-Indian rodeo association, the All-Indian Rodeo Cowboys Association. In 1962 Pius Real Bird, the arena manager of Crow Fair, followed suit and declared Crow Fair's rodeo to be an all-Indian rodeo. The all-Indian rodeo circuit really began to take shape, as Native organizers formed the All American Indian Activities Association in the mid 1960s to promote Native rodeo in the northern Great Plains. Shortly thereafter, Lakotas declared the Rosebud Sioux Fair and Oglala Sioux Fair to be AAIA-sanctioned all-Indian rodeos. As part of their movement toward Native solidarity and independence, Indian leaders realized that they needed to revitalize their reservations. To improve their economies, Crows and Lakotas promoted non-Indian tourism at their reservation fairs and all-Indian rodeos like the Crows' Teepee Capital of the World. In addition to being pan-Indian events and tourist attractions, all-Indian rodeos remained unifying events on the Crow, Northern Cheyenne, Pine Ridge, and Rosebud Sioux reservations, where a significant number of rodeo families had emerged.

With the federal Indian policy of Native American self-determination in effect after 1970, American Indians instituted the all-Indian rodeo as a nationwide pan-Indian activity. As northern Plains Indian involvement in rodeos increased, so too did the all-Indian rodeo circuit. In 1976 Indian rodeo competitors required an Indian National Finals Rodeo to determine their "world champions." By the mid-1990s, the all-Indian rodeo circuit had expanded to include fourteen regions, with each required to produce at least ten rodeos per year and to have a minimum of 100 members. The average number of members per region was about 150 to 200. Thus, up to 2,400 Indian cowboys have competed in about 150 all-Indian rodeos in recent years. Since its inception in 1976, the Indian National Finals Rodeo has remained the culmination of the all-Indian rodeo circuit and of the Native unity it nurtured.[2] Within tribal groups, Northern Plains Indian cowboys and audiences continued to participate vigorously in all-Indian rodeos on a community level at reservation celebrations, memorial and charity events, and above all tribal fairs. Through persistent training and exposure of younger family and tribal members to rodeo, Lakota, Northern Cheyenne, and Crow cowboys and cowgirls ensured that rodeo would endure as a favored form of camaraderie and contest.

Ironically, ever since tribes of the West had been placed—voluntarily or otherwise—on reservations, Indian agents had viewed rodeo as an instrument of acculturation, yet northern Plains Indians used rodeo to resist assimilation and to strengthen their Native ties. In the late nineteenth century, Crows,

Northern Cheyennes, and Lakotas chose to rodeo because it offered them a chance for equestrian competition and reunion, as their summer gatherings had once done. Over the course of the twentieth century, they knitted rodeo into their collective consciousness and identity, residing in their shared experiences and memories. Old-timers reminisced about its early days, while younger Indian cowboys gradually acquired their own store of rodeo recollections. The consistent participation in rodeos of families like the Real Birds, the Bird-in-Grounds, and the Not Afraids on the Crow reservation; the Smalls on the Northern Cheyenne reservation; the Walns, the Colombes, and the Whipples on the Rosebud reservation; and the Hunters and the Sierras on the Pine Ridge reservation ensured that rodeo would persist in those places. As Indian rodeo cowboys and cowgirls continued to ride in the saddles of their fathers and mothers, they made rodeo into a newfangled Indian tradition, one that continued to bring them together. At all-Indian rodeos, enthusiastic Indian rodeo competitors and audiences demonstrated the perseverance of their Native solidarity. This was cause for celebration.

# *Notes*

## ABBREVIATIONS

| | |
|---|---|
| CRA | Bureau of Indian Affairs, Cheyenne River Agency, File 518325–26, Box 185, RG 75 |
| CA | Bureau of Indian Affairs, Crow Agency, File 047, Box 99, RG 75 |
| HSC-CWS | Harold Schunk Collection: Center for Western Studies, Augustana College, Sioux Falls, South Dakota |
| LBHCA | Little Big Horn College Archives, CA, Montana |
| MGBP | Merrill G. Burlingame Papers, Montana State University, Bozeman |
| MHSA | Montana Historical Society Archives, Helena |
| NA-CPR | National Archives and Records Administration, Central Plains Region, Kansas City |
| NA-RMR | National Archives and Records Administration, Rocky Mountain Region, Denver |
| OLCA | Oglala Lakota College Archives, Kyle, South Dakota |
| PRA | Bureau of Indian Affairs, Pine Ridge Agency, File 047, Box 166, RG 75 |
| PRRA | Pine Ridge Rodeo Association |
| RG | Records Group |

## INTRODUCTION

1. While this study broadly delineates the origins and growth of rodeo within Native communities in the West, its principal focus remains on several groups of northern Plains Indians within the continental United States. Because of their long-standing equestrian, cattle ranching, and rodeo traditions, special attention is given throughout to the Crows and Northern Cheyennes of Montana as well as to those Lakotas residing on the Pine Ridge, Rosebud, and Cheyenne River Sioux reservations in South Dakota.

2. This belief in imminent Indian doom had become a recurring theme in late-nineteenth- and early-twentieth-century art, typified in Edward S. Curtis's photograph taken in 1904 of a Navajo Indian titled "The Vanishing Race." That

photograph was one of forty thousand that Curtis took as part of his ambitious project, *North American Indian*, which attempted to record on film and in text what he regrettably believed to be a culture and people on the verge of extinction. A discussion of "Indian doom" iconography is found in Schimmel, "Inventing the Indian."

3. White, *"It's Your Misfortune and None of My Own,"* 92.

4. Iverson, *When Indians Became Cowboys*, 84.

5. Ibid., 4.

6. Ibid, 53–54. Iverson discusses the ways in which many Plains Indians used cattle, just as they had the horses that preceded them, to demonstrate personal attributes such as generosity and equestrian skills, which were extolled by their communities. He states, "By giving cattle or beef to one's relatives, by feeding people at a celebration, and in other comparable ways, a person could be seen as generous, thoughtful, and properly mindful of the well-being of others." Iverson echoes this in *Riders of the West*, 5.

7. Iverson, *When Indians Became Cowboys*, 53. Of the enthusiasm with which many Plains Indians adopted cattle ranching, Iverson says, "The love of the outdoors, of horses, and of movement all contributed to the positive chord struck by the new industry." Iverson restates this in *Riders of the West*, 5.

8. Lowie, *The Crow Indians*, 329.

9. Ibid., , 5–11.

10. Hoxie, *Parading through History*, 5.

11. Ibid., 5.

12. Frey, *The World of the Crow Indians*, 3.

13. Ibid., 3–4.

14. Ibid., 5–11.

15. Ibid., 27.

16. Stands in Timber and Utley, *Cheyenne Memories*, 36n.

17. Hurt, *Sioux Indians II*, 13–14.

18. Hassrick, *The Sioux*, 6.

19. Medicine Crow, *From the Heart of Crow Country*, 11.

20. Stands in Timber and Utley, *Cheyenne Memories*, 91–92, 94, 98.

21. Ibid.

22. Lowie, *The Crow Indians*, 226–27.

23. Medicine Crow, *From the Heart of Crow Country*, 11.

24. Lowie, *The Crow Indians*, 61.

25. Ibid., 98–103.

26. Iverson, *Riders of the West*, 1, 4.

27. Stands in Timber and Utley, *Cheyenne Memories*, 116–17.

28. Fowler, *Shared Symbols, Contested Meanings*, 26; Ewers, *The Horse in Blackfoot Indian Culture*, 18, 212, 305, 308, 310, 312, 314–16, 319, 334, 338.

29. Pony Boy, *Horse Follow Closely*, 13.

30. Iverson, *Riders of the West*, 2.

31. Pony Boy, *Horse Follow Closely*, 6.

32. Iverson, "Native Peoples and Native Histories," 16.

33. Iverson, *Riders of the West*, 1. Iverson recounts the origin stories of horses told by several American Indian groups of the West that reveal the degree to which Indians have incorporated horses into their cultures. As Indians wove horses into their lives and stories, they came to view them less as European implants and more as part of their own heritage. Iverson retells the Blackfeet story of an orphan boy who dove into a lake at the culmination of a long journey and with the aid of a spirit chief retrieved an elk-dog. The boy then brought the horse back to his people. Likewise, the Navajos believed that the holy people created horses and the Sun and the Moon rode them and eventually presented them as a gift to the Diné.

34. Lawrence, *Rodeo*, 263.

35. Medicine Crow, *From the Heart of Crow Country*, 2.

36. Magdeline Medicine Horse, archivist at Little Big Horn College and Archives, interview with author, CA, Montana, October 6, 1994.

37. Schaafsma, "The Horse in Rock Art," 5.

38. Pony Boy, *Horse Follow Closely*, 9.

39. Pony Boy, *Out of the Saddle*, 34, 49, 59, 76.

40. Iverson, *Riders of the West*, 4.

41. Slatta, *Cowboys of the Americas*, 128. Other relevant articles by Slatta include "Cowboys and Gauchos," and "Cowboys, Gauchos, and Llaneros," 8–23. See also LeCompte, "The Hispanic Influence on the History of Rodeo," 21–38.

42. Sweet, "The Horse, Santiago, and a Ritual Game," 71.

43. Underwood, "The Vaquero in South Texas," 93–99.

44. Slatta, *Cowboys of the Americas*, 129–39.

45. Sweet, "The Horse, Santiago and a Ritual Game," 71.

46. Young and Morgan, *The Navajo Language*.

47. Kluckhohn et al., *Navajo Material Culture*, 388.

48. Roe, *The Indian and the Horse*, 186.

49. Eagle/Walking Turtle, *Indian America*, 31–34.

50. Roe, *The Indian and the Horse*, 125.

51. The author discussed riding bucking broncs at buffalo hunting rendezvous with Laurence Flatlip, a Crow oral historian, February 23, 1995. One of the many references to trading-post horse races is found in Wagner and Allen, *Blankets and Moccasins*, 193–95.

52. Roe, *The Indian and the Horse*, 82.

53. Wagner and Allen, *Blankets and Moccasins*, 193–95.

54. Shawn Real Bird, interview with the author, February 24, 1995, Garryowen, Montana.

55. Flatlip, interview.

56. Shawn Real Bird, interview.

57. White, *"It's Your Misfortune and None of My Own,"* 92. Historian Frederick Hoxie, in *A Final Promise*, argues that from 1890 to 1920 the assimilationist policy that had been in place throughout the 1880s shifted. He asserts that government expectations of Native Americans became more pessimistic, viewing Indians only as potential wageworkers on the periphery of American society but workers who needed to be made into independent individuals nonetheless.

58. Prucha, *The Great Father*, 618–19.

59. Ibid., 646.

60. Ibid., 688.

61. Iverson, *"We Are Still Here,"* 31–32.

62. Hoxie, "From Prison to Homeland," 72.

63. Fowler, *Shared Symbols, Contested Meanings*, 54–55.

## CHAPTER ONE

1. White, *"It's Your Misfortune and None of My Own,"* 92.

2. Hoxie, "From Prison to Homeland," 72.

3. Iverson, *When Indians Became Cowboys*, 53. Iverson asserts that northern Plains Indians' proclivity toward cattle ranching was born of their "love of the outdoors, of horses, and of movement."

4. Moses, *Wild West Shows and the Images of American Indians*, xiii, 221. Moses uses the term show Indians to describe Indians employed in Wild West shows. He also employs the term in the context of all American Indian performance, including agricultural displays at tribal and county fairs, historical tableaux, and Indian student exhibits at fairs and expositions. All were designed by the Indian Office to demonstrate to spectators the "progress" of American Indians, but often held different meanings for the Indian actors.

5. Iverson, *When Indians Became Cowboys*, 54. On the western Native tradition of gathering for and wagering on equestrian competitions, Iverson concludes, "Well before the days of the Navajo rodeo, the Diné raced their horses against each other, with people traveling long distances to watch, to wager and compete."

6. Fowler, *Shared Symbols, Contested Meanings*, 73–74.

7. West, *The Way to the West*. West looks at the ecology of the Plains in the nineteenth century under Indian, white, and animal pressures. He explains that "the 'push' of displacement and the 'pull' of new opportunities combined to scramble the tribal populations of the plains," 10.

8. White, "The Winning of the West," 253.

9. Thornton, *American Indian Holocaust and Survival*, 95–99.

10. Hoxie, *Parading through History*, 87.

11. Ibid., 92.

12. Hoxie, "Searching for Structure," 293; "Bureau of Indian Affairs List of Indian Agents and Superintendents in Charge of Crow Indian Agencies," compiled in 1968, Joseph Medicine Crow Collection. Little Big Horn College Archives, CA, Montana.

13. Hoxie, "Searching for Structure," 293.

14. Ibid.," 293–94.

15. Frank Bird Linderman, *Plenty-Coups*, 73–74.

16. Iverson, *When Indians Became Cowboys*, 53.

17. Hoxie, *Parading through History*, 282

18. *Oglala Light*, November 1916.

19. Ibid., June 1915.

20. Ibid., November 1916.

21. Mikkelson, "Indians and Rodeo," 14–15.

22. McGinnis and Sharrock, *The Crow People*, 53.

23. Hoxie, *The Crow*, 99–100.

24. Hoxie, *Parading through History*, 269.

25. Ibid., 267. This is also the central argument in Hoxie, *A Final Promise*.

26. *Oglala Light*, January 1908.

27. Hoxie, *Parading through History*, 267–70.

28. Ibid., 318–22.

29. Herbert T. Hoover, "The Sioux Agreement of 1889 and Its Aftermath," 58.

30. *Oglala Light*, January–February 1907.

31. *Oglala Light*, May 1906.

32. Iverson, *When Indians Became Cowboys*, 39–40, 69–70.

33. Hoxie, "From Prison to Homeland," 60–62.

34. Moses, *Wild West Shows*, 63.

35. Roth, "The 101 Ranch Wild West Show," 416.

36. Fredrikson, *American Rodeo*, 4.

37. Lawrence, *Rodeo*, 44–45.

38. Arpad and Lincoln, *Buffalo Bill's Wild West*, 22.

39. L. G. Moses, "Indians in Wild West Shows" (lecture given at the Buffalo Bill Historical Center, Cody, Wyoming, June 3, 1994).

40. Moses, *Wild West Shows*, 8. This is one of Moses' central arguments, which refutes the belief that Wild West shows exploited Indians by asserting that in fact the Indians quite self-consciously used the shows for their own personal benefit.

41. Ibid., 77.

42. U.S. Indian agent, CA, Montana, to W. H. Smead, U.S. Indian Agent, Jocko, Montana, June 2, 1902, Hoxie Crow Collections, Box 3, LBHCA.

43. *Oglala Light*, April 1908.

44. Moses, *Wild West Shows*, 168.

45. Ibid., 8.

46. *Oglala Light*, October 1909.

47. Moses, *Wild West Shows,* 196–205.

48. Ibid., 25.

49. *Oglala Light,* April 1911.

50. Director of the American Wild West Show in Brussels to R. G. Valentine, commissioner of Indian affairs, June 2, 1910; Bud Atkinson to Superintendent Brennan, Pine Ridge Agency, October 26, 1912; R. G. Valentine, commissioner of Indian affairs, to Joseph C. Miller, president, 101 Ranch Wild West Show, August 2, 1911; assistant commissioner to Joseph C. Miller, August 17, 1911; J. C. Miller to E. W. Jermark, U.S. Indian agent, May 10, 1927; Col. Cummins and Vernon C. Seavers, contract permitting David Red Star to perform in Young Buffalo Bill Wild West Co., April 17, 1914, "Show Correspondence, U.S. and Foreign"; George Arlington, general manager, Miller Bros. and Arlington 101 Ranch Real Wild West, to Major J. R. Brennan, August 3, 1915, "Fairs and Expositions: Young Buffalo Bill Show"; Bert Bowers, manager of Robinson's Famous Shows, to J. R. Brennan, superintendent Pine Ridge Indian Agency, May 12, 1915, "Fairs and Expositions: 1915"; Superintendent Brennan to commissioner of Indian affairs, April 21, 1916, "Fairs and Expositions: 1915"; all in PRA NA-CPR.

51. Moses, *Wild West Shows,* 252.

52. Ibid., 255.

53. Fredrikson, *American Rodeo,* 21.

54. Ibid., 22.

55. Big Foot Historical Society, *Reservation Round-Up: Stories of Pioneer Days in the Setting of the Pine Ridge Reservation Area,* Big Foot Historical Society: Shannon County, S. Dak., 9. SC, Box 1, Folder 3, Martha Whiting Collection, OLCA.

56. Iverson, *When Indians Became Cowboys,* 74.

57. *Lewiston Morning Tribune,* September 6, 1990.

58. Dempsey, *Tom Three Persons.*

59. *Lewiston Morning Tribune,* August 19, 1991.

60. *The (Calgary) Albertan,* May 1949.

61. Ibid.

62. Mikkelson, "Indians and Rodeo," 14–15.

63. Cheyenne Frontier Days, 1972 Souvenir Program, American Heritage Center, University of Wyoming, W994-t-ch-fd.

64. Shirley Flynn, Cheyenne, Wyoming, local historian, letter to author, October 14, 1994; Program, 42nd Cheyenne Frontier Days, July 1938, American Heritage Center, University of Wyoming, W994-t-ch-fd.

65. *Wyoming Tribune,* September 6, 1905. Unfortunately, the first rodeo rider to die at Cheyenne Frontier Days was a Creek from Oklahoma named Eddie Burghes. Atop his coffin during the funeral procession was an empty boot, his saddle, bridle, and lariat.

66. *Oglala Light,* June 1910.

67. Contract between Stockmen's Club of Denver and eighteen unnamed Indian performers, April 5, 1911, BIA, "Fairs and Expositions: 1911," File 047, Box 160, RG 75, NA-CPR.
68. Moses, *Wild West Shows*, 196.
69. Iverson, *When Indians Became Cowboys*, 76.
70. *Oglala Light*, May 1905.
71. Ibid., June 1909.
72. *Dupree Leader*, July 7, 1910.
73. *Faith Gazette*, June 10, 1910.
74. *Dupree Leader*, June 1, 1911.
75. Ibid., July 6, 1911.
76. Ibid., July 6, 1916.
77. Ibid., September 18, 1919.
78. Ibid., July 15, 1920.
79. Superintendent, CA, to commissioner of Indian affairs, June 19, 1925, Hoxie Crow Collections, Box 3.,
80. E. H. Becker, Indian agent, CA, to A. L. Babcock, Billings, Montana, September 24, 1898, Hoxie Crow Collection, Box 3.
81. S. G. Reynolds, U.S. Indian agent, CA, to Plenty Coups and Bell Rock, Pryor, Montana, September 5, 1902, Hoxie Crow Collection, Box 3.
82. S. G. Reynolds to Van Hoose, Pryor, Montana, September 16, 1905, Hoxie Crow Collection, Box 5.
83. Fred Miller, clerk in charge, CA to S. H. Glidden, Bridger, Montana, September 15, 1906, Hoxie Crow Collection, Box 3.
84. Indian Agent, CA to C. J. Burt, Belfry, Montana, June, 6, 1907, Hoxie Crow Collections, Box 3.
85. Indian Agent, CA to E. Gilette, Sheridan, Wyoming, June, 30, 1908, Hoxie Crow Collection, Box 3; S. G. Reynolds, CA, to Sheridan, Wyoming, June 10, 1909, Hoxie Crow Collections, Box 3.
86. Moses, *Wild West Shows*, 218.
87. *Hardin (Mont.) Tribune*, August 1, 1913; September 19, 1913.
88. McLaughlin, "The Big Lease," 19. Although buffalo riding may have occurred among Indians for sport, it was perhaps more common at off-reservation county fairs and rodeos, where it was a tourist attraction.
89. Acting superintendent, Cheyenne River Agency, South Dakota, to John E. Derby, Cherry Creek, South Dakota, August 30, 1915, "Fair 1915–1921," CRA, NA-CPR.
90. *Dupree Leader*, July 8, 1915.
91. Supplement to the Supplement, "State Fairs, 1924–1927," File 130, Box 83, Item 15, Hoxie Crow Collection, Box 3.
92. Premium List for 1913 Montana State Fair, Hoxie Crow Collection, Box 5; *Hardin Tribune*, September 15, 1913.

93. Moses, *Wild West Shows*, 206.

94. Maroukis, "Yankton Sioux Tribal Fairs."

95. *Oglala Light*, December 1905.

96. Moses, *Wild West Shows*, 207–9.

97. Maroukis, "Yankton Sioux Tribal Fairs."

98. Moses, *Wild West Shows*, 218.

99. Richardson, "The Crow Indian Fair," 3.

100. Superintendent S. G. Reynolds, CA, to the commissioner of Indian affairs, October 25, 1909, Hoxie Crow Collection, Box 5.

101. Moses, *Wild West Shows*, 208.

102. Program, 1907 Crow Indian Fair, Joseph Medicine Crow Collection, LBHCA.

103. Moses, *Wild West Shows*, 209.

104. Superintendent S. G. Reynolds, CA, to the commissioner of Indian affairs, July 31, 1912. Hoxie Crow Collection, Box 5.

105. Ibid., October 25, 1909, Hoxie Crow Collection, Box 5.

106. Ibid., October 1, 1912, Hoxie Crow Collection, Box 5.

107. Ibid., October 25, 1909, Hoxie Crow Collection, Box 5.

108. Ibid.

109. Ibid.

110. Flatlip, interview.

111. Eloise White Bear Pease, interview with author, March 9, 1995.

112. Flatlip, interview.

113. Ibid.

114. Superintendent S. G. Reynolds, CA, to Plenty Coups, September 1905, Hoxie Crow Collection, Box 5; *Great Falls (Mont.) Tribune*, August 28, 1955.

115. Hoxie, "Searching for Structure," 289–94.

116. Superintendent S. G. Reynolds, CA, to the commissioner of Indian affairs, October 1, 1912, Hoxie Crow Collection, Box 5.

117. Program, 1907 Crow Indian Fair, Joseph Medicine Crow Collection.

118. Hoxie, *Parading through History*, 307–8

119. *Hardin Tribune*, September 25, 1908.

120. Thomas Bull over Hill, interview for New Deal in Montana Oral History Project, May 27, 1987. Montana Historical Society, Helena.

121. Richardson, "The Crow Indian Fair," 3.

122. Program, 1907 Crow Indian Fair, Joseph Medicine Crow Collection.

123. *Hardin Tribune*, September 25, 1908.

124. Superintendent S. G. Reynolds, CA, to Joseph K. Dixon, Philadelphia, September 25, 1909, Hoxie Crow Collection, Box 5.

125. *Hardin Tribune*, October 3, 1913.

126. Ibid., September 3, 1915.

127. Ibid., October 5, 1917.

128. Program and Premium List, Thirteenth Annual Crow Fair, September 23, 1918, "Crow Fair 1918," CA, NA-RMR.

129. *Hardin Herald*, June 20, 1974.

130. Mikkelson, "Indians and Rodeo," 15.

131. Whyte, *Indians in the Rockies*, 71.

132. Ibid., 76.

133. Parker, *The Feather and the Drum*, 82–83.

134. Superintendent John R. Brennan, Pine Ridge, to the Sioux People, *Oglala Light*, September–October 1911.

135. Superintendent John R. Brennan, Pine Ridge, to the district farmers, *Oglala Light*, September–October 1911.

136. *Dupree Leader*, August 8, 1912.

137. Ibid., September 12, 1912.

138. *Oglala Light*, October 1917; Program, Fifth Annual Pine Ridge Indian Fair, September 25–26–27, 1919, "Local Fair and Rodeo Correspondence," PRA, NA-CPR.

139. *Dupree Leader*, August 8, 1912.

140. Ibid., August 8, 1912.

141. Jack Bull Eagle, Save Eagle Chasing, Fish Guts, and Ed Swan, Cherry Creek, South Dakota, to F. C. Campbell, Cheyenne River Agency, August 3, 1915, "Fair 1915–1921," CRA, NA-CPR.

142. Hoxie, *Parading through History*, 363. Frederick Hoxie explains of the Crows that such early-twentieth-century "cultural innovations" as community celebrations and tribal fairs "allowed groups to gather in explicitly secular settings that local whites would find acceptable. The result was the emergence of a range of 'Indian' activities that both reinforced local affiliations and forged new ties among native groups."

## CHAPTER TWO

1. This is a reference to Supreme Court Justice John Marshall's 1832 ruling in *Worcester v. Georgia* that defined the unique status of American Indian tribal groups within the United States as "nations within a nation," possessing sovereign powers, which were limited only by the federal government's power to "protect" them. While this ruling allowed for considerable federal interference in Indian affairs, American Indians would eventually use it to their advantage in their drive for self-determination after World War II.

2. Hoxie, *Parading through History*, 295, 306.

3. Superintendent Asbury, CA, to O'Neil, April 12, 1929, CA, NA-RMR.

4. Ibid.

5. Superintendent Asbury, CA, to Bert Hammond, July 14, 1924, Hoxie Crow Collection, Box 5.

6. Superintendent Asbury, CA, to commissioner of Indian affairs, June 6, 1925, Hoxie Crow Collections, Box 5.

7. Superintendent Asbury, CA, to Clara Belle Locke, Minnesota, December 8, 1930, CA, NA-RMR.

8. Superintendent Asbury, CA, to J. H. Bohling, Commercial Club, Miles City, Montana, January 14, 1928, CA, NA-RMR. By scoffing at the display of the Indians' so-called feather feature, Asbury revealed his preference that Indians present themselves to outsiders as progressive agriculturists rather than as "backward" traditionalists who performed in reenactments, entry parades, and dances bedecked in feathers and regalia.

9. Superintendent W. O. Roberts, Cheyenne Agency, S.D., to C.A. McCormack, President, Faith Fair and Rodeo, August 1927, CRA, NA-CPR.

10. Superintendent Asbury, CA, to commissioner of Indian affairs, November 26, 1926, Hoxie Crow Collections, Box 5.

11. E. M. Kelly, secretary, to Superintendent Asbury, February 27, 1928; Mrs. B. C. Keough, superintendent of the Indian Department at the Midland Empire Fair, to Superintendent Asbury, July 9, 1928, CA, NA-RMR.

12. Superintendent Asbury, CA, to district farmers, September 4, 1928, CA, NA-RMR.

13. Flyer, Midland Empire Fair, September 3–7, 1928, CA, NA-RMR.

14. Superintendent Asbury, CA, to district farmers, September 4, 1928, CA, NA-RMR.

15. Clark J. Nation to Superintendent Asbury, July 27, 1931, CA, NA-RMR.

16. Prucha, *The Great Father*, 275.

17. Moses, *Wild West Shows*, 253.

18. Commissioner of Indian affairs to Superintendent Asbury, with enclosed letter from Senator Warren, chair of Indian Committee on Appropriations, June 19, 1925, Hoxie Crow Collections, Box 5; Parman, *Indians and the American West*, 76.

19. Moses, *Wild West Shows*, 261, 264.

20. Telegram, E. Pat Kelly, Livingston, Montana, to Superintendent Asbury, June 2, 1929; telegram, Superintendent Asbury to E. Pat Kelly, June 3, 1929, CA, NA-RMR.

21. Roy L. Stith, surveyor, Terry, Montana, to Indian agent; Chairman chamber of commerce and American Legion committee, June 1, 1932; Superintendent James H. Hyde to Roy L. Stith, June 6, 1932, CA, NA-RMR.

22. *Hardin Tribune*, August 11, 1922.

23. Ibid., September 7, 1923.

24. *Billings Gazette*, August 4, 1928.

25. *Hardin Tribune-Herald*, September 11, 1925.

26. Ibid., September 3, 1926.

27. Ibid., September 24, 1926.

28. Ibid., September 14, 1928.

29. Ibid., September 13, 1929.

30. Ibid., August 9, 1928.

31. Ibid., July 8, 1927.

32. C. A. McCormack, president, Faith Fair & Rodeo to W. O. Roberts, super-intendent, Cheyenne Agency, S.Dak.August 8, 1927, CRA, NA-CPR.

33. Program, Faith Fair and Rodeo, August 31–September 2, 1927, CRA, NA-CPR.

34. Moses, *Wild West Shows*, 255.

35. Joe Yellowhead, interview by Steve Plummer, June 8, 1971, tape no. 695, American Indian Research Project, South Dakota Oral History Center, University of South Dakota, Vermillion.

36. Roberts to commissioner of Indian affairs, July 11, 1927; Commissioner of Indian Affairs Charles Burke to William Williamson, July 5, 1927, CRA, NA-CPR.

37. Roberts to commissioner of Indian affairs, July 11, 1927, CRA, NA-CPR.

38. Superintendent Asbury, CA, to O'Neil, April 12, 1929, CA, NA-RMR.

39. District Farmer R. C. Halgate, CA, to Luke Rock, Simon Bulltail, and all concerned, Pryor, Montana, May 16, 1926, Hoxie Crow Collections, Box 5.

40. *Hardin Tribune*, July 1, 1921.

41. Ibid., July 7, 1922.

42. *Hardin Tribune-Herald*, July 2, 1926.

43. Ibid., July 6, 1928.

44. Ibid., July 20, 1930.

45. Superintendent Asbury, CA, to Erle Howe, Lodge Grass, June 8, 1931; Reg Pearce, farmer, to Superintendent Asbury, 1931, CA, NA-RMR.

46. Hoxie, *Parading through History*, 306–7, 321.

47. Superintendent Asbury to district farmers, September 22, 1921, Hoxie Crow Collections, Box 5.

48. Chief Plenty Coups, CA, to Superintendent Asbury, July 25, 1922, Hoxie Crow Collections, Box 5.

49. Superintendent Asbury to commissioner of Indian affairs, July 18, 1922, Hoxie Crow Collections, Box 5.

50. Superintendent Asbury to O'Neil, April 12, 1929, CA, NA-RMR.

51. *Hardin Herald*, August 25, 1922.

52. Ibid., August 25, 1922, and September 15, 1922.

53. 1922 Premium List of Unclaimed Prizes, Hoxie Crow Collections, Box 5.

54. *Hardin Tribune*, August 25, 1922.

55. Superintendent Asbury, CA, to Fred Collins, Sheridan, Wyoming, August 15, 1923, Hoxie Crow Collections, Box 5.

56. *Hardin Tribune*, August 31, 1923.

57. Shiek, CA, to Superintendent Asbury, June 28, 1924, Hoxie Crow Collections, Box 5.

58. Bull over Hill, interview.

59. Superintendent Asbury, CA, to J. Clyde Williams, Bozeman, Montana, August 15, 1923, Hoxie Crow Collections, Box 5.

60. *Hardin Tribune-Herald*, September 25, 1925.

61. Ibid., September 25, 1926, and June 20, 1974.

62. Ibid., September 25, 1926, and June 20, 1974.

63. Ibid., September 25, 1926; Superintendent Asbury, CA, to Robert Yellowtail, July 16, 1926, Hoxie Crow Collections, Box 5.

64. *Hardin Tribune-Herald*, September 25, 1926; Superintendent Asbury, CA, to Robert Yellowtail, July 16, 1926, Hoxie Crow Collections, Box 5.

65. *Hardin Tribune-Herald*, September 25, 1926, and June 20, 1974.

66. Bull over Hill, interview , May 27, 1987.

67. John Bull Tail, interview for New Deal in Montana Oral History Project, June 13, 1989, Montana Historical Society, Helena.

68. District Superintendent F. C. Campbell, CA, to Clara Belle Locke, Minnesota, December 8, 1930, CA, NA-RMR.

69. Superintendent Asbury, CA, to Sheridan Commercial Club, Sheridan Wyoming, June 3, 1929, CA, NA-RMR.

70. B. C. Keough, CA, to Superintendent Asbury, June 19, 1929, CA, NA-RMR.

71. Commissioner C. J. Rhoads to Superintendent Hyde, September 24, 1932, and June 19, 1929, CA, NA-RMR.

72. *Hardin Tribune-Herald*, August 29, 1931.

73. Commissioner Rhoads to Superintendent Hyde, September 24, 1932, CA, NA-RMR.

74. *Oglala Light*, September–October 1912, p. 9.

75. Ibid., p. 10.

76. Program, Fourth Annual Pine Ridge Indian Fair, September 26–28, 1918, PRA, NA-CPR.

77. *Oglala Light*, October 1917; Program, Fifth Annual Pine Ridge Indian Fair, September 25–27, 1919, PRA, NA-CPR.

78. Iverson, *When Indians Became Cowboys*, 70.

79. Charles H. Burke to E. W. Jermark, June 23, 1927, PRA, NA-CPR.

80. Petition to Honorable Charles H. Burke, composed by James Ryan, Martin, South Dakota, June 23, 1927, PRA, NA-CPR.

81. Minutes, PRRA, February 6, 1928, PRA, NA-CPR; W.O. Roberts to farmers, Cheyenne River Reservation, [1928], CRA, NA-CPR.

82. McGregor to Frank Goings, June 2, 1932, PRA, NA-CPR.

83. E. W. Jermark to commissioner of Indian affairs, June 25, 1930, PRA, NA-CPR.

84. Minutes, PRRA, February 6, 1928, PRA, NA-CPR.

85. Ibid., January 22, 1929.

86. Lou Walker to Pine Ridge Agency, July 20, 1929; E. W. Jermark to Mrs. H. B. Billingley, July 29, 1929; W. O. Roberts to William Center, July 27, 1937; P. L.

Hallam to W. O. Roberts, July 28, 1938; and R. Walter White to Pine Ridge Agency, May 24, 1938; all in PRA, NA-CPR.

87. Case to Hermus Merrival, president, Pine Ridge Rodeo Association, July 29, 1929, PRA, NA-CPR.

88. "Pine Ridge Rodeo a Success," Rushville, Nebraska, newspaper clipping, 1932, PRA, NA-CPR.

89. King to E. W. Jermark, July 1929, PRA, NA-CPR.

90. Notice of receipt of $114.00 from Rodeo Association, Cheyenne River Agency, September 23, 1927, CRA; E. W. Jermark to Hermus Merrival, September 12, 1929, PRA; Frank Goings to James H. McGregor, September 16, 1933, PRA; and Dempster and O'Connell Hardware, Gordon, Nebraska, to Pine Ridge Agency, July 26, 1930, PRA; all in NA-CPR.

91. Goings to James H. McGregor, August 30, 1933, PRA, NA-CPR.

92. B. G. Courtright, field agent in charge, to Hermus Merrival, June 18, 1931; Merrival to E. W. Jermark, August 4, 1928; Dorothy Arnold to James H. McGregor, August 7, 1933; E. E. Kobernusz to mayor of Pine Ridge, June 17, 1929; and anonymous to Mr. President (Hermus Merrival), Pine Ridge, January 19, 1929; all in PRA, NA-CPR.

93. Minutes, PRRA, February 12, 1928, PRA, NA-CPR.

94. Anonymous to Mr. President, January 19, 1929, PRA, NA-CPR.

95. Minutes, PRRA, November 16, 1928, PRA, NA-CPR.

96. Ibid., January 22, 1929.

97. McGregor to Merrival, July 11, 1933; Jermark to Charles Yellow Boy, July 22, 1930; McGregor to Goings, May 17, 1932; all in PRA, NA-CPR.

98. Minutes, PRRA, February 6, 1928, PRA, NA-CPR.

99. Pine Ridge Rodeo Association, Consideration on Basis for Pine Ridge Rodeo, 1928, PRA, NA-CPR.

100. Jermark to commissioner of Indian affairs, June 25, 1930, PRA, NA-CPR.

101. Courtright to Merrival, June 18, 1931, PRA, NA-CPR.

102. Program, Pine Ridge Sioux Rodeo, August 2, 1929; Official Rules, Pine Ridge Sioux Rodeo, 1928; both in PRA, NA-CPR.

103. Program, Pine Ridge Sioux Rodeo, August 2, 1929; *Shannon County News*, August 6, 1931.

104. Merrival to Pine Ridge Rodeo Association, July 21, 1933; McGregor to Charles Gerber, August 15, 1933; Goings to McGregor, May 10, 1934, and May 28, 1934; all in PRA, NA-CPR.

105. Hoxie, *Parading through History*, 295, 306.

106. Iverson, *When Indians Became Cowboys*, 140; R. E. Coulter, Pine Ridge agricultural extension agent, to Guy McDonald, Agricultural Extension Service, August 30, 1939, PRA, NA-CPR; Hoxie, *Parading through History*, 342; Superintendent Hyde, CA, to Commissioner C. J. Rhoads, September 19, 1933, CA, NA-RMR.

## CHAPTER THREE

1. Lawrence C. Kelly, *Assault on Assimilation*. The provisions of the Indian Reorganization Act and the Crows' rejection of it are described later in this chapter.

2. Hoxie, *Parading through History*, 328.

3. Ibid., 326–27.

4. Joseph Medicine Crow, *From the Heart of Crow Country*, 107–8.

5. Hoxie, *Parading through History*, 328–33.

6. Ibid., 333–34.

7. Ibid., 334–35.

8. Ibid., 341.

9. Ibid., 339–341

10. Ibid., 335.

11. Robert Yellowtail, Copy of remarks before the National Emergency Council, Billings, Montana, April 10, 1936.     Robert Yellowtail Speeches, Montana Historical Society Archives, Helena. The IECW (Indian Emergency Conservation Work) was an agency established to provide support for Indians through New Deal agencies like CCC-ID (Civilian Conservation Corps—Indian Division).

12. Ibid., 4.

13. Superintendent Robert Yellowtail, CA, to J. Thomas, Editorial Department, August 28, 1936, CA, NA-RMR.

14. Ibid., 2.

15. *Absaroka kkuxce, The Crow Helper* no. 1 (1932), Joseph Medicine Crow Collection.

16. Ibid., 4.

17. Ibid., 4–5.

18. Hoxie, *Parading through History*, 336.

19. Ibid., 336.

20. Ibid., 333–34.

21. Ibid., 333–34.

22. Ibid., 342; Hoxie asserts that Crow processions symbolized that the Crows were a people who had adapted their traditional cultural, religious, and economic practices to a new setting, and were led by politicians, who protected their independence. Statements regarding the status of Crow military veterans and their defense of Crow independence as Crows as well as Americans are the author's own assessment.

23. Superintendent Robert Yellowtail to J. E. Shields, principal, Riverside Indian School, Anadarko, Oklahoma, July 6, 1937, BIA, "Crow Tribal Fair 1937," CA, NA-RMR.

24. West, *The Enduring Seminoles*, xv.

25. Circular marketing Crow Tribal Fair, 1938, "Crow Tribal Fair 1938," CA, NA-RMR.

26. Hoxie, *Parading through History*, 331; *Hardin Tribune-Herald*, May 4, 1934.

27. Superintendent Robert Yellowtail to J. E. Shields, principal, Riverside Indian school, Anadarko, Oklahoma, July 6, 1937, BIA, "Crow Tribal Fair 1937." NA-RMR

28. Robert Yellowtail, "A Conscious Citizenship," undated, BIA, "Folder: 045 Addresses and Speeches," Box 98, RG 75, NA-RMR; Parman, *Indians and the American West*, 76.

29. Robert Yellowtail, "A Conscious Citizenship," "Folder: 045 Addresses and Speeches," Box 98, RG 75, NA-RMR.

30. *Hardin Tribune-Herald*, September 7, 1934.

31. Ibid., August 16, 1935; August 7, 1936

32. Superintendent Robert Yellowtail to H. L. Fitton, manager, Midland Empire Fair, July 21, 1937, "Crow Tribal Fair 1937," CA, NA-RMR.

33. Superintendent Robert Yellowtail, CA, to commissioner of Indian affairs, CA, NA-RMR.

34. Superintendent Robert Yellowtail, CA, to Governor Roy E. Ayres, Helena, Montana, June 26, 1937, CA, NA-RMR.

35. Superintendent Robert Yellowtail, CA, to editor, *Hardin Tribune-Herald*, August 22, 1938, CA, NA-RMR; *Hardin Tribune-Herald*, August 25, 1938.

36. Circular, To Whom It May Concern from Superintendent Robert Yellowtail, CA, August 20, 1940, CA, NA-RMR; *Hardin Tribune-Herald*, August 8, 1940.

37. "Governor Ayres Leads Crow Fair Parade," (newspaper unknown), August 28, 1940, CA, NA-RMR.

38. *Hardin Tribune-Herald*, August 29, 1940.

39. Ibid., August 30, 1935.

40. Superintendent Robert Yellowtail, CA, to Mr. Croonquest, secretary, Dude Ranchers' Association, Billings, Montana, August 21, 1936, CA, NA-RMR.

41. Walter C. Nye, Dude Ranchers' Association, to Superintendent Robert Yellowtail, July 30, 1938, CA, NA-RMR.

42. Superintendent Robert Yellowtail, CA, to secretary of the chamber of commerce, Bozeman, Montana, August 31, 1936, CA, NA-RMR.

43. H. L. Buck, secretary-manager, Billings Commercial Club, Billings, Montana, to Superintendent Robert Yellowtail, June 3, 1937, CA, NA-RMR.

44. Superintendent Robert Yellowtail, CA, to the merchants of CA, August 15, 1938; Superintendent Robert Yellowtail, CA, to the merchants of Hardin, August 15, 1938; both in "Crow Tribal Fair, 1938," CA, NA-RMR.

45. Superintendent Robert Yellowtail, CA, to Indian Office employees August 30, 1938, CA, NA-RMR.

46. Superintendent Robert Yellowtail, CA, to manager, Sheridan Press, Sheridan, Wyo., August 20, 1940, CA, NA-RMR.

47. Letter to Mr. Paul J. Malone, sports editor, *Billings Gazette*, Billings, Montana, May 23, 1939, "Crow Tribal Fair, 1939," CA, NA-RMR.

48. Superintendent Robert Yellowtail, CA, Montana, Letter to Mr. Bob Frazier, Billings Hudson Company, Billings, Montana, July 30, 1941, "Crow Tribal Fair, 1939," CA, NA-RMR.

49. Memorandum for the Press, Department of Interior, July 13, 1937, "Advertising in relation to Crow Tribal Fair," CA, NA-RMR.

50. Circular marketing Crow Tribal Fair, 1938, "Crow Tribal Fair 1938," CA, NA-RMR.

51. Superintendent Robert Yellowtail, CA, to J. E. Shields, principal, Riverside Indian School, Anadarko, Oklahoma, July 6, 1937, "Crow Tribal Fair 1937," CA, NA-RMR.

52. Florence Lee White, New York City, to Superintendent Robert Yellowtail, July 16, 1938, "Crow Tribal Fair, 1938," CA, NA-RMR.

53. *New York Times*, August 28, 1938.

54. Superintendent Robert Yellowtail, CA, to J. Thomas, Editorial Department, Letters, New York, August 28, 1936, "Fairs and Expositions, Indians for," CA, NA-RMR.

55. Superintendent Robert Yellowtail, CA, to Nathan Tufts, Ruthrauff and Ryan, Inc., New York City, July 28, 1941, "Crow Fair, year of 1941" CA, NA-RMR.

56. Superintendent Robert Yellowtail, CA, to Oscar Boy, Browning, Montana, August 10, 1936, "Fairs and Expositions, Indians for," CA, NA-RMR.

57. Superintendent Robert Yellowtail, CA, to J. E. Shields, principal, Riverside Indian School, Anadarko, Oklahoma, July 6, 1937, "Crow Tribal Fair 1937," CA, NA-RMR.

58. Superintendent Robert Yellowtail, CA, to Marian E. Hall, editor, *Indians at Work*, Washington, D.C., July 16, 1938, "Crow Tribal Fair 1937," CA, NA-RMR.

59. Circular, Superintendent Robert Yellowtail, CA, to superintendents of reservation agencies, August 20, 1940, "Crow Tribal Fair, 1939," CA, NA-RMR.

60. Superintendent Robert Yellowtail, CA, to Stuart Hazlett, chairman, Blackfeet Tribal Council, Browning, Montana, August 10, 1938, "Crow Tribal Fair 1938," CA, NA-RMR.

61. Superintendent Robert Yellowtail, CA, to Mr. Smith, August 1, 1938, "Crow Tribal Fair 1938," CA, NA-RMR.

62. Superintendent Robert Yellowtail, CA, to Paul J. Malone, *Billings Gazette*, Billings, Montana, May 23, 1939, "Crow Tribal Fair 1939," CA, NA-RMR.

63. Superintendent Robert Yellowtail, CA, to Lawrence Two Axe, Oakland, California, June 16, 1939, "Crow Tribal Fair 1939," CA, NA-RMR.

64. Circular, for League of Nations of North American Indians Third Annual National Council of Chiefs, Crow Reservation, CA, Montana, 1939, "Crow Tribal Fair 1939," CA, NA-RMR.

65. Superintendent Robert Yellowtail, CA, to Basil D. Peone, Worley, Idaho, July 28, 1939, "Crow Tribal Fair 1939," CA, NA-RMR.

66. Circular, Superintendent Robert Yellowtail, CA, to superintendents of reservation agencies, August 14, 1939, "Crow Tribal Fair, 1939," CA, NA-RMR.

67. *Hardin Tribune-Herald*, August 8, 1940.

68. Superintendent Robert Yellowtail, CA, to M. J. Thomas, Editorial Department, New York, August 28, 1936; Superintendent Robert Yellowtail, CA, to Oscar Boy, Browning, Montana, August 10, 1936, "Fairs and Expositions, Indians for," CA, NA-RMR.

69. *Hardin Tribune-Herald*, September 1, 1938.

70. Superintendent Robert Yellowtail, CA, to Wades in the Water, Browning, Montana, August 21, 1936, "Fairs and Expositions, Indians for," CA, NA-RMR.

71. Superintendent Robert Yellowtail, CA, to Thomas Main, Hays, Montana, July 16, 1938; Superintendent Robert Yellowtail, CA, to James P. Williams of Ponca City, Oklahoma, August 10, 1938; both in "Crow Tribal Fair 1938," CA, NA-RMR.

72. *Hardin Tribune-Herald*, August 28, 1936.

73. Ibid., August 7, 1936.

74. Ibid., July 23, 1937.

75. *Hardin Tribune-Herald*, September 7, 1934.

76. Ibid., August 30, 1935.

77. Superintendent Robert Yellowtail, CA, to Oscar Boy, Browning, Montana, August 10, 1936, "Fairs and Expositions, Indians for," CA, NA-RMR.

78. *Hardin Tribune-Herald*, July 23, 1937.

79. Ibid., September 4, 1936.

80. Program, The Plains Indian Pow-Wow, Pageant: The Crow Tribal Fair-Rodeo, August 29–September 12, 1938, "Crow Tribal Fair 1938," CA, NA-RMR.

81. *Hardin Tribune-Herald*, August 25, 1938.

82. Program, Crow Fair and Rodeo, September 1, 1938, Joseph Medicine Crow Collection.

83. Superintendent Robert Yellowtail, CA, to general manager, Sheridan Iron Works, Sheridan, Wyoming, July 23, 1938, "Crow Tribal Fair 1938," CA, NA-RMR; *Hardin Tribune-Herald*, August 25, 1938.

84. Program, The Plains Indian Pow-Wow, Pageant: The Crow Tribal Fair-Rodeo, August 29–September 12, 1938, "Crow Tribal Fair 1938," CA, NA-RMR.

85. *Hardin Tribune-Herald*, August 7, 1936.

86. Ibid., September 7, 1934.

87. Ibid., August 7, 1936.

88. Superintendent Robert Yellowtail, CA, to Ruthrauff and Ryan, Inc., New York City, July 21, 1941, "Crow Fair, year of 1941," CA, NA-RMR.

89. Program, Crow Indian Fair and Rodeo Program, August 26–30, 1940, "Crow Tribal Fair 1940," CA, NA-RMR; *Hardin Tribune-Herald*, August 22, 1940.

90. Ibid., August 28, 1936.

91. Barrett, G. E., "Crow Indians Hold Second Annual Tribal Fair," *Scenic Trails*, October 1937, 11.

92. Hugh B. Nash, C. E. Erikson Company, Specialty Manufactures, Rapid City, South Dakota, to Superintendent Robert Yellowtail, April 11, 1938, "Crow Tribal Fair 1938," CA, NA-RMR.

93. Superintendent Robert Yellowtail, CA, to H. W. Willcutt, Hardin, Montana, July 16, 1938, "Crow Tribal Fair 1938," CA, NA-RMR.

94. Superintendent Robert Yellowtail, CA, to Paul J. Malone, *Billings Gazette*, Billings, Montana, May 23, 1939, "Crow Tribal Fair 1939," CA, NA-RMR.

95. Program, The Plains Indian Pow-Wow, Pageant: The Crow Tribal Fair-Rodeo, August 29–September 12, 1938, "Crow Tribal Fair 1938," CA, NA-RMR.

96. *Hardin Tribune-Herald*, August 21, 1941.

97. Superintendent Robert Yellowtail, CA, to Mr. H. B. Sanderson, Deputy Game Warden, Greybull, Wyoming, August 19, 1941, "Crow Fair, year of 1941," CA, NA-RMR.

98. Commissioner of Indian affairs to Superintendent Robert Yellowtail, April 8, 1941, "Crow Fair, year of 1941," CA, NA-RMR.

99. Superintendent Robert Yellowtail, CA, to commissioner of Indian affairs, April 11, 1941, "Crow Fair, year of 1941," CA, NA-RMR.

100. Superintendent Robert Yellowtail, CA, to Paul J. Malone, *Billings Gazette*, Billings, Montana, May 23, 1939, "Crow Tribal Fair 1939," CA, NA-RMR.

101. Announcement, 1936 Crow Fair and Rodeo, "Fairs and Expositions, Indians for," CA, NA-RMR.

102. Superintendent Robert Yellowtail, CA, to J. E. Shields, principal, Riverside Indian School, Anadarko, Oklahoma, July 16, 1938, "Crow Tribal Fair 1937," CA, NA-RMR.

103. Superintendent Robert Yellowtail, CA, to Wades in the Water, Browning, Montana, August 21, 1936, "Fairs and Expositions, Indians for," CA, NA-RMR.

104. *Hardin Tribune-Herald*, August 7, 1936.

105. Program, The Plains Indian Pow-Wow, Pageant: The Crow Tribal Fair-Rodeo, August 29–September 12, 1938, "Crow Tribal Fair 1938," CA, NA-RMR.

106. Robert Lowie, 1883–1957, was an anthropologist who studied the Crows extensively. His works focusing explicitly on the Crows include *Myths and Traditions of the Crow Indians* (New York: Farrar and Rinehart, 1918); *The Crow Indians* (New York: Holt, Rinehart & Winston, 1935); and *The Crow Language, Grammatical Sketch and Analyzed Text* (Berkeley: University of California Press, 1941).

107. Schimmel, "Inventing the Indian."

108. *Hardin Tribune-Herald*, August 28, 1936.

109. Superintendent Robert Yellowtail, CA, to commissioner of Indian affairs, July 16, 1938, "Crow Tribal Fair 1938," CA, NA-RMR.

110. *Hardin Tribune-Herald*, August 28, 1936.

111. Superintendent Robert Yellowtail, CA, to. J. E. Shields, principal, Riverside Indian School, Anadarko, Oklahoma, July 6, 1937, "Crow Tribal Fair 1937," CA, NA-RMR.

112. Superintendent Robert Yellowtail, CA, to Mr. Croonquest, secretary, Dude Ranchers' Association, Billings, Montana, August 21, 1936, "Fairs and Expositions, Indians for," CA, NA-RMR.

113. *Hardin Tribune-Herald*, July 23, 1937.

114. Superintendent Robert Yellowtail, CA, to manager, Sheridan Press, Sheridan, Wyoming, August 20, 1940, "Crow Tribal Fair, 1940," CA, NA-RMR.

115. Prucha, *The Great Father*, 218.

116. Press release, "Nation Wide Hookup To Advertise Events of the Crow Fair," from Superintendent Robert Yellowtail, CA, Montana, August 4, 1941, "Crow Fair, year of 1941," CA, NA-RMR.

117. Superintendent Robert Yellowtail, CA, to Nathan Tufts, Ruthrauff and Ryan, Inc., New York, July 28, 1941, "Crow Fair, year of 1941," CA, NA-RMR.

118. *Hardin Tribune-Herald*, July 23, 1937.

119. Program, The Plains Indian Pow-Wow, Pageant: The Crow Tribal Fair-Rodeo, CA, August 29–September 12, 1938, "Crow Tribal Fair 1938," CA, NA-RMR.

120. Superintendent Robert Yellowtail, CA, to Ruthrauff and Ryan, Inc., New York City, July 21, 1941, "Crow Fair, year of 1941," CA, NA-RMR.

121. Flatlip, interview.

122. Kelleher, "Something to Crow About."

123. Voget, *The Shoshoni-Crow Sun Dance*; Thomas Yellowtail, *Yellowtail, Crow Medicine Man and Sun Dance Chief*.

124. *Hardin Tribune-Herald*, August 21, 1941.

125. Superintendent Robert Yellowtail, CA, to H. B. Sanderson, Deputy Game Warden, Greybull, Wyoming, August 19, 1941, "Crow Fair, year of 1941," CA, NA-RMR.

126. Superintendent Robert Yellowtail, CA, to Ruthrauff and Ryan, Inc., New York City, July 21, 1941, "Crow Fair, year of 1941," CA, NA-RMR.

127. Ibid.

128. Superintendent Robert Yellowtail, CA, to Private Stephen M. Driftwood Jr., Casper, Wyoming, July 1, 1943, "Requests for furloughs Sun Dance, 1943," CA, NA-RMR.

129. Bull over Hill, interview.

130. Hoxie, *Parading through History*, 342.

131. Program, Crow Fair and Rodeo, September 1, 1938, Joseph Medicine Crow Collection; Program, The Plains Indian Pow-Wow, Pageant: The Crow Tribal Fair-Rodeo, CA, August 29–September 12, 1938, "Crow Tribal Fair 1938," CA, NA-RMR.

132. Program, The Plains Indian Pow-Wow, Pageant: The Crow Tribal Fair-Rodeo, CA, August 29–September 12, 1938, "Crow Tribal Fair 1938," CA, NA-RMR.

133. Frey, *The World of the Crow*, 27.

134. Klein and Ackerman, eds., *Women and Power in Native North America*, 8–9. Lowie, *The Crow Indians*, 61.

135. Program, The Plains Indian Pow-Wow, Pageant: The Crow Tribal Fair-Rodeo, CA, August 29–September 12, 1938, "Crow Tribal Fair 1938," CA, NA-RMR.

136. Maeser-Lemieux, 125. Acoose, *Iskwewak-Kah' Ki Yaw Ni Wahkomakanak*, 43–44.

137. Banet-Weiser, *The Most Beautiful Girl in the World*.

138. Kelly Crow, "Princess and the Pageantry," 40.

139. Program, The Plains Indian Pow-Wow, Pageant: The Crow Tribal Fair-Rodeo, CA, August 29–September 12, 1938, "Crow Tribal Fair 1938," CA, NA-RMR.

140. Medicine Crow, *From the Heart of Crow Country*, 11.

141. *Hardin Tribune-Herald*, August 28, 1936.

142. Ibid., July 23, 1937.

143. Program, The Plains Indian Pow-Wow, Pageant: The Crow Tribal Fair-Rodeo, CA, August 29–September 12, 1938, "Crow Tribal Fair 1938," CA, NA-RMR.

144. Program, Crow Indian Fair and Rodeo, August 26–30, 1940, "Crow Tribal Fair 1940," CA, NA-RMR; *Hardin Tribune-Herald*, August 22, 1940.

145. Lowie, *The Crow Indians*, 226–27. See chapter one for Lowie's detailed description of the Crow warriors' homecoming ceremony.

146. Hoxie, *Parading through History*, 84.

147. *Hardin Tribune-Herald*, August 19, 1943; August 24, 1944; August 23, 1945; August 20, 1942; July 15, 1943.

148. Ibid., August 20, 1942.

149. Ibid., August 7, 1936.

150. Ibid., August 28, 1936.

151. Superintendent Robert Yellowtail, CA, to commissioner of Indian affairs, April 11, 1941, "Crow Fair, year of 1941," CA, NA-RMR.

152. *Hardin Tribune-Herald*, August 30, 1935; August 7, 1936.

153. Barrett, "Crow Indians Hold Second Annual Tribal Fair."

154. Loeb, "Crow Beadwork, the Resilience of Cultural Values."

155. Ibid., 46 and 32.

156. Mae Takes Gun, interview for New Deal in Montana Oral History Project, May 10, 1989, Montana Historical Society, Helena.

157. Superintendent Robert Yellowtail, CA, to Oscar Boy, Browning, Montana, August 10, 1936, "Fairs and Expositions, Indians for," CA, NA-RMR.

158. Program, Crow Indian Fair and Rodeo, August 26–30, 1940, "Crow Tribal Fair 1940," CA, NA-RMR; *Hardin Tribune-Herald*, August 22, 1940.

159. R. E. Coulter, agricultural extension agent, Pine Ridge, South Dakota, to Guy McDonald, Agricultural Extension Service, Brookings, South Dakota, August 30, 1939, "Local Fair and Rodeo: Correspondence and Programs," PRA, NA-CPR.

160. Superintendent W. O. Roberts, Pine Ridge, to Charles N. Granville Jr., Chicago, January 23, 1941, PRA, NA-CPR.

161. Philip S. Byrnes, secretary, Oglala Sioux Fair and Festival Committee, to "Fellow-worker," August 27, 1940, PRA, NA-CPR.

162. Superintendent W. O. Roberts, Pine Ridge, to Charles N. Granville Jr., Chicago, January 23, 1941, PRA, NA-CPR.

163. Souvenir Program and Premium for the Oglala Sioux Fair and Festival, Pine Ridge, September, 4, 5, 6, 1940, PRA, NA-CPR.

164. *Todd County Tribune*, September 12, 1935.

165. Ibid., August 15, 1935.

166. Ibid., July 11, 1940.
167. Ibid., June 26, 1941.
168. Ibid., July 16, 1942.
169. Ibid., September 23, 1944.
170. Ibid., June 28, 1945.
171. Ibid., September 10, 1936.
172. Ibid., September 1, 1938, and September 7, 1939.
173. Ibid., August 22, 1940.
174. Puten, Roberts, and Ferris, *Contrary Warriors.*

## CHAPTER FOUR

1. In a 1945 article for *Reader's Digest* entitled "Set the Indians Free!" Indian policy reformer O. K. Armstrong urged Congress to "emancipate" American Indians by removing the roadblocks imposed by federal trusteeship. He suggested that only then would Native American communities be liberated to soar to new heights now denied them. The call for the "emancipation" of Native Americans from a restrictive Bureau of Indian Affairs eventually took the form of the federal Indian policy known as termination. Iverson, *We Are Still Here,* 120–21.
2. Iverson, "Building toward Self Determination," 163–73;
3. O'Brien, *American Indian Tribal Governments,* 86–87.
4. Ibid., 86. The Bureau of Indian Affairs Relocation Program was instituted with the passage of Public Law 959 in 1956. It provided "funds for institutional and on-the-job training for Indians.... The act, however, did not make these opportunities available on the reservation. To obtain training, Indians had to relocate to urban areas.... Although an estimated 35,000 individuals relocated in the late 1950s, the act's goal of abolishing Indians' ties to their reservations and cultures was not realized. More than one-third returned home within a few years."
5. Iverson, *We Are Still Here,* 159.
6. Iverson and MacCannell, *Riders of the West,* 8.
7. LeCompte, *Cowgirls of the Rodeo,* 15.
8. Fact Sheet, All-Indian Rodeo Cowboys Association, Inc., 1994, in author's possession.
9. Pius Real Bird, founder of all-Indian rodeo at Crow Fair, telephone interview with author, April 11, 1995; *Hardin Tribune-Herald,* August 9, 1962.
10. LeCompte, *Cowgirls of the Rodeo,* 14.
11. Baillargeon, *Legends of Our Times,* 234–235.
12. Ibid., 234.
13. Iverson, *We Are Still Here,* 120.
14. Ibid., 121.
15. Ibid., 120.
16. Holm, "Fighting a White Man's War, 149–65.

17. Iverson, *We Are Still Here*, 120–21.

18. Holm, "Fighting a White Man's War," 149–65.

19. Ibid., 164–65.

20. Iverson, *We Are Still Here*, 120.

21. Iverson, "Building toward Self Determination," 163–73.

22. "The American Indian," (supplement to the *Shannon County News*), August 28, 1947.

23. Fowler, *Shared Symbols, Contested Meanings*, 145.

24. Cornell, *The Return of the Native*; Stewart, "Urbanization, Peoplehood and Modes of Identity"; Thomas, "Pan Indianism"; Stewart, "Peyotism in Montana"; Morris W. Foster, *Being Comanche*; Black Bear and Theis, *Songs and Dances of the Lakota*; William K. Powers, *War Dance*.

25. *Todd County Tribune*, July 1, 1968.

26. Iverson, *When Indians Became Cowboys*, 158–59.

27. Iverson, *We Are Still Here*, 121. It should be noted that some Indians subscribed fully to the idea of assimilation. As Peter Iverson points out, many Indians recognized that the postwar economic boom was centered in urban America, and they were eager to seize the opportunities offered there. But most wanted relocation to be voluntary and not required, and resented the heavy-handed tactics of congressional proponents, who had advocated reform through policies of termination and relocation.

28. From John Wooden Legs: My Message as President of the Northern Cheyenne Tribal Council to My People, 1964, 1963–69, File 2-1, Box 2, RG 25, Montana Office of the State Coordinator of Indian Affairs, MHSA.

29. Iverson, *We Are Still Here*, 107.

30. Iverson, *When Indians Became Cowboys*, 161.

31. General Report, Northern Cheyenne Tourist Center Enterprise, October 1962, 1965–68, File 2-6, Box 2, RG 25, Montana Office of the State Coordinator of Indian Affairs, MHSA.

32. Prucha, *The Great Father*, 1010-11.

33. General Report, Northern Cheyenne Tourist Center Enterprise, October 1962, 1965–68, File 2-6, Box 2, RG 25, Montana Office of the State Coordinator of Indian Affairs, MHSA.

34. From John Wooden Legs: My Message as President of the Northern Cheyenne Tribal Council to My People, 1964, 1963–69, File 2-1, Box 2, RG 25, Montana Office of the State Coordinator of Indian Affairs, MHSA.

35. *Rosebud Sioux Herald: Eyapaha*, June 21, 1965.

36. *Shannon County News*, May 21, 1964.

37. Ibid., June 2, 1968

38. Robert Yellowtail, Lodge Grass, Montana, to Bergan, state coordinator of Indian affairs, Helena, Montana, May 5, 1965, 1965–68, File 2-6, Box 2, RG 25, Montana Office of the State Coordinator of Indian Affairs, MHSA.

39. *Hardin Tribune-Herald*, August 28, 1947.

40. Ibid., August 3, 1950.

41. Ibid., August 23, 1962.

42. *Great Falls Tribune*, August 28, 1955, Collection 2245, Box 35, "Burlingame Papers—Indians: Crow Fair," 37: 13, MGBP.

43. Ibid.

44. Ibid.

45. Phillip Bull Mountain, secretary of Crow Indian Fair and Rodeo, to Eugene Fisher, president of the Northern Cheyenne Tribe, July 23, 1953, "Crow Fair and Rodeo, 1953–54," CA, NA-RMR.

46. *Hardin Herald-Tribune*, August 5, 1948.

47. Ibid., July 28, 1949.

48. Ibid., August 27, 1953; August 23, 1956.

49. Ibid., August 30, 1956.

50. Ibid., August 1, 1957.

51. Robert Yellowtail, statement before Senate Committee on Interior and Insular Affairs, on S. 2619, To Allow The Indians a Voice in the Selection of the Commissioner of Indian Affairs, April 8, 1952. Folder 2-17, 1951–69. MHSA.

52. *Great Falls Tribune*, August 28, 1955, Collection 2245, Box 35, "Burlingame Papers—Indians: Crow Fair," 37: 13. MGBP.

53. *Hardin Tribune-Herald*, August 5, 1948; Phillip Bull Mountain, secretary of Crow Indian Fair and Rodeo, to lessees, permittees and friends, July 22, 1953, "Crow Fair and Rodeo, 1953–54," CA, NA-RMR; Program, Crow Fair Race Meet, Sunday, July 11, 1953, "Crow Fair and Rodeo, 1953–54," CA, NA-RMR; Program, Crow Fair Race Meet, August 20, 1959, "Crow Fair and Rodeo, 1953–54," CA, NA-RMR; "Lodge Grass Youth Given Big Job; He's President of Annual Crow Fair," (unknown periodical), "Crow Reservation, 1951–69," Folder 2-17, Box 2, RG 25, Montana Office of the State Coordinator of Indian Affairs, MHSA.

54. *Hardin Tribune-Herald*, August 30, 1956.

55. "Lodge Grass Youth Given Big Job; He's President of Annual Crow Fair," (unknown periodical), "Crow Reservation, 1951–69," Folder 2-17, Box 2, RG 25, Montana Office of the State Coordinator of Indian Affairs," MHSA.

56. *Hardin Tribune-Herald*, August 30, 1956.

57. Ibid., August 20, 1959.

58. Ibid., August 23, 1956.

59. K. W. Bergan, coordinator of Indian affairs, Helena, Montana, to Daniel LaForge, Lodge Grass, Montana, January 30, 1962, "Crow Reservation, 1951–69," Folder 2-17, Box 2, RG 25, Montana Office of the State Coordinator of Indian Affairs." MHSA.

60. Daniel LaForge, Lodge Grass, Montana, to K. W. Bergan, coordinator of Indian affairs, Helena, Montana, January 31, 1962, "Crow Reservation, 1951–69,"

Folder 2-17, Box 2, RG 25, Montana Office of the State Coordinator of Indian Affairs." MHSA.

61. Baillargeon and Tepper, *Legends of Our Times*, 183.

62. *Hardin Tribune-Herald*, August 28, 1952; August 27, 1953.

63. Ibid., September 19, 1946.

64. Ibid., July 6, 1950.

65. Ibid., June 17, 1948; June 8, 1950; July 3, 1953; June 26, 1952; July 9, 1959.

66. *Hardin Tribune-Herald*, August 20, 1959.

67. Ibid.

68. Ibid., August 22, 1946.

69. *Hardin Tribune-Herald*, September 14, 1928; September 13, 1929.

70. Ibid., June 29, 1950.

71. Ibid., August 21, 1952.

72. Ibid., June 6, 1957.

73. McLaughlin, "The Big Lease"; Photo #PAC-89-1: Crow Indian Sampson Bird in Ground riding a buffalo at the Miles City Roundup, 1915, MHSA.

74. *Hardin Tribune-Herald*, June 5, 1958; June 6, 1959.

75. Ibid., June 17, 1948; June 6, 1957; June 14, 1951.

76. Ibid., June 10, 1948; June 28, 1951; June 19, 1952; June 24, 1954; June 20, 1957; June 6, 1959.

77. Ibid., September 19, 1946; June 5, 1958; June 6, 1959; August 20, 1959.

78. Ibid., July 6, 1950; July 19, 1951.

79. Ibid., August 5, 1948; August 27, 1953; August 26, 1954; August 30, 1956; August 1, 1957.

80. Ibid., August 23, 1956; August 20, 1959.

81. Ibid., August 9, 1962.

82. Pius Real Bird, telephone interview.

83. Borland, *When the Legends Die*.

84. *Hardin Tribune-Herald*, August 9, 1962.

85. Ibid., August 9, 1962; August 23, 1962; August 13, 1964.

86. Ibid., August 18, 1962; August 23, 1962; August 1, 1963; August 29, 1963.

87. Ibid., , August 13, 1964; August 27, 1964; August 19, 1965; August 26, 1965; August 27, 1964.

88. Ibid., August 17, 1967.

89. Program, Crow Celebration and All-Indian Rodeo, August 16, 17, 18 and 19, 1968, Joseph Medicine Crow Collection.

90. *Hardin Tribune-Herald*, August 24, 1967.

91. Ibid., August 15, 1968.

92. Ibid., August 14, 1969.

93. Ibid., September 4, 1958.

94. *Birney Arrow*, September 28, 1959; October 12, 1959.

95. Ibid., October 12, 1959.

96. Ibid., July 18, 1960.

97. Betty Clark, Association on American Indian Affairs, New York, to Bergan, state coordinator of Indian affairs, Helena, Montana, May 21, 1964, "Northern Cheyenne, 1962–67," File 4-16, Box 4, RG 25," Montana Office of the State Coordinator of Indian Affairs, "MHSA.

98. Iverson, "We Are Still Here," 179.

99. 1968 Pow Wow—Greatest Ever, unidentified periodical, "Northern Cheyenne–St. Labre Mission, 1958–70," File 4-20, Box 4, RG 25, Montana Office of the State Coordinator of Indian Affairs, MHSA.

100. *Todd County Tribune*, July 1, 1948; July 10, 1948; July 28, 1949; June 23, 1949; July 28,1949; August 26, 1954.

101. Ibid., August 3, 1950.

102. Ibid., September 1, 1960.

103. Ibid., July 4,1957; *Rosebud Sioux Herald: Eyapaha*, September 13, 1965.

104. *Todd County Tribune*, September 13, 1965.

105. Ibid., July 11,1957.

106. *Rosebud Sioux Herald: Eyapaha*, July 20, 1961.

107. Ibid., September 13, 1965.

108. *Todd County Tribune*, September 2, 1948; September 9, 1948; August 20, 1953; August 3, 1950.

109. Ibid., September 9, 1948; August 18, 1949; July 26, 1951; August 20, 1953.

110. Ibid., August 30, 1956; August 23, 1956; September 3, 1959.

111. Ibid., September 1, 1960; August 19, 1963; September 1, 1960; September 13, 1965; September 12, 1966.

112. Iverson, "We Are Still Here," 125–26.

113. *Shannon County News*, August 22, 1963.

114. Ibid., August 5, 1963.

115. Reinhardt, "Spontaneous Combustion," 229, 231. Reinhardt used this description to characterize the constituencies, which supported either Gerald One Feather or Richard "Dick" Wilson in their 1972 bids for the tribal chairmanship of Pine Ridge.

116. Ibid., 231.

117. *Shannon County News*, July 19, 1967.

118. Ibid., July 1,1968.

119. *Rosebud Sioux Herald: Eyapaha*, September 15, 1969.

120. Ibid., June 18, 1964.

121. Ibid., September 1, 1966.

122. Ibid., June 10, 1963.

123. Ibid., September 23, 1965.

124. *Shannon County News*, September 1, 1966.

125. *Rosebud Sioux Herald: Eyapaha*, August 9, 1962.

126. Ibid., September 1, 1969.

## CHAPTER FIVE

Note: Chapter title from Curtis Real Bird, Talking Broncs: interview with Curtis Real Bird, Little Big Horn College Oral History Project, February 7, 1995, LBHCA.

1. *Calgary (Alberta) Herald*, 10 February 1994.

2. Ibid.

3. Josephy, Nagel, and Johnson, eds., *The American Indian's Fight for Freedom*, 101.

4. Reinhardt, "Spontaneous Combustion," 229, 231. Two constituencies had emerged on the Pine Ridge reservation by 1972 that supported either Gerald One Feather or Richard "Dick" Wilson in their bids for the tribal chairmanship. Wilson's subsequent victory served to exacerbate tensions between the two groups, contributing to the friction that would ultimately ignite the seventy-one day standoff at Wounded Knee, which pitted Wilsonite tribal officials aided by "various arms of the United States government" against a group of traditionalist Lakota residents of the Pine Ridge reservation supported by members of the American Indian Movement, who had taken over the reservation town of Wounded Knee, South Dakota.

5. "Preamble of American Indian Hall of Fame Proposal," (unidentified source, found in the papers of Harold Schunk, superintendent of Rosebud reservation, 1959–68), HSC-CWS.

6. Father Paul Quinn, Herreid, South Dakota, to Father Stan, January 1, 1973, HSC-CWS.

7. List of Outstanding American Indian Athletes (unidentified source), HSC-CWS.

8. AIHF, A Preliminary Report on the American Indian Hall of Fame, for the American Indian by the American Indian, HSC-CWS.

9. "Sioux Nation Rodeo," *American Cowboy*.

10. Ibid.

11. *Sioux Nation Cowboy News* (January 1980), Oglala Lakota College Archives, Kyle, South Dakota.

12. "Oglala Sioux Nation Honors Rodeo Greats," *Lakota Times/Indian Country Today*, 1996.

13. Clem McSpadden, general manager and cofounder of the Indian National Finals Rodeo, at the 1996 Indian National Finals Rodeo in Saskatoon, Saskatchewan, interview with the author, November 1, 1996. Clem McSpadden recalled six or seven all-Indian rodeo associations that had formed in the 1970s.

14. Iverson, *Riders of the West*, 18–20.

15. Ibid., 20–21

16. *Mellette County News*, August 11, 1977.

17. Ibid., 20–21.

18. Ibid., 20–23; Clem McSpadden, letter to author, October 20, 1994.

19. Baillargeon, *Legends of Our Times*, 235–36.

20. *Rosebud Sioux Herald: Eyapaha*, September 21, 1970.

21. Iverson, *Riders of the West,* 23.

22. Clem McSpadden, general manager and cofounder of the Indian National Finals Rodeo, at the 1996 Indian National Finals Rodeo in Saskatoon, Saskatchewan, November 1, 1996.

23. Iverson, *When Indians Became Cowboys*, 194; Iverson, *Riders of the West,* 23.

24. *Sioux Nation Cowboy News* (January 1980), OLCA.

25. Iverson, *Riders of the West*, 23–24.

26. Ibid., 24.; Indian National Finals Rodeo Fact Sheet, 1994. Given to author by Clem McSpadden, October 20, 1994.

27. *Lakota Times*, June 24, 1982.

28. Ibid., September 28, 1983.

29. *Rapid City Journal*, 30 January 1994.

30. Ibid., 3.

31. McSpadden, interview, November 1, 1996.

32. Ibid.

33. Ibid.

34. Ibid.

35. *Rapid City Journal,* January 30, 1994.

36. McSpadden, interview, November 1, 1996.

37. Ibid.

38. Program, 1996 Indian National Finals Rodeo, Federation of Saskatchewan Indian Nations, October 31–November 3, 1996, 10. In possession of author.

39. Ibid., 3.

40. McSpadden, interview, November 1, 1996.

41. Mike Not Afraid, Northern Cheyenne barrel racer; Sharon Small, Pine Ridge Lakota bull rider; Smiley Sierra; and Guy Colombe, Rosebud Lakota bareback riders, interview with the author at the 1996 Indian National Finals Rodeo, October 31–November 3, 1996, Saskatoon, Saskatchewan.

42. McSpadden, interview, November 1, 1996.

43. "Howard Hunter, the Cowboy from Wounded Knee," unidentified source, 1976, "Indian cowboy, Howard Hunter, Ca., 1970s," Folder 2, Box 1, SC 70, OLCA.

44. Ibid.

45. *Indian Country Today,* 1996.

46. *Rapid City Journal*, January 30, 1980.

47. "Indian Cowboy Howard Hunter," *Western Horseman*, 1975. SC 10, Box 1, Folder 2, "Indian cowboy, Howard Hunter, Ca., 1970s, OLCA.

48. *Minneapolis Tribune*, December 7, 1972.

49. *Rapid City Journal*, January 30, 1980.

50. *Minneapolis Tribune*, December 7, 1972.

51. "Indian Cowboy Howard Hunter," *Western Horseman*, 1975, SC 10, Box 1, Folder 2, "Indian cowboy, Howard Hunter, Ca., 1970s, OLCA.

52. One of state's top cowboys," (unknown journal), 1971, SC 10, Box 1, Folder 2, "Indian Cowboy, Howard Hunter, Ca. 1970s," OLCA.

53. *Minneapolis Tribune*, December 7, 1972.

54. "Indian Cowboy, Howard Hunter," *Western Horseman*, 1975, SC 10, Box 1, Folder 2, "Indian cowboy, Howard Hunter, Ca., 1970s, OLCA.

55. *Minneapolis Tribune*, December 7, 1972.

56. "Indian Cowboy, Howard Hunter," *Western Horseman*, 1975, SC 10, Box 1, Folder 2, "Indian cowboy, Howard Hunter, Ca., 1970s," OLCA.

57. *Shannon County News*, September 21, 1973.

58. "Indian Cowboy, Howard Hunter," *Western Horseman*, 1975, SC 10, Box 1, Folder 2, "Indian cowboy, Howard Hunter, Ca., 1970s," OLCA.

59. "Kyle cowboy top winner," unknown source, 1974, SC 10, Box 1, Folder 2, "Indian cowboy, Howard Hunter, Ca., 1970s," OLCA.

60. "Howard Hunter, the Cowboy from Wounded Knee," unknown source, 1976, SC 10, Box 1, Folder 2, "Indian cowboy, Howard Hunter, Ca., 1970s," OLCA.

61. "San Antonio Rodeo, Hunter Rides On!" unknown source, 1976, SC 10, Box 1, Folder 2, "Indian cowboy, Howard Hunter, Ca., 1970s," OLCA.

62. "Howard Hunter," *Hoof and Horn*, 1977.

63. *Rapid City Journal*, January 30, 1980.

64. Ibid., January 30, 1980.

65. "Howard Hunter, the Cowboy from Wounded Knee," unknown source, 1976, SC 10, Box 1, Folder 2, "Indian cowboy, Howard Hunter, Ca., 1970s," OLCA.

66. "Howard Hunter," *Hoof and Horn*, 1977.

67. *Rapid City Journal*, January 30, 1980.

68. "One of state's top cowboys," unknown source, 1971, SC 10, Box 1, Folder 2, OLCA; "Indian Cowboy, Howard Hunter," *Hoof and Horn*, 1977.

69. Howard Hunter," *Hoof and Horn*, 1977.

70. Ibid.

71. *Lakota Times/Indian Country Today*, 1996.

72. "Howard Hunter," *Hoof and Horn*, 1977, OLCA.

73. *Lakota Times*, April 29, 1982.

74. *Rosebud Sioux Herald: Eyapaha*, July 6, 1970.

75. Ibid., June 29, 1970.

76. *Lakota Times*, April 29, 1982.

77. Ibid.

78. Ibid.

79. McSpadden, interview, November 1, 1996.

80. *Lakota Times*, July 16, 1981.

81. Iverson, *We Are Still Here*, 160–162.

82. *Oglala Wicahpi*, A publication of the Media Communications Program at Oglala Lakota College, February 1985, SC13-36, Box 1-6, Jeanne Smith's Research Collection, No. 1, OLCA.

83. Phillip Whiteman Jr., Busby, Montana, letter to author, October 21, 1994.

84. *Indian Country Today*, October 12, 1994.

85. Programs, Crow Fair, Joseph Medicine Crow Collection.

86. Schedule, Crow Fair and Rodeo, August 18–22, 1994, Joseph Medicine Crow Collection.

87. For a discussion of pre-reservation "clan bonds and responsibilities" that required Crows to "giveaway" when "honoring and repaying" clan members, thereby fulfilling one's obligation to "contribute material wealth . . . to his own matrilineal and clan relatives," see Voget, *The Shoshone-Crow Sun Dance*, 32–33.

88. Frederick Hoxie, *Parading through History*, 195, 219, 225. Hoxie explains the Crows' development of "religious pluralism" that ensured that traditional cultural expressions would continue despite the arrival of Christianity on the reservation."

89. Della Big Hair, interview.

90. Randy Falls Down, Crow rodeo cowboy, letter to author, October 28, 1994.

91. Willis Tsosia, letter to author, October 27, 1994.

92. Albert Caphill Jr., letter to author, October 14, 1994.

93. Marlon B. Passes, letter to author, October 14, 1994.

94. Lloyd Pickett, letter to author, October 20, 1994.

95. Kelly Passes, letter to author, October 17, 1994.

96. Marlon B. Passes, letter to author, October 14, 1994.

97. Lonn A. Fitzler, letter to author, November 7, 1994.

98. Albert Caphill Jr., letter to author, October 14, 1994.

99. Sarah Bird, *Virgin of the Rodeo*, 30.

100. McSpadden, interview, November 1, 1996.

101. Ibid.

102. *Mellette County News*, September 1, 1977.

103. Ibid., July 13, 1978.

104. Program, 64th Annual Crow Fair, August 18–22, 1982, Joseph Medicine Crow Collection.

105. Kelly Passes, letter to author, October 17, 1994.

106. Willis Tsosia, October 27, 1994.

107. Marlon Passes, interview.

108. Lloyd Pickett, letter to author, October 20,1994.

109. Albert Caphill Jr., letter to author, October 14, 1994.

110. *Mellette County News*, August 11, 1977.

111. McSpadden, interview, November 1, 1996.

112. Kelly Passes, letter to author, October 17, 1994.

113. Lonn A. Fitzler, Crow cowboy, letter to author, November 7, 1994.

114. Marlon B. Passes, letter to author, October 14, 1994.

115. McSpadden, interview, November 1, 1996.

116. *Melette County News*, August 15, 1974.

117. Ibid., July 13, 1978.

118. Ibid., June 26, 1980.

119. *Lakota Times*, September 24, 1981.

120. *Indian Country Today*, July 22–29, 1996.

121. *Todd County Tribune* and *Rosebud Sioux Herald: Eyapaha*, August 23, 1973.

122. Ibid., August 17, 1972.

123. *Mellette County News*, August 21, 1975.

124. Ibid., July 29, 1976.

125. Ibid., August 11, 1977.

126. Ibid., August 24, 1978; August 16, 1979.

127. Ibid., August 28, 1980.

128. Ibid., August 14, 1980.

129. *Lakota Times*, August 17, 1983.

130. *Mellette County News*, August 21, 1975.

131. Ibid., September 7, 1978.

132. Ibid., August 16, 1979.

133. *Mellette County News*, July 29, 1976.

134. Ibid., August 19, 1976.

135. Ibid., August 11, 1977.

136. *Todd County Tribune*, August 17, 1972; *Todd County Tribune* and *Rosebud Sioux Herald: Eyapaha*, August 23, 1973; August 22, 1974; *Mellette County News*, August 21, 1975; August 24, 1978.

137. *Mellette County News*, August 11, 1977.

138. Father Paul Quinn, Herreid, South Dakota, to Father Stan, January 1, 1973, HSC-CWS.

139. *Mellette County News*, August 11, 1977.

140. Ibid., August 11, 1977.

141. Ibid., August 29, 1974.

142. Ibid., August 19, 1976; Iverson, *When Indians Became Cowboys*, 74. The claim that the Rosebud Fair and Rodeo, or a precursor to it, began in 1877 is uncertain but not doubtful. Iverson documents that in 1897 a bronc ride concluded a six day celebration in Parmelee on the Rosebud reservation.

143. Ibid., August 24, 1978.

144. Program, Crow Fair, "The Tepee Capital of the World," 1992, Joseph Medicine Crow Collection.

145. Della Big Hair, 1995 Miss Crow Nation, interview with author, February 22, 1995.

146. Program, Crow Fair, "The Tepee Capital of the World," 1992, August 12–17, 1992, Joseph Medicine Crow Collection. LBHCA.

147. Souvenir Program, Crow Indian Fair, Rodeo and Race Meet, August 14–19, 1975, Joseph Medicine Crow Collection. LBHCA.

148. Pius Real Bird, interview.

149. Curtis Real Bird, interview with author at the Real Birds' home and ranch in Garryowen, Montana, February 27, 1994.

150. Charles Real Bird, interview with the author at the Real Birds' home and ranch in Garryowen, Montana, February 24, 1995.

151. Shawn Real Bird, interview.

152. Curtis Real Bird, Talking Broncs: interview with Curtis Real Bird, Little Big Horn College Oral History Project, February 7, 1995, LBHCA.

153. Curtis Real Bird, interview with the author at the Real Birds' home and ranch in Garryowen, Montana, February 24, 1995.

154. Shawn Real Bird, interview.

155. Curtis Real Bird, interview, February 24, 1995.

156. Paul Hill, interview with the author at the Real Birds' home and ranch in Garryowen, Montana, February 24, 1995.

157. Joseph Medicine Crow, *From the Heart of Crow Country*.

## CONCLUSION

1. Hoxie, *Parading through History*, 295, 306.

2. Clem McSpadden, letter to the author, November 18, 1994.

# Bibliography

PRIMARY SOURCES

*Manuscript Collections*

American Indian Research Project, University of South Dakota, Vermillion.

Big Bat Pourier Collection, 1868–1969, Oglala Lakota College Archives, Kyle, South Dakota.

Cheyenne Frontier Days Souvenir Programs, American Heritage Center, University of Wyoming, Laramie.

Dorothy Mack Black Crow Collection, Oglala Lakota College Archives, Kyle, South Dakota.

Eloise White Bear Pease Collection, Little Big Horn College and Archives, Crow Agency, Montana.

Greenough Family Rodeo Collection, Carbon County Museum, Red Lodge, Montana.

Harold Schunk Collection, Center for Western Studies, Augustana College, Sioux Falls, South Dakota.

Howard Hunter, Indian Cowboy Collection, Oglala Lakota College Archives, Kyle, South Dakota.

Hoxie Crow Collection, Little Big Horn College and Archives, Crow Agency, Montana.

Jake Herman Collection, Indian rodeo clown, Oglala Lakota College Archives, Kyle, South Dakota.

Jeanne Smith's Research Collection: family and community histories of the Pine Ridge Reservation, 1800–1976, Oglala Lakota College Archives, Kyle, South Dakota.

Joseph Medicine Crow Collection, Little Big Horn College Archives, Crow Agency, Montana.

Martha Whiting Collection, ca. 1891–1983, Oglala Lakota College Archives, Kyle, South Dakota.

Merrill G. Burlingame Special Collections, Montana State University Library, Bozeman.

Montana Office of State Coordinator of Indian Affairs, 1930, 1948–71, Montana Historical Society and Archives, Helena, Montana.

National Archives, Regional Archives System—Central Plains Region, Kansas City, Missouri; Rocky Mountain Region, Denver, Colorado.
New Deal in Montana Oral History Project, Montana Historical Society and Archives, Helena.
Robert Yellowtail Speeches, 1936–57, Montana Historical Society and Archives, Helena.
Sioux Music and Pan-Indianism Collection, Oglala Lakota College Archives, Kyle, South Dakota.
U.S. Bureau of Outdoor Recreation: Lee Metcalf Papers, 1934–78: Crow Indian Reservation, Montana Historical Society and Archives, Helena.

*Newspapers*

*A'Atomone* (Ashland, Mont.), 1972–73, Merrill G. Burlingame Special Collections, Montana State University Library, Bozeman.
*Absaloka'a News* (Crow Agency, Mont.), Merrill G. Burlingame Special Collections, Montana State University Library, Bozeman.
*Absaroka* (Crow Agency, Mont.), 1968–70, Merrill G. Burlingame Special Collections, Montana State University Library, Bozeman.
*Absaroka kkuxce, The Crow Helper*, 1932, Joseph Medicine Crow Collection.
*Albertan (Calgary)*, May 1949.
"American Indian," a supplement to the *Shannon County News*, 1947.
*American Indian Journal* (Billings, Mont.), 1928, Montana Historical Society and Archives, Helena.
*Arrow* (Ashland, Mont.), 1934–36, Merrill G. Burlingame Special Collections, Montana State University Library, Bozeman.
*A'tome: Northern Cheyenne Press* (Lame Deer, Mont.), 1974–75, Merrill G. Burlingame Special Collections, Montana State University Library, Bozeman, Montana.
*Baawalaatpuuche* (Crow Agency, Mont.), 1977–80, Merrill G. Burlingame Special Collections, Montana State University Library, Bozeman.
*Billings (Mont.) Gazette*, 1978–94.
*Birney Arrow* (Birney and Busby, Mont.), 1958–71, Montana Historical Society and Archives, Helena.
*Calgary (Alberta) Herald*, 1991–94.
*Chicago Tribune*, 1987. *Dupree (S. Dak.) Leader*, 1910–24, South Dakota Historical Society, Pierre.
*E.D.P. (Economic Development Program) News:* Northern Cheyenne Tribe (Lame Deer, Mont.), 1971, Merrill G. Burlingame Special Collections, Montana State University Library, Bozeman.
*Eagle Butte (S. Dak.) News*, 1939–96, South Dakota Historical Society, Pierre, South Dakota.
*Faith (S. Dak.) Gazette*, 1910, South Dakota Historical Society, Pierre.

*Great Falls (Mont.) Tribune*, August 28, 1955.

*Hardin (Mont.) Tribune-Herald*, 1905–1996.

*The Indian*, 1969, Merrill G. Burlingame Special Collections, Montana State University Library, Bozeman.

*Lakota Times/Indian County Today*, 1981–92. Sinte Gleska College Archives. Mission, South Dakota, and South Dakota Historical Society Archives.

*Lakota Eyapaha*, 1977–81, South Dakota Historical Society, Pierre.

*Lewiston Morning Tribune*, July 12, 1990, and September 6, 1990.

*Mellette County News* (White River, S.Dak.), 1961–96, South Dakota Historical Society, Pierre, South Dakota.

*Minneapolis Tribune*, December 7, 1972.

*Morning Star News* (Lame Deer, Mont.), 1967. Merrill G. Burlingame Special Collections, Montana State University Library, Bozeman.

*Morning Star People* (St. Labre Indian School, Ashland, Mont.), 1965–96. Merrill G. Burlingame Special Collections, Montana State University Library, Bozeman.

*New York Times*, August 12, 1938, and June 18, 1989.

*Official Rumors* (Northern Cheyenne Agency, Lame Deer, Mont.), October 1970. Montana Historical Society and Archives, Helena.

*Oglala Light*, Pine Ridge, South Dakota, 1905–20, South Dakota Historical Society, Pierre.

*Rapid City Journal*, 1994.

*Rosebud Farmer*, 1916–17, South Dakota Historical Society, Pierre.

*Rosebud (S. Dak.) Sioux Herald: Eyapaha*, 1963–71, merged with *Mellette County News* (White River, S. Dak.), 1971–74, South Dakota Historical Society, Pierre.

*San Francisco Examiner*, April 10, 1994.

*Shannon County News* (Pine Ridge, S.Dak.), 1930–73, South Dakota Historical Society, Pierre.

*Sunset* (Albuquerque, N.Mex.), August 1986.

*Times* (Calgary, Alberta), August 14, 1980. Glenbow Museum, Art Gallery, Library, and Archives, Calgary.

*Todd County Tribune* (Mission, S. Dak.), 1921–96 , South Dakota Historical Society, Pierre.

*Western Horseman*, 1975.

*West River Progress* (Dupree, S. Dak.), 1936–96, South Dakota Historical Society, Pierre.

*Wyoming Tribune*, September 6, 1905.

## Interviews and Personal Communications

Benson, Michael. Letter to Governor Apodoca of New Mexico, June 13, 1976. State Commission of Public Records and Archives, Santa Fe.

Big Hair, Della, Miss Crow Nation. Interview by author, February 22, 1995.

Bull over Hill, Thomas. Interview for New Deal in Montana Oral History Project, 1987. Montana State Historical Society, Helena.

Bull Tail, John. Interview for New Deal in Montana Oral History Project, 1989. Montana State Historical Society, Helena.

Caphill, Albert Jr., Crow rodeo cowboy. Letter to author, October 14, 1994.

Colombe, Guy, Rosebud Lakota bareback rider. Interview by author at the 1996 Indian National Finals Rodeo, Saskatoon, Saskatchewan, October 31–November 3, 1996.

Craton, Lisa, Blood Indian rodeo cowgirl. Letter to author, October 7, 1994.

Cummins, John, team roper. Interview by author, February 24, 1995.

Cummins, Nicole, former Miss Crow Nation and prize barrel racer. Interview by author, February 24, 1995.

Falls Down, Randy, Crow rodeo cowboy. Letter to author, October 28, 1994.

Fitzler, Lonn A., Crow rodeo cowboy. Letter to author, November 7, 1994.

Flatlip, Laurence, Crow oral historian. Interview by author at Western Heritage Center, Billings, Montana, February 23, 1995.

Flynn, Shirley, Cheyenne, Wyoming, local historian. Interview by author, October 14, 1994.

Gray, Terry, Rosebud Sioux rodeo cowboy and Sinte Gleska University archivist. Interview by author at Sinte Gleska University, Mission, South Dakota, October 23, 1996.

Hill, Paul, novice bronc rider. Interview by author, February 24, 1995.

Hoover, Herbert T., professor of history at the University of South Dakota. Interview by author, South Dakota History Conference, Sioux Falls, South Dakota, May 31, 1997.

Legg, Jim, Bureau of Land Management official responsible for recording cattle grazing on the Pine Ridge reservation. Interview by author, South Dakota History Conference, Sioux Falls, South Dakota, May 31, 1997.

McSpadden, Clem, general manager of Indian National Finals Rodeo. Letter to author, November 18, 1994.

———. Interview by author at the Indian National Finals Rodeo, Saskatoon, Saskatchewan, November 1, 1996.

Medicine Horse, Magdeline, archivist at Little Big Horn College and Archives, Crow Agency, Montana. Interview by author, October 6, 1994.

Moses, L. G. "Indians in Wild West Shows." Lecture at the Buffalo Bill Historical Center, Cody, Wyoming, June 3, 1994.

Not Afraid, Mike, Crow steer wrestler. Interview by author at the 1996 Indian National Finals Rodeo, Saskatoon, Saskatchewan, October 31–November 3, 1996.

Passes, Kelly D., Crow rodeo cowboy. Letter to author, October 17, 1994.

Passes, Marlon, 1993 Crow Fair Rodeo manager. Interviews by author, October 14, 1994 and February 22, 1995.

Pease, Eloise White Bear. Interview by author, March 9, 1995.

Pickett, Lloyd, Crow rodeo cowboy. Letter to author, October 20, 1994.

———, Crow rodeo cowboy. Interview by author, February 22, 1995.

Powers, Wila, Heard Museum: Native Cultures and Arts, Phoenix. Interview by author, October 19, 1994.

Pretty-on-Top, Burton, Crow Fair public relations manager. Interview by author, April 12, 1995.

Pullen, Roberta, Lewiston, Montana, Historical Society. Letter to author, October 26, 1994.

Real Bird, Charles, Crow rancher and former rodeo cowboy. Interview by author at Garryowen, Montana, February 24, 1995.

Real Bird, Cotton, seven-year-old future bronc rider. Interview by author at Garryowen, Montana, February 24, 1995.

Real Bird, Curtis, bronc rider. Interview by author at Garryowen, Montana, February 24, 1995.

———. Interview for Little Big Horn College Oral History Project, Crow Agency, Montana, February 7, 1995.

Real Bird, Ken, 1982 Crow Fair Rodeo manager, bronc rider, and artist. Interview by author at Garryowen, Montana, February 24, 1995.

Real Bird, Krystal, eleven-year-old rodeo fan. Interview by author at Garryowen, Montana, February 24, 1995.

Real Bird, Kylie, twelve-year-old rodeo fan. Interview by author at Garryowen, Montana, February 24, 1995.

Real Bird, Pius, founder of all-Indian rodeo at Crow Fair. Interview by author at Garryowen, Montana, April 11, 1995.

Real Bird, Shawn, steer wrestler and war dancer. Interview by author at Garryowen, Montana, February 24, 1995.

Redhouse, John, National Indian Youth Council. Letter to Legislative Finance Committee, December 2, 1977. State Commission of Public Records and Archives, Santa Fe.

Sierra, Smiley, Pine Ridge Lakota bull rider. Interview by author at the 1996 Indian National Finals Rodeo, Saskatoon, Saskatchewan, October 31–November 3, 1996.

Small, Sharon, Northern Cheyenne barrel racer. Interviews by author at the 1996 Indian National Finals Rodeo, Saskatoon, Saskatchewan, October 31–November 3, 1996.

Smith, Alvin, president, Navajo National Rodeo Cowboy Association. Interview by author, November 23, 1994.

Takes Gun, George. Interview for New Deal in Montana Oral History Project, 1989. Montana State Historical Society, Helena.

Takes Gun, Mae. Interview for New Deal in Montana Oral History Project, 1989. Montana State Historical Society, Helena.

Tashquinth, Eugene, Tohono O'dham rodeo announcer. Interview by author, October 2, 1994.

Tsosia, Willis, Crow rodeo cowboy. Letter to author, October 27, 1994.

Walks over Ice, Carson, Little Big Horn College librarian and member of Mad Dog Drum Group. Interview by author, February 22, 1995.

Ward, Kelli Powers, president of Great Plains Indian Rodeo Association. Letter to author, November 15, 1994.

White Clay, Delano. Interview by author, April 11, 1995.

Whiteman, Phillip Jr., Northern Cheyenne rodeo cowboy. Interview by author, October 21, 1994.

Yellowhead, Joe, seventy-six-year-old from Cheyenne River Sioux reservation, Eagle Butte, South Dakota, June 8, 1971. Interview for American Indian Research Project, University of South Dakota, Vermillion.

## SECONDARY SOURCES

Acoose, Janet. *Iskwewak-Kah' Ki Yaw Ni Wahkomakanak: Neither Indian Princesses Nor Easy Squaws*. Toronto, Canada Women's Press, 1995.

Alcorn, Rowena L., and Gordon D. Alcorn. "Jackson Sundown: Nez Pierce Horseman." *Montana* 33 (autumn 1983): 46–51.

Arpad, Joseph J., and Kenneth R. Lincoln. *Buffalo Bill's Wild West*. Palmer Lake, Colo.: Filter Press, 1971.

Baillargeon, Morgan, and Leslie Tepper. *Legends of Our Times: Native Cowboy Life*. Seattle: University of Washington Press, 1998.

Banet-Weiser, Sarah. *The Most Beautiful Girl in the World: Beauty Pageants and National Identity*. Berkeley: University of California Press, 1999.

Barrett, G. E. "Crow Indians Hold Second Annual Tribal Fair." *Scenic Trails*, October 1937, 10–19.

Barth, Fredrik. *Ethnic Groups and Boundaries: The Social Organization of Culture Difference*. Boston: Little, Brown, 1969.

Bederman, Gail. *Manliness and Civilization: A Cultural History of Gender and Race in the United States, 1886–1917*. Chicago: University of Chicago Press, 1995.

Begaye, Gabrielle Arviso. "The Indian Cowboy and Cowgirl in Indian and Professional Rodeo." Paper completed for an undergraduate course in American Indian history at Arizona State University. Copy in possession of the author.

Biolosi, Thomas. *Organizing the Lakota: The Political Economy of the New Deal on the Pine Ridge and Rosebud Reservations*. Tucson: University of Arizona Press, 1992.

Bird, Sarah. *Virgin of the Rodeo*. New York: Doubleday, 1993.

Black Bear, Ben, and R. D. Theis. *Songs and Dances of the Lakota*. Rosebud, S. Dak.: Sinte Gleska College, 1976.

Boeheme, Sara E. "The North and the Snow: Joseph Henry Sharp in Montana." *Montana* 40 (fall 1990): 32–47.

Borland, Hal. *When Legends Die*. New York: Harper and Row, 1963.

Brin, Sylvester. "The Indian Cowboy in the Rodeo Circuit." *Journal of Ethnic Studies* 5 (January 1977): 51–57.

Calloway, Colin G. "The Only Way Open to Us: The Crow Struggle for Survival in the Nineteenth Century." *North Dakota History* 53 (summer 1986): 24–34.

———. "Sword Bearer and the Crow Outbreak, 1887." *Montana* 36 (fall 1986): 38–51.

Carter, George E., and James R. Purkee, eds. *Identity and Awareness in Minority Experiences.* LaCrosse: Institute for Minority Studies, University of Wisconsin, 1975.

Chavis, Ben. "All-Indian Rodeo: A Transformation of Western Apache Tribal Warfare." *Wicaza Saturday Review* (1993).

Cohen, Abner. *Two Dimension Man: An Essay in the Anthropology of Power and Symbolism in Complex Society.* Berkeley: University of California Press, 1974.

Collier, John. *The Indians of the Americas.* New York: Norton, 1947.

Cornell, Steven. *The Return of the Native: American Indian Political Resurgence.* New York: Oxford University Press, 1988.

Crenshaw, John. "Rodeo: A Spectator's Guide." *New Mexico Magazine* (August 1979): 19–20.

Crow, Kelly. "Princess and the Pageantry: The Serious World of Indian Pageants." *Oklahoma Today* (May/June 2000): 40.

Crummett, Michael. "Tepee Capital of the World." *Americana* 32 (July–August 1981): 32–37.

Demallie, Raymond J. "Pine Ridge Economy: Cultural and Historical Perspectives." In *American Indian Economic Development*, edited by Sam Stanley. The Hague: Mouton, 1978.

Dempsey, Hugh A. *Tom Three Persons.* Saskatoon, Saskatchewan: Purich Publishing, 1997.

Deward, Walker E. Jr., ed. *The Emergence of Native Americans: A Reader in Culture Contact.* Boston: Little, Brown, 1972.

Eagle/Walking Turtle. *Indian America: A Traveler's Companion.* 3rd ed. Santa Fe: John Muir Publications, 1993.

Ewers, John C. *The Horse in Blackfoot Indian Culture.* Bureau of American Ethnology Bulletin 159. Washington, D.C.: Smithsonian Institution, 1955

Fife, Austen E. *Exploring Western Americana.* Ann Arbor: UMI Research Press, 1988.

Foster, Morris W. *Being Comanche: A Social History of an American Indian Community.* Tucson: University of Arizona Press, 1991.

Foucault, Michel. *Power/Knowledge: Selected Interviews and Other Writings, 1972–1977.* New York; Pantheon Books, 1980.

Fowler, Loretta. *Shared Symbols, Contested Meanings: Gros Ventre Culture and History, 1778–1984.* New York: Cornell University Press, 1987.

Frazier, Patrick. "Crow Indian Fair." *Travel*, July 1973, 24–29, 75.

Fredrikson, Kristine. *American Rodeo: From Buffalo Bill to Big Business*. College Station: Texas A&M University Press, 1985.

Frey, Rodney. *The World of the Crow Indians: As Driftwood Lodges*. Norman: University of Oklahoma Press, 1987.

Geertz, Clifford. *The Social History of an Indonesian Town*. Cambridge: MIT Press, 1965.

————. *The Interpretation of Cultures*. New York: Basic Books, 1973.

Getty, Harry T. *The San Carlos Apache Cattle Industry*. Tucson: University of Arizona Press, 1963.

Gruneau, Richard S. "Sport, Social Differentiation, and Social Inequality." In *Sport and Social Order*, edited by Donald W. Ball and John W. Loy. Reading, Mass.: Addison-Wesley, 1975.

————. *Class, Sports, and Social Development*. Amherst: University of Massachusetts Press, 1983.

Gutman, Allen. *From Ritual to Record: The Nature of Modern Sports*. New York: Columbia University Press, 1978.

Haines, Francis P. *Horses in America*. New York: Crowell, 1971.

Hargreaves, John. "Sport and Hegemony: Some Theoretical Problems." In *Sport, Culture, and the Modern State*, edited by Hart Canteon and Richard Gruneau. Toronto: University of Toronto Press, 1982.

Hassrick, Royal B. *The Sioux: Life and Customs of a Warrior Society*. Norman: University of Oklahoma Press, 1977.

Hertzberg, Hazel. *Search for an American Indian Identity: Modern Pan Indian Movements*. Syracuse: Syracuse University Press, 1971.

Holm, Tom. "Fighting a White Man's War: The Extent and Legacy of Indian Participation in World War II." In *The Plains Indians of the Twentieth Century*, edited by Peter Iverson. Norman: University of Oklahoma Press, 1985.

"Howard Hunter," *Hoof and Horn*, 1977. Oglala Lakota College Library, Kyle, South Dakota.

Hoover, Herbert T. "The Sioux Agreement of 1889 and Its Aftermath." *South Dakota History* 19 (spring 1989).

Hoxie, Frederick E. *A Final Promise: The Campaign to Assimilate the Indians, 1880–1920*. Lincoln: University of Nebraska Press, 1984.

————. "From Prison to Homeland: The Cheyenne River Indian Reservation before World War I." In *The Plains Indians of the Twentieth Century West*, edited by Peter Iverson. Norman: University of Oklahoma Press, 1985.

————. "Review of Fred W. Voget's The Shoshoni-Crow Sun Dance." *Western Historical Quarterly* 17 (January 1986): 75–76.

————. *The Crow*. Edited by Frank W. Porter III. Broomall, Penn.: Chelsea House.

————. "Searching for Structure: Reconstructing Crow Family Life during the Reservation Era." *American Indian Quarterly* 15 (March 1991): 287–309.

————. *Parading through History: The Making of the Crow Nation in America, 1805–1935*. Cambridge: Cambridge University Press, 1995.

Hurt, Wesley R. *Sioux Indians II: Dakota Sioux Indians*. New York: Garland Publishing, 1974.

Iverson, Peter. "Building toward Self Determination: Plains and Southwestern Indians in the 1940s and 1950s." *Western Historical Quarterly* 16 (April 1985): 163–73.

————. *The Plains Indians of the Twentieth Century*. Norman: University of Oklahoma Press, 1985.

————. "Cowboys, Indians, and the Modern West." *Arizona and the West* 28 (February 1986): 107–24.

————. "The Cowboys Are Indians: Indian Cattle Ranching in the American West." *Storia Nord Americana* (Italy) 5 (January 1988): 115–24.

————. *When Indians Became Cowboys: Native Peoples and Cattle Ranching in the American West*. Norman: University of Oklahoma Press, 1994.

————. "Native Peoples and Native Histories." In *The Oxford History of the American West*, edited by Clyde A. Milner, Carol A. O'Connor, and Martha A. Sandweiss. New York: Oxford University Press, 1994.

————. *"We Are Still Here": American Indians in the Twentieth Century*. Wheeling, Ill.: Harlan Davidson, 1998.

Iverson, Peter, and Linda MacCannell. *Riders of the West: Portraits from the Indian Rodeo*. Seattle: University of Washington Press, 1999.

Jensen, Joan M. "Native American Women and Agriculture: A Seneca Case Study." In *Unequal Sisters: A Multicultural Reader in U.S. Women's History*, edited by Ellen Carol DuBois and Vicki Ruiz. New York: Routledge Press, 1994.

Jensen, Margaret. "Indian Fair." *American Tourists* 69 (May 1963).

Jordan, William. "Indians in the Cattle Business in the Early Days." In *Early Dakota Days*, edited by Winifred Reuter. Stickney, S.Dak.: Argus Printers, 1962.

————. *Eighty Years on the Rosebud*. Pierre: South Dakota Historical Collections, 1970.

Josephy, Alvin M. Jr., Joane Nagel, and Troy Johnson, eds. *Red Power: The American Indian's Fight for Freedom*. Lincoln: University of Nebraska Press, 1999.

Kelleher, Robert. "Something to Crow About." *American West* 28 (fall 1990): 12–15.

Kelly, Lawrence C. *Assault on Assimilation: John Collier and the Origins of Indian Policy Reform*. Albuquerque: University of New Mexico Press, 1983.

Kesey, Ken, and Ken Babbs. *Last Go Round*. New York: Viking Press, 1994.

Klein, Laura F., and Lillian A. Ackerman, eds. *Women and Power in Native North America*. Norman: University of Oklahoma Press, 1995.

Kluckhohn, Clyde, et al. *Navajo Material Culture*. Cambridge: The Belknap Press of Harvard University Press, 1971.

Koester, Pat. "Crow Fair." *Trailer Life*, August 1987: 33.

Kroeber, A. L. *An Anthropologist Looks at History*. Berkeley: University of California Press, 1963.

Lawrence, Elizabeth Atwood. *Rodeo: An Anthropologist Looks at the Wild and the Tame*. Knoxville: University of Tennessee Press, 1982.

———. *Hoofbeats and Society: Studies of Human-Horse Interactions*: Bloomington: Indiana University Press, 1995.

Lears, T. J. Jackson. "The Concept of Cultural Hegemony: Problems and Possibilities." *American Historical Review* 90 (June 1985): 567–93.

LeCompte, Mary Lou. "The Hispanic Influence on the History of Rodeo, 1823–1922." *Journal of Sport History* 12 (spring 1985): 21–38.

———. *Cowgirls of the Rodeo: Pioneer Professional Athlete*. Urbana: University of Illinois Press, 1993.

Linderman, Frank B. *Plenty-Coups, Chief of the Crows*. Lincoln: University of Nebraska Press, 1930.

———. *Red Mother* (later published as *Pretty-Shield, Medicine Woman of the Crows*). New York: John Day, 1932

Loeb, Barbara. "Crow Beadwork: The Resilience of Cultural Values." *Montana* 40 (fall 1990): 48–59.

Lowie, Robert H. *The Crow Indians*. New York: Holt, Rinehart and Winston, 1935.

———. *Myths and Traditions of the Crow Indians*. New York: Holt, Rinehart and Winston, 1935.

———. *The Crow Language, Grammatical Sketch and Analyzed Text*. Berkeley: University of California Press, 1941.

Maroukis, Thomas C. "Yankton Sioux Tribal Fairs: The Early Twentieth Century." *Institute of American Indian Studies: The Bulletin: University of South Dakota*. (August 1992).

Marquis, Thomas B. *Memoirs of a White Crow Indian (Thomas H. Leforge)*. Lincoln: University of Nebraska Press, 1974.

———. *Custer, Cavalry and the Crows: The Story of William White as Told to Thomas Marquis*. Fort Collins, Colo.: Old Army Press, 1976.

Maeser-Lemieux, Angelika. "The Metis in the Fiction of Margaret Laurence: From Outcast to Consort." In *The Native in Literature: Canadian and Comparative Perspectives*, edited by Thomas King, Cheryl Calver, and Helen Hoy. Winnipeg: ECW Press, 1987.

Marshall, Howard W. *Buckaroos in Paradise: Cowboy Life in Northern Nevada*. Lincoln: University of Nebraska Press, 1981.

———. *Paradise Valley, Nevada: The People and Buildings of an American Place*. Tucson: University of Arizona Press, 1995.

McGinnies, William G., Bram J. Goldman, and Patricia Paylore, eds. *Food, Fiber, and the Arid Lands*. Tucson: University of Arizona Press, 1971.

McGinnis, Dale K., and Floyd W. Sharrock. *The Crow People*. Phoenix: Indian Tribal Series, 1972.

McLaughlin, Castle. "The Big Lease: Confined-Range Ranching on the Fort Bert-
hold Indian Reservation, 1910–1950." *North Dakota History: Journal of the
Northern Plains* 61 (fall 1994).

Medicine Crow, Joseph. "Notes on Crow Indian Buffalo Jump Traditions." *Plains
Anthropologist* 23 (1978), 82.

———. *From the Heart of Crow Country: The Crow Indians' Own Stories.* New
York: Orion Books, 1992.

"Medicine Robes and Black Cowboys." *New Yorker*, March 17, 1986, 30–32.

Mikkelson, Glen. "Indians and Rodeo." *Alberta History* 35 (March 1987): 13–19.

Morrison, Joan. "Indian Rodeo." *Native Peoples* 2, no.4 (summer 1989): 22–23.

Moses, L. G. *Wild West Shows and the Images of American Indians, 1883–1933.* Albuquerque: University of New Mexico Press, 1996.

"Multi-Cultural Mix-ups: Post Modern Cowboys and New Age Indians." *Utne
Reader*, March/April 1993, 127.

Nabokov, Peter. *Two Leggings: The Making of a Crow Warrior.* Lincoln: University
of Nebraska Press, 1967.

Nelson, Barney. "Ranching on the Reservations: The Crows in Montana." *Western
Horseman*, April 1993, 94–97.

O'Brien, Sharon. *American Indian Tribal Governments.* Norman: University of
Oklahoma Press, 1989.

Ortner, Sherry. "Theory in Anthropology since the Sixties." *Comparative Studies
in Society and History* 26 (1984).

Parfit, Michael. "A Gathering of Tribes." *National Geographic*, June 1994, 91–113.

Parker, Patricia. *The Feather and the Drum: The History of Banff Indian Days,
1889–1978.* Calgary, Alberta: Consolidated Communications, 1990.

Parman, Donald Lee. *Indians and the American West in the Twentieth Century.*
Bloomington: Indiana University Press, 1994.

Pony Boy, GaWaNi. *Horse, Follow Closely: Native American Horsemanship.* Irvine,
Calif.: Bowtie Press, 1998.

———. *Out of the Saddle: Native American Horsemanship.* Irvine, Calif.: Bowtie
Press, 1998.

Porter, Constance J. "Robert Yellowtail: The New Warrior." *Montana* 39 (summer
1989): 36–41.

Powers, William K. *War Dance: Plains Indian Musical Performance.* Tucson: University of Arizona Press, 1990.

Prucha, Francis Paul. *The Great Father: The United States Government and the
American Indians.* Abridged ed. Lincoln: University of Nebraska Press, 1984.

Puten, Connie, Pamela Roberts, and Beth Ferris. *Contrary Warriors: A Film of the
Crow Tribe.* Santa Monica: Direct Cinema, 1986. Film.

Reinhardt, Akim. "Spontaneous Combustion: Prelude to Wounded Knee 1973."
*South Dakota History* 29, no.3 (fall 1999): 229–44.

Richardson, E. A. "The Crow Indian Fair." *Yellowstone Monthly*, December
1907, 1–6.

Richardson, Miles. *The Human Mirror: Material and Spatial Images of Man*. Baton
    Rouge: Louisiana State University Press, 1974.
Roe, Frank Gilbert. *The Indian and the Horse*. Norman: University of Oklahoma
    Press, 1955.
Roscoe, Will. "That is My Road: The Life and Times of a Crow Berdache." *Montana* 40 (winter 1990): 46–55.
Roth, Barbara Williams. "The 101 Ranch Wild West Show, 1904–1932." *Chronicles
    of Oklahoma* 43 (April 1966): 416–31.
Royce, Anya Peterson. *Ethnic Identity: Strategies of Diversity*. Bloomington: Indiana University Press, 1982.
Sahlins, Marshall. *Islands of History*. Chicago: University of Chicago Press, 1985.
Sanchez, George J. *Becoming Mexican American: Ethnicity, Culture, and Identity in
    Chicano Los Angeles, 1940–1945*. New York: Oxford University Press, 1993.
Savage, William W. *The Cherokee Strip Live Stock Association: Federal Regulation
    and the Cattle Man's Last Frontier*. Columbia: University of Missouri Press, 1973.
Schaafsma, Polly. "The Horse in Rock Art." *El Palacio* 81 (March 1975): 4–5.
Schimmel, Julie. "Inventing the Indian." In *The West as America: Reinterpreting
    Images of the Frontier*, edited by William H. Truettner. Washington, D.C.:
    Smithsonian Institution Press, 1991.
Schlereth, Thomas J. *Material Culture: A Research Guide*. Lawrence: University of
    Kansas Press, 1984.
Scott, Joan M. "Gender: A Useful Category of Historical Analysis." *American Historical Review* 91 (1986).
*Sioux Nation Cowboy News*, January 1980. Oglala Lakota College Archives, Kyle,
    South Dakota.
"Sioux Nation Rodeo." *American Cowboy*, November–December 1981.
Skags, Jimmy M., ed. *Ranch and Range in Oklahoma*. Oklahoma City: Oklahoma
    Historical Society, 1978.
Slatta, Richard W. "Cowboys and Gauchos." *Americas*, March 1981, 3–8.
———. "Cowboys, Gauchos, and Llaneros." *Persimmon Hill* 12:4 (1983): 8–23.
———. *Cowboys of the Americas*. New Haven: Yale University Press, 1990.
Slotkin, Richard. *Gunfighter Nation: The Myth of the Frontier in Twentieth Century
    America*. New York: Atheneum, 1992.
Smith, Burton M. "Politics and the Crow Indian Land Cessions." *Montana* 36 (fall
    1986): 24–34.
Stands in Timber, John, with the assistance of Robert M. Utley. *Cheyenne Memories*. Lincoln: University of Nebraska Press, 1967.
Stevens, Harry. "Cattle Raising on the San Carlos Reservation in Arizona." *Indians
    at Work* 7 (July 1939).
———. "Papagos Manage Their Own Fair and Rodeo." *Indians at Work* 7
    (December 1939).
———. "Hard Riding Cowboys Combine Old Time Skills with Modem Methods
    to Make Cattle Business Pay." *Indians at Work* 8 (December 1940).

Stewart, James H. "Urbanization, Peoplehood and Modes of Identity: Native Americans in Cities." In *Identity and Awareness in Minority Experience*, edited by George E. Carter and James R. Purkee. LaCrosse: Institute for Minority Studies, University of Wisconsin, 1975.

Stewart, Omer C. "Peyotism in Montana." *Montana* 33 (spring 1983).

Svingen, Orlan J. "Reservation Self-sufficiency: Stock Raising, Farming on the Northern Cheyenne Indian Reservation, 1906–1913." *Montana* 31, no. 4 (October 81): 6.

Sweet, Jill D., and Karen E. Larson. "The Horse, Santiago, and a Ritual Game: Pueblo Indian Response to Three Spanish Introductions." *Western Folklore* 53 (January 1994): 69–84.

Thomas, Robert K. "Pan Indianism." In *The Emergence of Native Americans: A Reader in Culture Contact*, edited by Deward E. Walker Jr. Boston: Little, Brown, 1972.

Thornton, Russell. *American Indian Holocaust and Survival: A Population History Since 1492*. Norman: University of Oklahoma Press, 1987.

Truettner, William H., ed. *The West as America: Reinterpreting Images of the Frontier*. Washington: Smithsonian Institution Press, 1991.

Underwood, Jerald. "The Vaquero in South Texas with an Interpretation by John Houghton Allen." *West Texas Historical Association Yearbook* 68 (1992): 93–99.

Voget, Fred W. *The Shoshoni-Crow Sun Dance*. Norman: University of Oklahoma Press, 1984.

Wagner, Glendolin Damon, and William A. Allen. *Blankets and Moccasins, Plenty Coups and His People, the Crows*. Lincoln: University of Nebraska Press, 1987.

West, Elliot. *The Way to the West: Essays on the Central Plains*. Albuquerque: University of New Mexico Press, 1995.

West, Patsy. *The Enduring Seminoles: From Alligator Wrestling to Ecotourism*. Gainesville: University of Florida Press, 1998.

White, Richard. "The Winning of the West: The Expansion of the Western Sioux in the Eighteenth and Nineteenth Centuries." *Journal of American History* 65 (September 1978): 319–43.

———. *"It's Your Misfortune and None of My Own": A New History of the American West*. Norman: University of Oklahoma Press, 1991.

Whyte, John. *Indians in the Rockies*. Canmore, Alberta: Altitude Publishing, 1985.

Xavier, Gwyneth Harrington. *The Cattle Industry of the Southern Papago Districts with Some Information on the Reservation Cattle Industry as a Whole*. Tucson: Bureau of Ethnic Research, University of Arizona.

Yellowtail, Thomas. *Yellowtail, Crow Medicine Man and Sun Dance Chief; An Autobiography as told to Michael Oren Fitzgerald*. Norman: University of Oklahoma Press, 1991.

Young, Robert W., and William Morgan Sr. *The Navajo Language: A Grammar and Colloquial Dictionary*. Rev. ed. Albuquerque: University of New Mexico Press, 1987.

# Index